Life's Little Edge

Life's Little Edge

Roselle Graskey

P.D. Publishing, Inc.
Clayton, North Carolina

ISBN-13: 978-0-9754366-0-8
ISBN-10: 0-9754366-0-0

First Printing 2005

9 8 7 6 5 4 3 2 1

Cover art and design by Talaran
Edited by Day Petersen/Stacia Seaman

Published by:

P.D. Publishing, Inc.
P.O. Box 70
Clayton, NC 27528

http://www.pdpublishing.com

Acknowledgements:

I could have never accomplished what I have without the love and support of my family and friends, who understand why I'm grumpy when I have writer's block, who don't even look embarrassed anymore when I start scribbling on napkins in a restaurant and have learned just not to talk to me when my eyes get that certain glazed over look.

Barb and Linda, thank you for letting me dream once more and for your guidance and for the wonderful team you put together for the finished product.

For two wonderful friends, Janet S. and Lori A., you both remind me what's important in life and you keep letting me not forget to have fun and dream. Thank you so much both of you.

Prologue

She came awake slowly, eyes blinking against the overhead light. She shifted a little and became suddenly aware that she was in a real bed, not in the seat of her HMMWV or on the hard nylon of an Army-issue cot. The almost-forgotten comfort only served to confuse her further.

"Oh good, you're awake," a woman's voice off to her right observed.

She slowly turned her head, wincing when a sore spot touched the pillow. Her eyes came to rest on a blurry figure in a battle dress uniform; silver bars gleamed in the light. She watched the nurse come closer, stethoscope looped around her neck. She tried to speak, but found her mouth and throat too dry to produce anything more than a slight groan. Suddenly a straw was offered to her lips.

"Go slowly. Don't shock your system all at once," the nurse ordered gently.

She nodded carefully and did as ordered. Slow, wonderfully wet sips cleared away the cotton-dry feeling in her mouth and throat. When she finished, the straw was pulled away, then she relaxed into her pillow.

"You might want these," the nurse offered, and carefully slipped a pair of prescription glasses in place.

Instantly the world came into sharper focus. The hospital room was like every other she'd ever been in, but this time the nurse, she thought, was infinitely better looking than most. Auburn hair framed a face delicate enough to belong to a porcelain doll and complemented eyes whose color reminded her of the green apples she used to pick at her aunt's farm.

"Thank you," she managed. "Ma'am."

The nurse chuckled. "Good thing you remembered that; I'd hate to have to have you drawn and quartered," she said as she moved the blanket and slipped the stethoscope under the hospital-issue gown. "Shh."

The patient in the bed endured the usual elements of examination, breaking into a sweat and feeling the edge of pain move to a slightly higher level when she leaned up to allow the nurse to listen to her lungs from the back. Warm hands helped guide her back to the bed when it was over. She lay there exhausted, the scratch of pen on paper indicating that the results were being recorded. "Now we get to play a game," *the nurse deadpanned as she flipped a page on the chart. She carefully watched the curious, pale blue eyes that stared back.* "Do you remember your name?"

"Staff Sergeant Callan G. O'Malley, ma'am," *the patient answered with half a smile, suddenly aware of the tightness in her face.*

"You've answered question two, so we'll move on to three: what day is it?"

Callan thought, trying to gauge how much time had passed since the lights had gone out. Unsuccessful, she refocused on the nurse. "The day I woke up from getting my ass handed to me, ma'am?" *She watched her nurse try to suppress a smile.*

"I'll give you that one."

"Excuse me, ma'am. What's your name?" *Callan asked in a soft voice.*

"Lieutenant Rivers. What's the G stand for?"

Callan frowned. "Grace."

Rivers chuckled. "I take it you don't like it."

"Do I look like a Grace, ma'am?" *Callan asked as she tried to shift in bed.*

"Not at the moment, no." *She read down the checklist.* "President of the United States?"

"Bush."

"Godzilla or Mothra?" *Lieutenant Rivers hid her smile.*

Callan blinked twice. "Would that be based on a rating of fighting skill or looks?" *she countered.*

This time Lieutenant Rivers let herself laugh. "Sergeant O'Malley, I think you are suffering no ill effects from that knock on the head." *She leaned forward, clutching the file to her chest.* "Kevlars are meant to keep your head intact. Next time, wear your brain bucket. That's an order."

Callan heard the rate of the heart monitor beeps jump as her anxiety level went off the chart. In her mind, she could hear the mine exploding under her vehicle and the shouts of near panic mixing with the distinct popping sound of gunfire.

Lieutenant Rivers moved quickly to Callan's side. "Sergeant O'Malley?"

"My guys." *Her eyes searched Rivers's face in desperation.* "Did they make it? Barnes was hit pretty bad."

"They made it," *the nurse assured her.* "Barnes and the rest are here and breathing." *Her voice took on a practiced soothing quality.* "You need to calm down. We don't want you messing up the surgeon's work."

"Surgeon?"

"That would be Major Thompkins. He's sort of like all the king's horses and all the king's men, only better." She smiled.

Callan winced against the pain. *"Call me Dumpty,"* she managed, then took a slow, steadying breath. *"Jesus, how bad did I get hit?"*

"Major Thompkins will explain it to you in a short while."

"Please, ma'am, I'd really like to know," Callan importuned. *"I won't tell on you, I promise."* She attempted a ghost of a smile.

"Okay." Rivers sighed and looked to the door, making sure the coast was clear. *"In English, you have shrapnel wounds to your arms, legs, and face. There is a back-to-front gunshot wound just under your right shoulder blade that resulted in broken ribs and a collapsed lung. The new haircut is courtesy of an eight-stitch, concussion-causing wound."* She watched carefully as her patient processed the information. *"You were transported off the field via evac to the medical facility in Turkey. Once you were stable, they flew you here to Ramstein. Sergeant O'Malley, you are a mess, but the important thing is that you have made it, and you will recover."*

Callan blinked a few times in response before her eyes locked onto Lieutenant Rivers's. *"I am never going to do Packard any more favors,"* she decided out loud, and closed her eyes.

"How's the pain?"

"Not too bad, ma'am," Callan lied.

"Sergeant O'Malley, you are exactly like every other MP I have ever treated. I can still order you drawn and quartered, you know."

Callan's eyes shot open. *"Ma'am?"*

"You will leave the macho bullshit at the door when I am around. You can admit it hurts, Sergeant; I won't tell your buddies. I cannot treat your pain if I don't know how bad it is. Am I coming in clearly?"

Callan sighed. *"Crystal clear, ma'am."*

The irritated tone was replaced by one of concern. *"On a scale of one to ten."*

"Right now, five and a quarter, ma'am."

Lieutenant Rivers arched an eyebrow. *"Tell me, Sergeant, do you always buck authority?"* she asked as she replaced the chart in its holder.

Callan smiled a bit. *"Only when I think I can get away with it, ma'am."*

"I'll make note of that. You get some rest. I'll check with the doctor about getting you some more pain meds on board." She turned to leave.

"Ma'am."

Rivers turned back. *"Yes?"*

"Godzilla, but only on fighting skill."

"Sergeant, you are going to be trouble. I can tell."

* ~ * ~ * ~ *

Callan G. O'Malley woke from her dream quickly, but without starting. She automatically reached for her pack of smokes. Tucking a cigarette between her lips, she swung her legs off the bed and then slowly slipped the matchbook free from the cellophane wrapper. She took her time lighting up, wondering at the same time when the dreams would stop. She closed her eyes and inhaled the smoke. When she opened them again, she let out a stream of smoke and stood.

The morning sounds of the prisoners at the county correctional facility reached her ears as she listened to the normal, everyday chaos beginning. When she could no longer put off the inevitable, she crushed out her cigarette. Slowly, she shed her prison uniform and dressed in musty-smelling jeans and a gray T-shirt.

At least my socks are clean, she thought, as she pulled the thick white cotton onto her feet. Her black boots were next. When she heard the call for breakfast and the cell doors unlocked electronically, she looked up. A few minutes later, prisoners on her tier started passing by her locked door. Some wished her luck, others said nothing, and there were, inevitably, some threats tossed her way, vivid descriptions of what they would do to her when they got out. She ignored them. Finally they were all gone, and the only sounds she could hear were the footfalls of the guard coming to escort her.

"Open two twelve," a female voice boomed, echoing down the tier. The lock disengaged and the door slid open. "Two twelve, step out."

O'Malley stepped out of the cell and onto the metal floor of the tier. She stood still, not moving a muscle. She waited while the uniformed guard inspected her cell to make sure it was free of any personal items and held nothing that could be used as a weapon by the next occupant.

Finally, the guard joined O'Malley on the tier. "Turn to your right and walk forward. You will proceed down the steps and follow the blue line. Do not stray from the blue line. Do you understand these instructions, O'Malley?" The guard sounded almost bored.

O'Malley resisted the urge to roll her eyes. "Yes, ma'am."

"Let's go. I don't have all day."

O'Malley nodded and turned to her right. She walked forward, and then down the metal steps. Together, guard and prisoner followed the blue line on the floor until they reached the release office. O'Malley wondered for a moment why they called it an office, since it was a counter with a warehouse space attached.

She produced her prison ID and signed several slips of official-looking paper. Once those were passed back, she waited for her personal items to be handed over to her. Another bored guard pushed over a manila envelope. O'Malley ripped it open and let the contents fall onto the counter. She picked up her wallet and slipped it into her back pocket.

"You're not going to count your cash?" the officer asked, sounding every bit as confused as he looked.

Pale blue eyes locked onto him. "Why, did you steal anything?" she asked as she fitted a stainless steel bracelet onto her right wrist.

"Of course not."

"Then I don't have to count it. If you can't trust the cops..." She let the sentence die as she wound her watch, then abandoned the effort when she discerned that the battery was dead. Absently she signed the statement confirming that everything was in order.

"Follow the blue line," she was ordered.

She turned and trailed the blue line to freedom. When she finally reached the metal door leading to the outside, she turned her ID over to the guard and signed out for the last time, then stepped out into the sunlight.

The door closed behind her and O'Malley took a long breath. She looked around and quickly located a Mexican woman standing across the street, her back pressed against a wall. O'Malley waved and darted across the street.

As O'Malley's feet touched the curb, Maria pushed away from the wall and launched into a tight hug. "That's jaywalking, O'Malley," she teased.

"So arrest me," O'Malley growled. She pulled out of the embrace. "You look good."

"You lost weight," Maria observed.

"Let's get out of here."

"Bike's around the corner. How 'bout I buy you breakfast?" Maria offered.

"Steak and eggs?" O'Malley hoped aloud.

"For you? Of course." Maria smiled as she led the way down the sidewalk.

Chapter 1

Maria kept an eye on the petite woman as she worked her way to the bar. She noted the look of fatigue on the still-young face even as she reached into the beer cooler. It took only a second for her to pull the cap off the beer, set it on the counter in front of the only empty seat, and toss the mangled cap over her shoulder. The young woman promptly filled the seat.

Maria pushed the ice-cold brew closer to the woman. "Here you go, Terri."

Terri picked up the beer and took a long sip. "God, thank you, Maria," Terri said gratefully as she set the bottle down. "All right. Where is the rat bastard?" she asked, almost too tired to be angry. Her feet hurt, and besides...her feet hurt.

Maria stifled a chuckle. The woman in front of her might look like a piece of fluff, but when she needed to be, she was all spitfire. "He's in the back, playing poker," she answered.

Terri took another sip of her beer. "How long?"

Maria turned and looked at the clock. "About five hours now."

Terri's milk-chocolate eyes hardened. "He been losing?"

"I'd have to say yes," Maria answered, and something close to panic flitted across Terri's face. She placed her hand gently on Terri's forearm. "*Chica,* you have to get away from him."

Terri turned away. "Easy to say, Maria, but getting away from him is hard to do. I tried that once, and he came looking for me and brought me back."

"A lot of the guys like you, maybe they could help."

Terri shook her head. "And what are they going to want in return? With Trey, at least I know what the score is. Besides, most of the guys think Trey's up Spyder's ass. Who's going to mess with Spyder or his yes-man?"

Maria didn't have to answer. None of the club members would

take on the leader or his appointed second. Spyder was one mean son of a bitch and had proven it on many occasions. It was a no-win situation. She watched quietly as Terri finished her beer.

"Who's he playing with?"

Maria sighed. "John, Mike, Gato, and O'Malley. You want another beer?"

"I better not. John, Mike, and Gato will let me pay over time, but I've never heard of this O'Malley. I hope whatever I have on me is enough to cover Trey's losses," Terri answered, all the while thinking that a second beer sounded like a small piece of heaven.

"Terri, I'll cover your beer. It's not like you've ever stiffed me on a tip or never bought me a round."

"I can't. I appreciate the gesture—"

Maria interrupted and finished the sentence for her. "But Trey would think you're holding out on him." For a long moment Terri was frozen, then she nodded slowly. "Okay, how 'bout a friend of mine buys you the beer? Can he argue with that?"

Terri's smile was tired as she teased, "Aren't you a little old for imaginary friends, Maria?" Half a second later, she started when a group of empty beer bottles was loudly clattered onto the countertop.

A voice to Terri's left sounded light and playful. "Maria, are you pretending you don't know me again?"

Maria grinned with joy. "What's your name again?"

The presence choked back a laugh. "Well, apparently last night it was 'oh God.' We need another round."

"I think we can do that. O'Malley, this is Terri; Terri, this is Callan O'Malley." She provided the introduction as she turned to raid the beer cooler again.

Terri turned and faced O'Malley. Worn and faded jeans, a green T-shirt from some pub, and black motorcycle boots: Callan O'Malley was pretty much what Terri had expected. What she had not expected was Callan O'Malley's gender.

"Hi," she managed without embarrassing herself.

"Hi there." There was a smile on the woman's face. "Just call me O'Malley." It sounded like a soft-spoken order. O'Malley didn't take her eyes off Terri. "Hey, Maria, Terri's next beer is on my tab."

Maria caught Terri's eye and winked. "You got it, baby," she answered as she set the new round of beers on the counter.

"You know, if Gato ever heard the way you talk to me, he'd kill me."

"Hell, O'Malley, he knows I love you. He's just glad he found me first and not you."

Terri watched O'Malley laugh and take the bottles of beer.

O'Malley flashed a grin at Maria and turned to Terri. "I'll see you around."

Struck mute by the woman standing beside her, Terri nodded, and then the woman was gone. Terri had seen a lot of women around the bikers, but never one who was obviously more than decoration for the back of a bike. Mildly stunned, she turned her focus back to the bar and the fresh bottle of beer sitting in front her.

Maria chuckled. "You know, this is the first time I've seen you speechless."

"I'm having an off day," Terri protested, then lapsed into silence.

"Don't worry about it. Just drink your beer and relax." Maria tossed the empty bottles into a trash can and turned back to wipe down the counter. The crowd was pretty low-key for a Wednesday night—mostly bikers and their partners, who would drink, get drunk, and try to make it home in one piece. One thing she could say for them was that, for the most part, they followed the rules. It was the Friday night rednecks who were more trouble than they were worth. She couldn't keep them out, and they seemed too stupid to not show up where they were most obviously not wanted. When she had left her life in the Air Force nine years earlier, her only desire was to own a bar, to be her own boss. When business was good, she couldn't imagine any other life. When chaos reigned, she wondered why the hell she didn't sell and get out.

The sound of an open palm striking flesh ripped her from her thoughts, and she looked around sharply. The sight of Terri leaning heavily against the bar, her hair hiding her face, was almost enough to propel Maria over the bar. Only exercising every bit of her restraint kept her in place. She was no match for the stocky man with whom Terri lived, and there were some things in a biker's society in which she had no place.

"Where the fuck have you been?" Trey Marks demanded of Terri. "You're late." He grabbed her arm and turned her to face him.

"I had to walk here," she explained quietly. "You didn't pick me up." She didn't bother looking up at him. She knew that his face would be almost purple with rage. The pupils of his hazel eyes would be pinpoint small; they always were when he was angry.

Trey glanced at Maria. "Gimme a beer." He tightened his grip on Terri's arm. "Well, now that you're here, you can watch this bitch O'Malley. She's cheating, and you're going to help me catch her."

Terri squirmed in his grip. "Trey, I don't know anything about cards," she said reasonably.

He slapped the back of her head again with his free hand. "She don't know that. How can you be so fucking stupid?" he asked, as he took his beer from Maria. "She'll settle up the tab later," he said casually to Maria as he tugged Terri off her seat. "C'mon, get your butt in gear."

She didn't bother to struggle; she knew she'd only get hurt in the process. She allowed herself to be led through the bar, trying to ignore the stares of pity that were flashed in her direction. No one would help her, and she didn't want them to. That would only make it worse for her later. He half dragged her into the back room where everyone played cards.

It was a tight-fitting room with a round card table and, like the rest of the bar, it smelled of stale smoke and spilled alcohol. Terri sank gratefully into the chair that Trey pointed out. She had a good view of the woman who had bought her beer—which, she realized with an inner groan, was still sitting out on the counter.

Terri watched the cardplayers look at her with a mixture of confusion and welcome. John, Mike, and Gato all knew her and flashed her smiles. O'Malley's eyes danced with something Terri could not identify.

Maria tapped Terri on the shoulder and handed her the forgotten beer and an opened second bottle. Terri could see the concern on Maria's face. She shook her head slightly, letting Maria know that she shouldn't press the issue. Maria pressed her lips together, turned around, and melted back into the mix of patrons.

"Hope you all don't mind if my lucky charm sits there," Trey said as he dropped himself back into his chair. He set his beer bottle on the table, completely ignoring the cardboard coasters Maria asked everyone to use.

Gato smiled from somewhere under his mustache. "Hi, Terri." He looked at Trey. "Hope she brings you better luck than you've been having."

"She will. Now deal, before we're all as old as you," Trey

snapped back.

Terri kept her eyes on the game, like she was supposed to, but she couldn't see where O'Malley was cheating. What she did notice was that for every five sips the guys had, the woman drank only once. Terri found herself looking more and more at O'Malley's face, rather than at her hands. The shortish dark hair was a deep contrast to the light-colored eyes. Every once in a while, Terri caught a glimpse of what looked like small scars on her face, but in the over-head light she couldn't be certain.

She watched as each pot grew and someone would take the game. Piles of chips seemed to wander around the table. She could feel Trey's eyes on her from time to time, but all she could do was shrug. She couldn't see anything that O'Malley was doing that raised suspicion. When she wasn't disappointing Trey, Terri was aware of O'Malley's eyes on her. She knew it was going to be a long night.

After two hours, Terri's butt was nearly numb and she had to go to the bathroom. As she rose, she watched in disbelief as Trey pushed all of his remaining chips into the middle of the table. The other players looked at him for a second, and then at their cards. Gato folded immediately. Terri hid a smile. Maria would let him bet only so much and if he lost more, there was hell to pay. Mike followed Gato's example and let his cards fall to the table, disgust written on his face. Terri knew he hated to lose to Trey.

Trey's face took on a triumphant expression. He looked at O'Malley.

Her cool eyes regarded him for a moment, then she leaned forward. "You're bluffing," she said, and pushed a stack of chips forward. "I'll see your bet, and raise you." She shoved her remaining chips into the pot.

"Terri, gimme what you got on you," Trey demanded.

Terri opened her mouth to protest. What she had in her purse was supposed to go toward rent.

"You got yourself into this, son. You match it, not the lady." O'Malley's voice was too flat not to be dangerous.

"She's mine, she'll do what I tell her," Trey snapped back.

Terri had no choice. She pulled the money from her jeans and handed it to Gato, who handed it over to Trey.

Trey tossed the money into the pile. He grinned and laid down his cards. "Two pair." Rubbing his hands together, he started to pull the chips toward him.

"Not so fast, slick." O'Malley set down one card, the jack of spades, followed by a nine, then another jack, and a second nine, and finally one more jack. "Now, where I come from, mine is bigger than yours." She reached out, grabbed the stack of cash, and quickly counted it. "And you're still short. I raised you a grand, and there's only five hundred here. What else you got?"

"I ain't putting up my bike," Trey whined.

O'Malley shrugged. "I didn't make the rules to the game, that was you. You said all bets paid at the end of the night."

"One more game to give me a chance to pull even," Trey suggested.

O'Malley shook her head. "Not with the way you play. Besides, you got nothing to bet since you won't put up the bike." O'Malley pushed out of her chair. "You got 'til tomorrow to come up with the other five hundred."

Trey shook his head. "I gotta pay rent. I can't come up with five by tomorrow."

O'Malley looked at Terri and saw that she was close to tears. She turned her attention back to Trey, who looked like a little kid playing biker. "Looks like she earned rent and you lost it." O'Malley stepped away from the table.

"One punch, winner take all," Trey said loudly.

"You got nothing left to bet," O'Malley reminded him.

"I got her." Trey pointed at Terri. "Or are you just some chicken-shit, yellow bitch?" he taunted.

O'Malley knew he was trying to push her buttons. She couldn't believe he would bet his girlfriend. A part of her wanted to just call it even, but another part of her knew that if she backed down, her credibility was shot. She had spent most of the previous eight hours sizing him up. Mentally she calculated how much he'd had to drink and decided that it was worth the risk. The worst that could happen was that she would lose and wake up with a hell of a headache in the morning. When it came to biker society, there was no disgrace in accepting a challenge and losing. It was the running with your tail between your legs that usually got you into trouble.

John, Mike, and Gato looked at Trey and O'Malley like they had both lost their minds. A grim look on his face, Mike slipped out of the room and went running to Maria.

Terri sat openmouthed at the bet, obviously stunned.

O'Malley looked at her and noted, not for the first time, the marks on her arm. They looked suspiciously like the imprint of a hand. Looking back at Trey's sneering face, she made her decision. "Get your ass outside, son. One punch, winner takes all."

Word didn't take long to travel around the bar. By the time the duo made it outside past the edge of the parking lot, there was a crowd following. As O'Malley peeled off her leather vest, Maria stepped in front of her.

"*Chica,* do you really know what you're doing?" she asked in a low tone. O'Malley met her eyes and nodded just once. "Okay. Just so you know, if you go down in one, the guys won't let him get in any more shots. He's done that before."

"Has he ever lost?" O'Malley asked casually as she handed over the vest.

"No," Maria answered grimly.

O'Malley's smile was almost frightening in its intensity. "Good. I get to be the first."

Maria folded the vest over her arm and walked back to Gato. He wrapped his arm around her shoulders as O'Malley and Trey stepped up to face each other. Terri stood next to Mike and watched through half-closed eyes.

Trey grinned as he popped the knuckles of both hands. "You ready to hurt like hell?"

O'Malley stood in front of him, totally relaxed. "Back out or punch me, but shut up." She watched his grin fade and knew instinctively when he was going to throw the punch by his squint. O'Malley took the blow on the side of her head, just under her left ear. She let her head snap to the side, let the force of the punch flow through her rather than trying to resist it. Her knees wanted to give out as her world started to spin, but she kept her feet. After a moment, she straightened.

As she looked at him, Trey's face lost its gloating. For just an instant, O'Malley thought she saw fear in his eyes. She had no doubt that he'd never seen anyone still standing after he'd hit them. She let him stew in his fear for a long moment before her fist moved. She did not squint, tense, or otherwise telegraph her blow. She connected full force on the point of Trey's chin. She knew Trey's mistake was relying on the strength of his arm; she'd used the force of her entire body. The only way she even knew that she had moved was the pain that flared in her fist.

* ~ * ~ * ~ *

Terri watched Trey as his eyes rolled back; he blinked once, his eyelids closed, and then he collapsed into the dirt. His head bounced once on the hard ground, and he lay still. Mike gave a low whistle, while others watched with a mixture of disbelief and outright joy. Terri's stomach sank to her ankles. She was free of Trey, but she didn't know O'Malley from Adam.

She started toward Trey, but Mike stopped her with a gentle hand on her shoulder. "He played the game, Ter, and he lost. There's nothing you can do about it. Even if you wanted to go back to him, you couldn't," he explained. "You better go with Maria for now. Everything will get sorted out in a little bit."

Terri let herself be guided toward Maria and Gato. A couple of bikers checked to make sure Trey was still breathing, then struggled to pick him up. She knew someone would make sure he lived through the night.

Maria took her arm and led her back into the bar. "You okay?" Maria asked as Gato looked over her shoulder.

"What just happened?" Terri asked through her daze.

O'Malley leaned against the bar next to Terri. "I think I just broke my hand on his face," she groaned. "Hey, Maria, you think I could get some ice for my hand, my face, and my drink?"

"Well, O'Malley, I see your hand and your face, but I sure don't see your drink," the bar owner teased.

"I knew I forgot to do something. How 'bout an Irish whiskey and Coke, tall glass, and whatever Terri's drinking. She looks like she needs one," O'Malley said as she sank down onto the stool.

"You got it, but only one. You took one hell of a shot out there. I'd hate for you to survive that and die 'cause I gave you too much to drink." Maria smiled to take the sting out of her words.

"I've got a thick Irish skull and I've been hit harder." O'Malley suddenly sounded quite somber. "But not by much," she admitted.

Maria whipped two bar towels from their cubbyhole, filled them with ice, tied them off with thick rubber bands, and handed them to O'Malley, who set one ice-filled towel on her right hand and pressed the other against the side of her head. Maria stifled a laugh as Gato expressed his merriment.

"Hey, O'Malley, don't ever hit me okay?" he managed as Maria glared at him.

"Just don't piss me off, Gato, and all will be fine," O'Malley answered. She shifted her gaze to Maria, watching as she placed the requested drink in front of her. A straw floated in the glass and with both of her hands occupied, O'Malley finally had to laugh at her predicament. She closed her eyes.

"You okay, O'Malley?" Terri's voice was soft with shock.

"Yeah. Just wondering what I've gotten myself into, that's all. You okay?"

"Yeah. I was just thinking the same thing, actually."

Maria cut in. "Technically, Trey's the one who got you both into this. You want a beer, Terri, or something stronger?"

"Just a beer. Anything stronger might kill me," she admitted slowly. "Or give me enough courage to kill that son of a bitch."

"Nah, don't kill him. Just take a good look at him after he wakes up. With that headache, I'm sure he's gonna wish he was dead." Maria chuckled. "It's gonna quiet down here quick enough, so I'll drive you two wherever in O'Malley's truck, and Gato will follow us." She held up a hand to forestall any arguments. "Neither of you can drive safely. You have a dented skull, O'Malley, and Terri, you just worked how many hours and walked the five miles here? I'm betting you're wiped out."

"Yeah," Terri admitted.

"Besides, this is a good excuse for me to leave early and have some extra time with my wild man." Maria leered at Gato.

"C'mon, Maria. Too much info," O'Malley groaned.

"Too much info, my ass. You stayed at my place how long after you got out? If I remember, her name was...Adrian?"

"Her name was Alice. Okay, I get the message." O'Malley relented and tried to smile. The smile stopped short. "Ouch."

"You big baby."

Even in her stunned state, Terri had to laugh, but she did so softly. They finished their drinks, and then the group slipped out of the bar. Terri noticed the stares; they were hard to miss. She could see the questions as if they had been written on paper: who was this O'Malley and what was Terri going to do now? *Funny, I'm having those same questions. Go figure,* her brain piped up in a tone dripping with sarcasm. She silently followed the group out to the truck.

"Maria, you know where Terri here lives?" O'Malley asked as she eased into the truck.

"Yeah. Why?"

"We stop there first, get her stuff, and then hit my place. I do not want to have to go there after he wakes up. I don't like getting hit in the head that much."

Maria chuckled and nodded. She waited until Gato came over with the car and told him of the change in plans. He agreed, and they set off. Maria drove, with Terri in the middle and O'Malley resting against the passenger door.

"How much stuff you got, *chica*?" Maria asked to have some noise during the trip.

"Not much, just my clothes and some small things. Trey's not real big on collecting stuff, you know," Terri answered quietly. She watched the road signs as they got closer to the rental house that she had called home for the past thirteen months. It wasn't much, but it was dry and the roach population was under control. She'd seen worse.

* ~ * ~ * ~ *

It didn't take Terri long to pack her things into the back of O'Malley's truck. She hadn't been lying when she said she didn't have much. They loaded three baskets of clothes and two boxes of books and personal stuff.

O'Malley looked around. She'd seen homeless people who had more personal belongings. *No one should have to live like this.* In a little under half an hour, the group was back on the road and driving to O'Malley's.

O'Malley was sulking, staring out the window and dealing with the pain in her hand and face when she felt the smaller woman's head lean against her shoulder. She looked over without moving her shoulder much. Terri was dead to the world. For a second, she let herself enjoy the odd moment. She caught sight of Maria's sidelong glance.

"Now that's cute. Brings back some old memories," Maria said quietly.

"Yeah, it does. Thanks for your help tonight." O'Malley ignored Maria's sigh and changed the subject. "Just accept the thank you and let it go, Maria."

"I will not just let it go," Maria hissed. "I know you haven't. Otherwise you wouldn't be here in the middle of all of this."

"Maria, *cariña*, what's done is done. You know why I'm here."

O'Malley sounded tired.

"Yeah, I do. I can still be mad," Maria said.

"I'm mad, too, but I can't afford to show it. I'm too close to finishing this."

"But will it make a difference?"

"I don't know, but the payback will more than make up for the 'suck it up and drive on' we've had to do."

"Suck it up and drive on," Maria echoed. "God, I haven't heard that in a long time."

"I haven't said it in a long time," O'Malley said. "Just pull up on the lawn. We'll get her stuff into the house and just pile it somewhere."

Maria pulled into the driveway and rolled the truck onto the cut grass in front of the door. "How's that for service?"

"You are the best, Maria. You get the door, I'll get Sleepy here into the house."

O'Malley managed to rouse Terri enough to get her inside and guide her into the bedroom. She pulled off Terri's shoes and socks, then covered her with the blanket. That done, she returned to the truck and helped Gato and Maria unload Terri's things into the living room. Gato went out to wait in the car.

"You know they're gonna expect you to sleep with her. You own her now," Maria pointed out.

"Yeah, I know, but I'll figure it out later. It'll work out. Right now, all I want is some aspirin and sleep. Now get out of here and go play with your wild man," she teased. The two friends shared a hug at the door, and O'Malley watched until their taillights could no longer be seen before she closed the door and quietly turned the dead bolt. "Now what, genius?" she asked herself.

~~*~*

Callan's eyes opened automatically when the door to her room opened. She didn't have to look at the clock on the wall. She knew it would be her favorite nurse. She could set her watch by the woman. She turned her head and smiled as the Air Force officer closed the door and walked to the side of the bed.

"Bugs or Marvin?" Lieutenant Rivers asked as she reached for the blood pressure cuff.

"Oh please. Marvin, of course." Callan didn't know why their little game gave her so much pleasure, but it did. She endured the check of her vitals

and braced herself for the pain of movement that she knew would be coming.

"You are such an odd duck. Marvin." She shook her head. "I like his dog, though." The lieutenant smiled and slid the stethoscope from her neck. "You ready for this?"

Callan gripped the bed rail with her good hand and nodded. "Let's hit it."

With help, she sat forward, sucking in a hard breath around the pain. Once she was settled, Lieutenant Rivers listened to her lungs, stethoscope pressed against Callan's back. Callan breathed when ordered. She felt the sweat popping up on her forehead and neck from the effort. When it was over, the nurse helped her back into a lying position.

Lieutenant Rivers resettled her pillow under her head. "Now your front." Her voice was even and sure. She pulled the ties of the hospital gown open and freed the Velcro ends of the rib wrap. She looked first at the incisions to make sure they showed no signs of infection, then ran her eyes over the mending ribs.

"Things are looking good. The respiratory tech told me you're giving her a hard time. You tin-canned a lung, Sergeant; let her do her job to fix it. That means breathing exercises. It's a pain in the ass, I know, but if you want to meet your PT standards and stay Army, then you do what she says. I know you don't think so, but you're progressing well." She listened to Callan's lungs, and then rewrapped her ribs. Her fingers were shaking as she tied the gown back together.

"You're looking tired, LT," Callan said.

"Been a long day, O'Malley," Rivers answered as she scribbled notes in Callan's chart.

"More guys coming in?"

She nodded. "Yeah. War sucks, you know?"

"Tell me about it." Callan let the sarcasm leak through.

Lieutenant Rivers looked up from her chart. "I didn't mean it like that, Callan."

Callan managed to keep the smile off her face. "I know you didn't, Mabel."

"Mabel?" The lieutenant let the chart fall back into its tray.

"Well, I don't know your first name," Callan pointed out.

The nurse laughed. When she'd caught her breath, she looked at Callan. "It's Ellen."

"Nice to meet you, Ellen." O'Malley couldn't hide the warmth in her voice. "If it wasn't for you doing this job, some of us wouldn't be getting back home. So don't go thinking that because you're not in the sand, you're not important."

"*Thank you for saying so.*" *She looked at the sergeant.* "*The stitches in your face, arms, and legs will be coming out soon.*"

"*There is a God. They itch like crazy. When do I get out of here?*" *Callan wormed around in the bed, mindful of her nearly useless arm.*

Ellen laughed again. "*It's going to be a while. Let's make sure you can salute with that arm before you go.*"

Callan groaned. "*Well, where's the fun in that?*" *she asked in a teasing tone.* "*When do I get to move around? I don't think I've been this still in years.*"

"*You must have been a fun kid. I feel sorry for your parents,*" *Ellen said wryly.* "*You feel up to sitting in a chair tomorrow?*"

"*Hell, how about today?*"

"*Baby steps, Sergeant. Your body went through a blender. It got you back home, now you have to be good to it to say 'thank you, nice body.'*"

"*Yes, ma'am,*" *Callan managed. She was acutely aware of the lieutenant's choice of words, and a small glow started in her chest.* "*So, what's on the agenda for the rest of the day, ma'am?*"

"*Well, you get to lie here and heal, and I get to go and spread cheer and joy for another five hours. I'll check back on you later in the day. You want the TV on?*"

Callan turned her head to the window at the suggestion. "*No, ma'am, thank you. I don't think I can watch any more. It's full of what I should be out there doing.*"

"*Sergeant, look at me,*" *Ellen said, and watched her patient remain stubbornly in position.* "*Callan.*" *Pale blue eyes turned to her.* "*You and your Army dogs on the ground are heroes to a lot of us. You got hit, Callan, there's no disgrace in that. I talked to Barnes yesterday. He told me you took that bullet dragging him out of the combat zone, two and a half miles. With all the blood you were losing and the shell fragments in your legs, I don't know how you did it, but you did. You might think you are superhuman, but your body knows you aren't. It gave out because of the damage; it had nothing to do with anything else.*"

"*You a shrink, too?*" *Callan asked. Part of her knew the lieutenant's words were true, but part of her felt like a failure.*

Ellen shook her head. "*Nope, just a good judge of character. You're a good soldier, Sergeant O'Malley. If you weren't, you would be dead and so would your men. But if you want to talk to a shrink, I can arrange it.*"

Callan shook her head. "*No, ma'am. I'll deal with this on my own. But thanks for the offer.*"

There was an edge in her voice that let Ellen know that the subject was closed. "Okay, your call, O'Malley. I'll check on you later."

O'Malley opened her eyes and looked at the clock on the night-stand. The numbers stared back at her. *Four a.m.* She sighed, rolled over, and plumped her pillow. She knew sleep would be long in coming; it always was when her brain decided to take a trip down memory lane. She sighed again in the dark. *Damn, I miss you, Nurse.*

She lay in bed for the next half hour, watching the minutes tick by with agonizing slowness. Finally she got up and, feeling the pain from the night's activities, stumbled into the kitchen and fixed herself an ice pack and rummaged around for aspirin. She swallowed three pills dry and gingerly sat on the couch. Leaning her head back, she watched the early morning dark turn into sunrise.

Chapter 2

With a sigh, Terri slowly hung up the telephone. Looking around the strip club, she felt a wave of helplessness. She found herself in a situation for which she was not prepared, and for the first time in a long time, she was at a loss as to what to do. She leaned her head against the wall and closed her eyes. An ironic smile crossed her lips as she recalled waking up that morning. She'd been confused to find herself in an unfamiliar bed. Her confusion quickly changed to something close to fear when the previous night came rushing back. Fear changed to anger at Trey for betting her. She still wasn't sure she was angry that he'd lost. *Well, at least you won't get your ass kicked tonight,* her brain muttered.

She opened her eyes and checked the time. Her break was over, and she was expected to push the turmoil of her personal life aside and sling drinks to overgrown boys watching nearly naked women dance. Terri sighed again and pushed away from the wall. She did not miss two of Trey's friends eyeing her from a distance. She couldn't tell if their attention was a good thing or a bad thing. Terri returned to the bar and picked up her drink tray, then made the circuit of her tables and served drinks for the next four hours.

She was grateful for the hard bench in the women's dressing room. Her feet hurt, she was tired, and her stomach growled loudly. Terri sighed out her relief when she pulled off the none-too-comfortable shoes that Hank required her to wear. They were supposed to be sexy, but to her, they were just instruments of torture. Her fantasy of slowly killing Hank by making him hike miles on end in those same shoes was interrupted when two of the strippers came into the room.

"One of these days I'm so going to rip his head off," Candace fumed, then she stopped short when she saw her friend recovering on the bench. "Hey, Terri, want to join in on some male bashing?"

She flashed a tired smile as she tossed her bag across the room.

Terri hoped there was nothing breakable in the bag. "I'm too tired to male bash today. Pathetic, huh?" she answered with a groan.

"Don't tell me Morgan called in again today?" Rhea asked as she let the dressing room door close. She walked over to the mirrors and pulled out a chair.

Terri nodded. "Wonder how she manages that all the time." Her tone implied she already knew the answer. "I wouldn't mind so much, except her regulars don't tip for shit if she's not the one flashing her tits at them."

Candace couldn't keep the look of disgust off her face. "And they're fake. It's not even a good job. I guess you're just having a rotten week all the way around."

"We heard what Trey did," Rhea said quietly.

"I figured as much. Hank kept looking at me like it was my fault somehow. Hell, all I did was walk to the bar and turn over my rent money."

"So, how's O'Malley?" Candace asked as she pulled her dance costume out of her bag and started rummaging for her makeup.

Terri shrugged. "I dunno. She was gone when I got up this morning. I guess I'll find out what I'm in for soon enough."

Rhea checked her watch and settled in to relax. She had time. "You okay? I mean, she's got a killer rep with women."

"You know, I've done a lot of things in my life, but being with a woman isn't one of them," Candace said as she rubbed cleanser on her face with a washcloth. "That said, I have got to admit, if O'Malley was doing the teaching, I would be willing to learn."

"You and half the women in town, though most of 'em wouldn't be caught dead admitting it." Rhea chuckled as she lit a cigarette.

"Don't smoke that in here. Jesus, Hank will have a fit, and then the rest of us will pay all night long for it," Candace complained. Rhea smiled and deliberately blew out three almost perfect smoke rings. "Bitch."

"I gotta get my sick kicks somewhere." Rhea turned her attention back to Terri. "I hear O'Malley's okay. She had a girlfriend a couple of years ago, before she got sent up. They used to come to the club all the time. I never saw the girlfriend with a mark on her. Well, no bruises, anyway." She leered. "And damn, did her woman always look like she had a smile."

"C'mon, you're making her sound perfect," Candace carped as

she wiped the white foam off her face. "She hangs out with Spyder's little gang of overgrown delinquents, and where did she used to go disappearing to all the time? She doesn't have a job that we know about, so where does her money come from?"

Rhea's voice took on a warning edge. "Candy girl, you have got to learn to stop with the questions sometimes. You never know who might be listening."

"All I'm saying is that Terri should be careful. If you ever need anything, you know how to get hold of either one of us." Candace's reflection in the mirror looked at Terri. She held Terri's gaze until the waitress nodded.

"Believe me, after all this shit with Trey, I plan on being way more careful. And if I get in a bind and I need help, I'll get hold of you. But this is my problem, and I think I have to deal with it. I wouldn't want to get you involved in the bad side of anything, you know?" Terri slumped lower.

"Hey, what are you doing tonight?" Rhea asked suddenly.

"I was just going to go back to O'Malley's," Terri said. "I'll grab something to eat first and then head over."

"You want to go out after we're done? We haven't done that in ages. I miss having a designated driver."

Terri laughed. "You only want me to come along 'cause you lost your license."

"She so has your number." Candace grinned. "She's right though, Terri. You should come with us."

"I think I'm gonna have to pass this time. Gotta figure out O'Malley before I start breaking rules I don't know about. You know how bikers can be." The tone in her voice was far more revealing than she'd intended.

* ~ * ~ * ~ *

O'Malley chalked the cue and looked at the layout of the balls on the table. A quick glance at Maria's smirking expression, and she knew she was done for. She didn't have one good shot. Hell, she didn't even have a bad shot. To top it off, her hand was sore as hell and the side of her head occasionally gave her a sharp reminder of its recent abuse. She groaned and set the cue on the table, then dug into her jeans pocket, pulled out a bill, and handed it to the bar owner. O'Malley picked up her beer bottle as she sat down. She watched with amusement as Maria tucked the money into her bra.

"That'll teach you to play with me." Maria grinned and took a sip of her margarita.

"Yeah, but every time I lose I get to watch you play with your tits." O'Malley laughed and took a drink of her beer. "You remember the time you forgot you weren't wearing a bra?"

"That is so not funny, O'Malley," Maria answered with a small smile. "I lost fifty bucks that night."

O'Malley shook her head. "Actually, she found it and slipped it into your purse."

There was a momentary softness to O'Malley's eyes. "You should remember her more often." Maria's voice was gentle.

"Just a little longer and I'll have all the time in the world to remember." O'Malley become somber and her eyes took on their usual hard edge.

"You need to find someone. I don't mean one of your little side trips, either." Maria's glare cut off O'Malley's attempted reply. "I know all about those. You need someone you can love, Callan."

"I had someone," O'Malley said bitterly. "I prefer alone right now."

"You call being with those women being alone?"

"I call it physical release. Each one of them knew it was just a fuck or two, and then I was gone or they were. I'm not a total asshole. I was honest."

Maria shook her head. "God, you worry me sometimes."

"Maria, you've been a friend for a very long time and I don't want you to take this the wrong way, but stay out of what I need or don't need. I can't have the life I had before; it's way too late for that. And I really, really don't want to rehash it over and over." She covered Maria's hand with one of her own. "I know you worry about me, and I love you for it, but it's wasted emotion and energy."

"So you're just going to continue as you are? Do you really think that's the life she'd want for you? Don't you think she would have wanted you to find someone else?"

O'Malley sighed. "I know she would have wanted that. But this is more about what I want. I want her, only I can't have her, can I? I didn't get a say-so in that. Hell, I wasn't even home. I was off doing what I was expected to do, and it cost me everything. This time around, Maria, I call the shots and what I want goes. No exceptions and no discussion." O'Malley stopped abruptly as her eyes caught a reflection in the mirror.

She could see the livid bruise on Trey's face as he glared hard at the back of her head and detoured to the bar. She let out a relieved breath. The last thing she wanted was a fight in Maria's bar. O'Malley quickly drained her bottle of beer.

"What do you say we blow this joint and get drunk?" Maria offered with a smile.

"You're just trying to finally get me into your bed," O'Malley teased. They had been friends for a very long time and the teasing was just a natural occurrence between the two.

"You've been in my bed, O'Malley," Maria reminded her with a grin.

"Doesn't count. We were asleep," O'Malley countered.

"It does count. You were naked."

"Was not. I had my socks on."

"You were so drunk, how would you know?" Maria reminded her with an evil grin.

O'Malley's smile fell. "Okay, it does count. Come on. I'll buy the Scotch."

Maria slid out of the booth and batted her eyes. "Tequila."

"I hate tequila," O'Malley reminded her friend as they started out of the room.

"I know, that's why we're drinking it. It's the only thing I can outdrink you with."

O'Malley chuckled as they turned the corner into the main area of the bar. Her eyes quickly scanned the area. There were only six others present. She waited as Maria headed to the office to grab her purse. She could feel Trey's eyes boring into her back and found herself wishing that he would just say something and get it over with. She didn't have to wait long.

"You and Maria looked real tight back there." He finished his drink in one gulp and set the shot glass down on the bar. He did not look at O'Malley. His jaw tightened when she didn't reply. "I want my bitch back."

O'Malley forced herself to sound more casual than she felt. "You bet her, you lost her. Live with it."

"You didn't hear me right. I want her back. I'm not asking, I'm telling you." He turned to face the woman who had disgraced him.

"I really don't give a shit what you want. She belongs to me now." O'Malley turned her head away in dismissal. She listened as he ordered another shot, then caught sight of Maria closing the office door and sighed mentally.

Maria quickly joined her friend at the bar. "You ready to go?" she asked, sneaking a wary glance at Trey.

"Yeah." O'Malley turned to leave and found her way blocked by Trey's leg. "Move," she warned.

"Or what? You going to cheap shot me again?" The accusation could be a dangerous one if he could get any other bikers to believe it. He wasn't prepared for O'Malley's reaction.

She laughed out loud, and for a second neither Maria nor Trey could decide if she was going to laugh all night. She finally had to lean against the bar for support. Her arms held her up, and she cracked up again as she looked at him.

"You are so full of shit," she managed. "You bet her in front of how many people? You lost with witnesses, and you had the first shot. That's the best laugh I've had in years." She didn't blink when he stood up from his stool and leaned in close.

"Are you laughing at me?" His breath smelled of beer and stale pot.

O'Malley did not lose her smile. "You couldn't tell?" she asked with an evil gleam. "Do yourself a favor and chalk this one up to experience. Let it go."

"Or what? You gonna pull your war hero shit on me?" he sneered. Even in the dim light of the bar, he didn't miss her eyes turning arctic blue. "This ain't over."

"Come on, O'Malley. Let's go." Maria tugged on her friend's sleeve. The arm hardly moved.

"That's right, hero, let a woman save you," Trey gloated.

O'Malley lifted her eyes to meet his gaze. "I think I'll take that advice," she said in a bright tone, throwing him off balance. Maria in tow, she pushed past him, her arm around Maria's neck in a friendly embrace. They could both hear the snickers that came from the few nearby drinkers. O'Malley was sure that Trey could hear them as well. *Some people never learn.*

"You certainly like to live dangerously," Maria said in a low voice as they walked toward the door.

"Yeah, well, I do like to be all I can be. And my day wouldn't be complete without pissing someone off," O'Malley shot back.

*~ * ~ * ~ *

Terri shifted restlessly on the couch as she surfed the channels on TV. She wondered at the wisdom of paying for every station known to man when it seemed there was still nothing on that was any good. She turned off the TV and paced the living room. Her eyes stole to the clock. *Midnight, and still no sign of O'Malley.* She didn't know whether to be worried or relieved. The glare of headlights on the wall drew her attention.

She looked out the window and recognized Maria's car, with Gato in the driver's seat. She watched for a moment as Maria opened the rear passenger door and tugged O'Malley from the seat. They both weaved across the lawn on unsteady legs. Terri moved quickly and pulled the front door open as the two women tried to navigate the three steps.

O'Malley looked up at Terri. "She's drunker," she said as her foot slipped off the step. Only Maria's arm around her waist kept her from falling.

"Liar." There was a slight slur in Maria's voice.

Terri chuckled as she watched them finally manage the last step. She stepped back and opened the door wide so that the women could stumble into the house. When they reached the couch, they fell onto the cushions. They sat there for a while catching their breath.

"I take it you two had a good time," Terri teased as she closed the door.

"Oh yeah. I got to drink her under the table." Maria cackled with drunken glee. "She's gonna hate me in the morning."

"I hate you now," O'Malley shot back with a grin. "My whole world is spinning."

Terri looked down at O'Malley. "Um, try opening your eyes. It might help."

O'Malley slowly opened both eyes. "Oh, that's better." Her face took on a green hue. "Maria, see you tomorrow," she said quickly, and propelled herself off the couch and into her bedroom. A moment later, Terri heard the bathroom door slam.

"She'll just never learn: I can't lose with tequila." Maria chuckled and then took a deep breath. "See you later, Terri." She tried to move off the couch twice before looking at Terri. "I can't get off this damn thing. Help."

Terri didn't hold back her laughter as she reached down and

pulled Maria off the couch. She looped one of Maria's arms over her shoulder and helped her to the front door, struggled for a moment with the knob, and finally opened the door. Together they made their way down the steps and to the car.

Gato already had the passenger door open. "Thanks, Terri. I was gonna come get her in a minute." He didn't hide the amusement in his voice.

"No problem, Gato. Do they do this often?" She helped Maria into the seat and buckled her up.

"Only when they rehash their glory days. Sometimes I don't know if I believe all those stories. No one is that wild," he answered. "But then again, we are talking about Maria and O'Malley," he added. "Keep an eye on O'Malley, she had a lot of tequila."

"Most of which she's yacking up as we speak. I'll make sure she lives," Terri promised.

Gato laughed as he got into the car and started the engine. Terri waited until she was sure he wasn't weaving down the road, then made her way back into the house. She locked the front door and turned off most of the lights in the house before venturing into O'Malley's room.

O'Malley was spread out on the bed with one boot still on her foot. Her shirt was tossed by the side of the bed, and a pillow covered her face. She moaned from under the pillow and, after a second, shot off the bed. With one shod foot, she stumbled awkwardly into the bathroom and slammed the door.

"This is going to be a long night," Terri said.

* ~ * ~ * ~ *

Maria lifted her head at the soft tap on the open door of her office. Her eyes lit on O'Malley, who looked better than either of them had a right to. Maria's headache had finally gone away only an hour before. She let her pencil fall to the desk as she leaned back in her creaky chair and motioned for her friend to come in.

"What's up?" O'Malley asked as she pushed away from the door frame.

"O'Malley, sit down," Maria said softly. "Normally I wouldn't say anything, but you're a friend of mine and I like Terri, so I have to say something. Trey's been running his mouth."

O'Malley lifted an eyebrow. "That's nothing new. He's always running his mouth."

"Well, this time he's making really dangerous noise."

O'Malley sighed. "Maria, I am way too hungover to play word games. Is there a point to this?"

"You don't look hungover," Maria complained. "Last night he was saying that she is a cop."

O'Malley's confusion showed on her face. "She, who?"

"Terri," she answered, then took a sip of her tea. "Or you. He wasn't real clear on the definition of 'she.' Of course, I hear he was also skunk drunk."

"So, he's basing one of us being a cop on what?"

"You want me to translate or his version?" Maria worried about giving O'Malley the choice.

"You translate. He uses really small words and I like a challenge."

"Well, based on his observations of your usual conquests and your, um, systematic marking of said conquests, Terri isn't showing your typical brand. In his book, that's enough to claim that one of you must be a cop."

O'Malley yawned and instantly appeared to regret it. "What look?"

Maria rolled her eyes. "The freshly 'oh my God I'm satisfied' fucked look. You really are out of it."

"Your fault," O'Malley accused. "I'm never drinking tequila with you again." She groaned. "As far as eliciting that look goes, I prefer willing partners."

"As we used to say in the Air Force, that is not the prevailing attitude."

"We used to have a saying in the Army, too: fuck them."

"Normally I would agree with you, but this isn't just about you. Now you have Terri. If anyone thinks the garbage coming out of his mouth is true, she's a dead woman." Maria's expression was laced with worry.

O'Malley let out a slow breath. "So, basically, she's my responsibility and I've got to cover her and me." Maria nodded. "I do not need this shit," O'Malley grumbled. "Who ever heard of betting your girlfriend?"

"No one ever claimed these guys were bright."

"Well, I can't give her back. Him being a fuckhead aside, it would make me look like I couldn't handle her...."

Maria leaned forward in her chair. "I have an idea, which you probably won't like, but it's worth thinking about." Half-afraid of O'Malley's reaction, she watched O'Malley arch her eyebrows, a sure sign that her patience was beginning to wane. "Talk to Terri. She might not be willing to jump into your bed, but she might be willing to make it look that way. If for no other reason than to embarrass him."

"Okay, I'll bite. Embarrass him how?"

"He treated her like hell and she never looked satisfied, if you know what I mean. If she starts walking around now like she's having a good time, believe me, the others will notice and give him an earful."

"You figure she'll go for it?"

Maria shrugged. "I don't know. You'll have to talk to her."

"I think I can do that. You want her to know where I heard all of this?"

"Might as well. Everyone knows I hear all the gossip and rumors going around." Maria watched O'Malley stand, stretch a little, and groan. "Hey, O'Malley, watch your six, okay?"

"Always." O'Malley nodded once and turned to leave.

Chapter 3

Terri pushed open the exit door and stepped into the sunlight, squinting against the brightness. The club owners kept the place dark except for the areas around the stage. She looked around before she caught sight of O'Malley and one of the dancers talking next to O'Malley's truck. Curious as to why the biker would want to call her for lunch, Terri walked over and joined the twosome. She was struck again by O'Malley's odd combination of dark hair and pale blue eyes. For a second, she faltered, and just as quickly recovered. "Hey, O'Malley." She smiled.

O'Malley just looked at Terri for a moment, realizing that in the light of day, the woman in front of her was very desirable. She had spent the previous two days getting things ready for a road trip, which hadn't left her much time to spend with Terri.

"Hey, Terri." O'Malley grinned. "Thanks for the invite, Donna, but as you can see, my lunch date is here."

The dancer glanced at the cocktail waitress and quickly dismissed her as competition. "Oh yeah. I heard about that thing with Trey."

O'Malley opened the passenger door for Terri. "Yeah, well, you shouldn't bet what you don't want to lose. His loss, my gain." She smiled at Terri as she got into the truck and buckled up. O'Malley closed the door without looking back at the dancer. "See ya around, Donna," she called over her shoulder. She walked around to her door, opened it, and climbed in.

Terri watched the dancer mull over O'Malley's comment. Donna might have the body parts for dancing, but sometimes she was a little slow on the uptake. Terri caught herself feeling a little sorry for her. The rumble of the truck engine catching distracted her.

"So what do you want for lunch?" O'Malley asked as she pulled the truck out of the parking lot. She noticed the look of surprise on Terri's face. "One thing you should know is that I'm not a lot like that fuckhead you were with." She concentrated on pulling into traffic. "Most of the time, I'll give you a choice."

"But?" Terri's voice was tight.

"But sometimes I'm an asshole and you don't get a choice," she admitted. "We both know what kind of life we're living. I know it's not your choice and not even really my choice, but like it or not, you now belong to me." The truck pulled to a stop at a traffic light.

Terri thought about the ramifications of the statement. "I'd like lunch at Gus's," she answered finally. "And I have to be at my probie by two."

O'Malley checked the dashboard clock. "I can manage that." She didn't bother asking what Terri had done to get probation. "Most of the time, I can give you a ride to work or you can use the truck," O'Malley said as she moved with traffic. Her stomach growled.

"You'd trust me enough to loan me your truck?" Disbelief edged into Terri's voice.

O'Malley chuckled. "A truck is just that. Touch my bike, though, and I'll hunt you down."

Terri managed a smile. "Somehow I expected that answer." Terri fell silent, her brain trying to catch up with the last two days. She had never really thought the stories about some bikers selling their women off like property were true. She figured the stories were something akin to children's tales about the bogeyman: they might not be real, but then again, you couldn't take too many chances. *Now I know better.*

O'Malley pulled into Gus's parking lot. She killed the engine and opened her door. "C'mon." She stepped out of the truck and let the door close softly as she looked around. She waited for Terri at the bed of the truck, her eyes lingering over Terri's figure.

Terri looked up just in time to see O'Malley's expression—an open look of hunger. It made her feel like something between a deer in the headlights and the luncheon special. A shiver ran down Terri's back. She was surprised when the biker abruptly turned and headed for the front door of the hole-in-the-wall diner. Terri followed, confused. The little voice in her head told her to get used to the feeling.

She followed O'Malley into the diner and they found an empty booth near the back, away from most of the lunch crowd. They ordered coffee as they settled in, and in moments, each woman had a steaming cup. Without having to bother with a menu, O'Malley ordered breakfast. Terri ordered after a quick scan of the grimy, plastic coated pages. The waitress grunted and popped her gum as she walked away.

"So, what's the story with you and Trey?"

Terri shrugged. "I was drifting and he gave me a ride. I guess staying with him was better than being alone. Sort of safer," she answered after a moment. "He was okay at first, but when he hooked up with Spyder, he just got mean."

"Apparently." O'Malley took a sip of coffee and instantly her face relaxed. "And that's the life you want?"

"Listen, O'Malley, what I want won't happen, so I don't go lying to myself about it. Life sucks, and sometimes you have to take whatever you can get. Yeah, Trey is an asshole and he talks a lot with his fists, but I know guys who are way worse. I've seen them." Terri's voice edged toward anger and her eyes flashed at O'Malley. "Besides, I don't know you. You could be a hell of a lot worse."

O'Malley nodded. "Yeah, I could be. But then, I'm not the one running around saying you might be a cop." Terri's face paled at the accusation. "Keep in mind that if I were worse than the others, I would be treating you like a prize bitch and taking anything I want." The sentence hung in the air.

"Who said I was a cop?" Terri asked, her voice quavering.

"Maria heard it going around. Trey was running his mouth last night."

Terri opened her mouth to ask a question and closed it quickly as the waitress returned with a pot of coffee to refill their cups. She waited until the woman walked away. Spyder could have people anywhere, as she had learned in the past.

"I know he's pissed, but that kind of rumor could get me killed." She looked at O'Malley. "What the hell is he thinking?"

O'Malley shrugged. "He's trying to get back at both of us. I made him look bad by beating him at cards and one punch. You didn't bitch enough about me taking you away." She leaned back in the booth. "According to him, you are obviously not sharing my bed, so one of us must be a cop. I just did eighteen months in county for Spyder, so they'll think it's you."

"Great." Terri sighed and let her head rest in her hands. "I'm fucked. They'll kill me. Nice knowing you, O'Malley."

O'Malley turned to see the waitress returning with their order. She pushed her coffee cup aside to make room for breakfast. The waitress settled their plates on the table, and followed them with ketchup and steak sauce. Not bothering to ask if they needed anything else, she left.

O'Malley grabbed her knife and cut into her steak. "What if I said there's a way to deflect all that bullshit away from you and make him look like a fool?" she asked as she brought a piece of steak to her mouth.

"I'd say I have to hear what it is before I said yes or no." Terri pushed her scrambled eggs around the plate.

"Okay, now just hear me out before you scream at me. It's no secret that I prefer women." Terri nodded slowly. "What I'm suggesting is that we make it look like you're between my sheets and enjoying it." O'Malley bit down on her steak and almost moaned. Gus's might look like a dive, but they made a good breakfast steak.

Terri stopped short at O'Malley's suggestion. "We do that and he's going to be way pissed, you know that, don't you? I've seen him like that. He's going to do whatever he can to get back at us."

"Well, more like get back at me. You have no choice, right? You're mine now, and you have to do what I tell you. I can handle him," O'Malley promised with a grim expression.

"I'm going to need some time to think it over," Terri said softly.

O'Malley nodded. "Okay. Now eat your food." She tucked into her plate with enthusiasm.

Terri watched for a long moment before she started to eat. As she chewed, she ran the situation through her mind. She could keep going as she was and most likely find her life was worth the sum total of a bullet in the head, or she could put her existence in the hands of a woman she knew nothing about. True, this was a woman who had the brains to beat Trey at cards, and Terri knew he cheated. O'Malley had taken one of his harder punches to the side of the head and gave better than she got. Terri felt like she was the high-wire act, and instead of a safety net, there were hungry lions at the bottom of a long fall. Her mother never told her that life, on occasion, might be harder than it looked.

As O'Malley pushed her plate to the edge of the table, her sleeve rode up her forearm and Terri couldn't miss the Celtic banded tattoo circling O'Malley's arm and the initials *ER* just above the banding. She wondered if the needlework had hurt and who ER was.

When O'Malley pulled her sleeve over the exposed tattoo, the look on her face cut the question off before Terri could voice it. Apparently it was a subject that was off limits. Terri went back to eating her meal and was surprised when she noticed that, for the first time in a long time, her stomach wasn't in knots as she ate.

"What's that look on your face?" O'Malley asked after a sip of coffee.

"I just realized this is the first time my stomach's not doing flips while I'm eating," she answered truthfully. O'Malley's expression told Terri that she didn't understand. "It was one of Trey's favorite times to fight. Nothing was ever right," she explained.

O'Malley nodded. "Well, food-wise, I'm pretty easy. As long as it's dead and relatively cooked, I'll eat it."

Terri finished her breakfast and checked her watch. She still had time to make it to her appointment at the probation office. Pushing her plate to the end of the table, she watched as O'Malley checked the bill and fished out her wallet, dropped a twenty on the table, and started to slide out of the booth.

"Aren't you going to wait for your change?"

"Nah, I just leave it as a tip. It's only money." O'Malley stood up. "You ready?"

Terri nodded. She couldn't think of any reason to linger at the diner. "Sure." She followed O'Malley out of Gus's and into the daylight.

* ~ * ~ * ~ *

Terri watched O'Malley pull away from the curb and out of the parking lot. With quick, sure steps, she made her way to the elevators and waited impatiently along with the others milling around. She kept her gaze leveled straight ahead, ignoring the sidelong glances from the better-dressed people. In her worn jeans and casual blouse, she was definitely not an office employee or some well-off client. In their eyes, she could only be a probie.

She suffered the trip to the sixth floor in silence. The mixture of sweat and too-strong cologne made her stomach nervous. She was finally able to push her way to the front of the car as the doors almost closed before she could exit. She waited until the doors closed behind her before she turned and walked down the hall toward the probation office. She took a deep breath and entered.

Without a word, she signed the clipboard while the secretary picked up the office phone and announced her arrival. The secretary buzzed Terri into the inner hall.

Terri didn't bother knocking on the familiar door. She entered, closed the door, and walked over to the chair across from the man behind the desk. His suit was wrinkled enough for her to believe he'd slept in it. She sat while he listened to the other end of the telephone conversation. Once in a while, he made some sort of noise to assure the other party that he was listening, or at least conscious. Finally, he muttered an unenthusiastic "Yes, sir," and hung up, then rubbed his face vigorously before looking up at her.

"Would you like to explain what in the hell is going on?" He sounded tired.

"Before or after I skewer that rat-bastard little fu—"

He cut her off quickly. "Terri, calm down."

Terri inhaled deeply and let it out slowly. "Have you talked to Trey?"

"Why do you think I called you in? I couldn't understand a damn thing he said. He was on pain pills and damn drunk."

"Okay, *Reader's Digest* version. Trey spent eight hours losing at cards, including the five hundred I worked my ass off for at the club." She was mad and she let him see it. "Then he whines about losing and challenges some new biker woman to something archaic called one punch. Which, if you ask me, is just two idiots getting to hit each other in the head." She took a deep breath. "It gets better. Did I mention that he put me up for that part of the bet? He did, and he lost. So now I 'belong' to this woman, who, as a biker goes, doesn't seem to be a Neanderthal, except for that whole one punch thing. But wait, there's more."

The probation officer did not miss the sarcasm.

"It seems my new owner prefers the company of women in her bed, and because it's obvious that she didn't just toss me down and fuck me after she won me, Trey is telling anyone who will listen that one of us—me or the biker chick—must be a cop." Terri slumped in her seat. "Basically, I'm fucked, because everyone is looking at me like I'm a badge."

The probation officer waited for a moment to make sure she was finished and he could get a word in edgewise. "Terri, you *are* a cop," he reminded her gently.

"George, *we* know that. Trey is supposed to be one of us, so *he* knows that. The bad guys we're trying to catch aren't supposed to know that," she whispered loudly. "You need to pull him back in; he's getting damn close to crossing the line."

"Who's the biker?" he asked, ignoring her request.

Terri sighed. "A woman by the name of O'Malley. First name is pronounced Kalhan. I don't know how to spell it." She watched George scribble on a notepad. "From what I gather, she just did an eighteen-month stretch in county. I don't know what for."

"Full sentence or parole?" he asked distractedly.

"Full sentence, I think."

"Okay. Try to smooth over you being associated with her," he mumbled as he wrote. "Guess there's not much of a chance that she'd give you back to Trey?"

"Think snowball and hell," she muttered dryly. "And, George, I wouldn't go back if I was given the choice."

George sat forward and let his pen drop. The question was written on his face. "Spill it."

Terri managed to blink twice before confusion took over. "Spill it? George, haven't you been getting my reports for the last four months?"

He shook his head. "Trey said you were coming up dry, so I let it go," he admitted.

"Jesus," Terri exclaimed. "George, in the last four months, Trey's beaten me up twice, and his behavior has taken on a whole new swing. Each time he's claimed that it was necessary to keep our cover intact."

"Was it?"

Terri thought it over for a moment. "Not that I'm aware of." She checked her watch. "He's gotten closer to Spyder, but I don't believe that he's kept me in the loop."

George nodded again. "Well, so much for keeping you two together for cover." He looked at Terri with concern. "I don't have any idea what to tell you about the situation with this O'Malley."

"She offered a temporary solution. It's not perfect, but it would work for now, at least until you get more info on her." Even to her own ears, she sounded unsure.

"Care to share?"

"She suggested that we make it look like we actually do have a physical relationship. The upside is that Spyder and his cronies probably wouldn't look at me like I'm a cop. The downside is that it will probably really piss off Trey, and I can't predict his behavior."

Her boss's face was unreadable. "Are you prepared to go that far?"

Terri shrugged. "George, my options here are pretty limited. If you're asking can I convincingly make it look like I'm having a good time and great sex with this woman, then my answer is yes. I don't have a choice. I've got over a year sunk into this investigation. I'm not walking away."

"This could blow up in your face. You said she's done time."

"Give me some other option here; otherwise, I run with this one," she replied.

George shook his head. "I don't have one yet. How connected is she to the club?"

"Honestly, I'm not sure. She could be close to Spyder, but not the club. She doesn't wear club colors, and I don't see where she's an associate. I'll pick some brains when I can." She paused for a second to think through an idea. "You know, being with O'Malley might not be a bad thing. Being on the outside looking in, I might get a better big picture."

George sighed. "I'll get you what I can on O'Malley. Contact Heather for updates. She'll be your mom from now on."

Terri nodded. "Okay. I know we're playing this a little loose, but I'd rather Trey not be kept in my loop. As much as you'd like to ignore my request to pull him in, I'm not going to let him get me hurt. And I will keep suggesting that you pull him."

"I can't do that right now."

Terri swallowed her smart-ass retort. She knew that pushing George beyond his limits was a bad idea. Inwardly, she could appreciate her boss being between a rock and a hard place. His bosses wanted results. City officials wanted the motorcycle club's criminal activity to end, and to date they had little to show for the team's efforts. If Trey was crossing the line, it would probably mean an end to Lieutenant George Schmidt's career. He was a lifelong cop; it was in his blood. He needed his badge like people needed oxygen.

She changed the subject. "Okay. Have any news for me?"

He sighed. "No, it's been relatively quiet." He sounded worried. "It's an adventure sometimes."

"Yeah, but you told me adventures were nasty, icky things that make one late for dinner," she reminded him with a smile. "Next week?"

George nodded. "Yeah. Any changes, you contact me," he ordered.

"I will." Terri signed her probationary visit paperwork and left his office with a reassuring smile. Once she closed the door, she let the smile fall. She was not feeling all that reassured herself.

*　~　*　~　*　~　*

O'Malley pulled her truck to a stop in the driveway of Spyder's modest single-story house. She slowly shook her head as she pulled the keys from the ignition. The neighborhood, while not prestigious, was certainly better than the run-down streets on which most of the club members lived. *Business must be good.* She took a deep breath and exited her truck, closing the door loudly enough so that it could be heard in the house. It would be bad for her health if she surprised Spyder.

A tall blonde with a permanently mousy disposition answered her knock at the door. They greeted each other quietly, then the blonde pointed toward the living room and turned to what O'Malley knew was the kitchen. She knew from past experience that the woman would wait hand and foot on Spyder and his guests; nothing was too much for his circle. She shelved the observation and stepped into the living room, her face a mask of neutrality.

"O'Malley," Spyder said as she walked into the room. "I hear it didn't take you long to get back into the swing of things. Sit down, have a drink."

O'Malley nodded and took her favorite spot by the fireplace. She liked having a wall at her back. "I'm an overachiever," she muttered in a flat tone, letting her eyes rest on the gang leader. As always, she was surprised by how absolutely normal he looked. Good looking enough to attract women's attention, though not what anyone would consider handsome; in shape, yet not looking like he was a slave to the weights. He didn't match the typical picture of a man who ran a lucrative criminal enterprise.

Spyder laughed as his girlfriend walked into the room and handed them each a beer. O'Malley nodded her thanks. She took a long sip of beer as the blonde left, no doubt staying as far away from the room as possible. The rumors of Spyder's treatment of eavesdroppers were legendary. Looking into his eyes, O'Malley was sure those rumors were true.

"Just don't let it be a problem," he advised as he took a drink of his beer.

O'Malley shrugged. "That's up to Trey. I'm cool to let some things go. Making noise that I'm some fucking cop is not something I'm cool with." She leaned back against the wall. "I'm happy to do what I do and make money. I'm not happy about having to watch my back all the time."

"Trey has a point. If she's not fucking you, she could be a cop." His voice was even and calm.

"Jesus, Spyder, think about it. She's been with him how long? And he's never said nothing about her not being between his sheets." She tapped her head with a finger. "I think...he doesn't have his free ride anymore, so suddenly she's a cop."

Spyder nodded slowly. "That does make a certain amount of sense. But, O'Malley, what if she is a cop?"

O'Malley raised her gaze to meet his. "Then I'll put a bullet in her myself, and then I'll put a bullet in him. He brought her here, which means chances are he's a cop, too." O'Malley drained her beer. "I'm out of here for a few days. A friend has a line on some Berettas. You interested?" She set the beer bottle on the floor.

Spyder leaned back in his seat. "How much?"

"I won't know until I see them. If they're clean, it's higher; if they're junk, I won't buy real high. Call my cell phone in a couple of days. I'll know more by then."

He nodded. "Sounds good. Who's gonna keep an eye on the chick?"

She looked at him for a moment before answering. "She's going with me."

"You sure that's smart?"

"If she's a cop, she already knows what I do for a living. If she's not, it doesn't really matter. I'm supposed to be on vacation. She's just the window dressing if anyone has eyes on my friend."

Spyder smiled. O'Malley wasn't the reckless type. She always planned ahead and always checked out anyone she questioned. She liked her independence and freelance status, so she wasn't a member of the club and she didn't wear the colors despite his attempts to tie her to the club officially, if only to keep himself covered.

"Okay, day after tomorrow. Any other reason you're taking her?"

O'Malley smiled. "Yeah, it's a long fucking drive. This time I won't have to talk to myself. My conversations suck."

* ~ * ~ * ~ *

Terri was waiting at the bus stop bench when O'Malley's truck pulled up next to the curb. She quickly jumped into the cab of the vehicle and buckled up as O'Malley moved back into traffic. Terri could not read her expression.

"How'd it go?" O'Malley asked as she lowered the radio volume.

"It went. I have to be back next week."

"Is that normal?"

"Every time he and his wife fight, his probies get extra visits," Terri groused, and then she fell silent. She chewed her thumbnail for a while before she spoke again. "I was thinking while I was waiting for you."

"Yeah?" O'Malley was distracted by having to change lanes.

"Can I ask why you didn't...that first night? I mean, I'm grateful you didn't force...Shit. I'm saying this all wrong." Terri couldn't figure out why she was having a sudden problem with words. She blushed in embarrassment when she heard O'Malley chuckle.

"Look, Ter, I like women. A lot." O'Malley grinned. "But I also have this thing about women coming into my bed willingly. I don't know a great deal about what went on with you and Trey, but I can add two and two." She risked a glance at the woman sitting next to her.

"I was thinking that I'm okay with what you suggested. I won't live long if they think I'm a cop, and I don't think you can let me just leave. I'm never going back to Trey," Terri said in a rush. "But how do we go from me not sleeping with you to sleeping with you?"

O'Malley's cell phone cut off the answer. Grabbing the phone, she pressed the center button. "Yeah?" Her voice was rough. She listened for a second and a smile broke out on her face. "Barnes, you old war dog. How the hell are you?" After a moment, she laughed out loud and had to pull the truck back into her lane while Terri nearly had a heart attack. "No, man, that's cool. ... Yeah, I can still make it. ... Sure, but I'll have company." O'Malley had to wait for the questions on the other end to cease. "No, I'm not telling. ... I'll fill you in when we get there. But we have to be back here in a week."

Terri knew O'Malley was talking about the two of them and experienced a moment of fear that took every ounce of her training to keep from showing on her face. A trip was the last thing she had been expecting. *I hate to remind you, but this whole case isn't what you were expecting,* her mind supplied with a great deal of sarcasm.

"Yeah, it'll be good to see you, too. It's been way too long. ... See ya in a day or two." O'Malley shut down the phone and let it settle in the cup holder by her seat. "And to answer your question," she continued, "I was planning to visit an Army buddy. You come with me and while we're gone, our relationship just kinda happens."

"So, we go away practically strangers and come back as lovers," Terri clarified. "Where are we going?"

"Ever been to Texas?" O'Malley asked quietly.

Terri's stomach did a flip-flop. "I went to El Paso once. It was different."

O'Malley did not miss the tone of Terri's voice. Something about El Paso had obviously not been pleasant. She herself had been to the desert city and had enjoyed the surrounding mountains, climate, and especially the food. Most importantly, she had enjoyed the company.

"Army buddy, huh?" Terri shifted in her seat and was treated to O'Malley's profile. The thin white lines of scars marred the lean lines of her face. "What did you do in the Army?"

"Supply, mostly," O'Malley answered smoothly. "And avoided the military police," she finished with a smile. "Barnes and me, we still keep in touch from time to time. He's an okay guy." She changed the subject. "Is Hank going to give you shit about taking off from work?"

Terri groaned. "Yeah, he is."

"Don't worry about it. I'll talk to him tomorrow and then he won't have a problem with it."

"What do you mean?"

O'Malley turned her blue eyes on Terri. "I'll take care of it," she said.

Terri looked like she wanted to protest, but instead she shifted again in her seat and stared out the windshield. Both women spent the rest of the trip to O'Malley's rental house in silence, each absorbed in her own thoughts and fears.

They spoke little during an early dinner, and when Terri announced that she had to get to work, O'Malley handed her the truck keys without a word. She watched the petite woman struggle into the driver's seat and pull slowly out of the driveway, then closed the front door and poured herself a drink. After a few moments of solitude, she worked her way into a semblance of calm. She knew Terri had to be kept in the dark about her level of hatred for Hank Stillman. Even the name set her on a dangerous edge. She refilled her drink and sat in her favorite chair and watched the sun bleed into setting.

* ~ * ~ * ~ *

Callan strained against the pain and growled out loud. Her right hand shook with effort and fatigue. Letting out a harsh breath, she managed to bring the weight up to the designated point and ease it back down. She blinked several times as drops of sweat fell to the floor.

"One more, Sergeant," Stephens said in his no-nonsense manner.

"Damn it," she muttered under her breath, knowing that he heard her but not really caring. The pain of getting shot paled in comparison to that of the rehabilitation. Her entire body was one big lump of hurt. She swallowed the desire to cry and concentrated on the task at hand. Slowly, she urged her damaged muscles to move the weight upward. She could only bring it halfway up.

"Quit slacking on me," Stephens ordered in a harsh tone. A disgusted snort followed when she couldn't get the weight to move further. "How the hell did you make it out of the desert? Come on, halfway, finish it."

Callan knew she was beyond the point of being able. She eased her arm down. "You finish it," she rasped, and drew in several harsh breaths.

"So, you're just going to quit? Give up now, and all you'll have is a useless decoration for your shirts," he taunted.

"That will be quite enough." The strong voice caused both exhausted patient and physical therapist to turn in surprise. Lieutenant Rivers stalked into the room and planted herself in front of Stephens. Her normally smiling face was rigid with anger.

Callan took a second to wonder who had stolen her favorite nurse.

"Ma'am, the sergeant needs to finish these exercises without giving up," Stephens began. "You can't coddle her."

"How many?" Lieutenant Rivers demanded.

"Ma'am?" Stephens asked in confusion.

"How many reps did you have her do?" She enunciated each word slowly.

"Fifteen, ma'am. Standard procedure for rehabbing a shoulder wound."

"Standard for a shoulder wound without the complication of broken ribs."

Lieutenant Rivers watched the color drain from therapist's face. His normally ruddy complexion paled at the implications.

"I didn't know, ma'am—" he began.

Lieutenant Rivers cut him off harshly. "You do read, don't you, Stephens? I mean, you wouldn't have lied to the Air Force about being literate."

"No, ma'am. I mean, yes, ma'am, I can read," he stammered.

"Then why would you have this patient doing exercises that are beyond her current medical capacity? Did you read the file?" she demanded.

"No, ma'am," he admitted. "Henderson passed this case to me and gave me an overview. He's normally very thorough."

"I'm sure he is." Her words were clipped. "You are done for the day, Sergeant O'Malley. Stephens, you will be prepared to explain yourself to the CNO by end of the day. I suggest you find Henderson and bring him with you when the CNO calls."

He drew himself to attention. "Yes, ma'am."

She stepped close to him. "While you have been warm and comfortable and safe here in Ramstein, there are others who actually stepped onto Iraqi sand. Don't you ever let me hear of you berating them again," she ordered in a low, clear voice. "Dismissed."

She waited until the therapy room door closed before she turned to face Callan. "Are you okay?"

"You mean I didn't have to go through all that?" Callan asked. She watched Rivers shake her head sadly. Callan closed her eyes in frustration and pain. Every cell in her body rebelled and wanted to strike out. She opened her eyes and almost exploded. The tears tracking down Rivers's face stopped her in an instant. She exhaled a slow, calming breath. "Ma'am, could you get me out of this thing?"

Callan waited patiently while the lieutenant released the Velcro wrap holding the weight in her hand. Her relief lasted only seconds before more pain invaded. She closed and opened her fist slowly several times, halting only when the pain became almost too much. She was surprised when a soft, strong hand closed gently over hers.

"It will never happen again," Rivers promised quietly.

"I know, ma'am," Callan reassured her nurse. "Army dogs know Air Force pukes can't read," she joked, and her weak attempt at humor was rewarded with a groan. "Joke, ma'am, please don't order me drawn and quartered." This time she got the smile she was looking for and her heart swelled. Her mind took a moment to remind her to be careful.

"And Air Force pukes know Army dogs can't follow orders. Come on, *let's get you into your wheels and get you cleaned up," Rivers said. She offered her arm to help Callan up and over to the wheelchair, which the sergeant was under orders to travel in when moving any distance. In the week since her ribs were pronounced healed enough, Callan had worked her way up to three rolling laps around the ward hallways every other day.*

"I'll get the CNO to assign you to a new therapist. And I'll make sure that your file is read this time," she said as she released the brakes on the wheels.

"I guess you got my back?"

"I'm in the Air Force, Sergeant; we call it a six."

"Clock watcher," Callan teased.

O'Malley jolted awake, her eyes tracking steadily as her mind cleared of the fog. When the phone rang again, she understood there was no reason for alarm. She pushed the dream memory aside for the moment. Her brain would figure it out in time. She picked up the receiver and pressed it to her ear.

"Yeah?" She managed to sound almost awake.

"O'Malley?" Terri could barely hear over the music in the club.

"Terri? What's wrong?" A million worst-case possibilities ran through her head.

"Could you come get me? I'm at the club, and the truck has four flat tires." Terri's worry and fear came through the phone line loud and clear.

"Flat or slashed?" O'Malley asked, and waited for an answer. "Terri, just tell me the truth, I'm gonna find out anyway."

Terri sighed. "Slashed."

"Okay. I'll come get you on the bike. Do you see Trey anywhere around?"

"No. But that's when I worry the most." Terri sounded tired.

"Just hang at work 'til I get there. You see him, just call the cops."

"You have got to be kidding me," Terri shouted.

"Why would a cop call the cops if she were a cop?" O'Malley reasoned, and after a moment heard a small chuckle at the other end. "It's a normal thing to do if you're scared. I'll be there soon."

"Okay, and I'm sorry."

"Don't be. He's the one who's gonna find sorry." O'Malley didn't wait for a reply. She let the phone drop gently into its cradle, then placed a quick call on her cell phone to arrange for a tow and new tires for the truck. That done, she grabbed her leather jacket and snagged the bike keys from the counter. In no time, her Harley Sportster was out of the garage and on the road. She kept the anger deep inside as she drove. The irony of having an accident now would just make the Fates smile. She had no desire to please the Fates.

It took O'Malley fifteen minutes to get to the strip club. She parked her bike in full view of the bouncer at the front door. As she swung her leg over the bike, she could see her truck and the four flat tires. She could only laugh at the petulant act. Everyone knew that if they really wanted to piss her off, they should go after her bike.

He's trying to scare Terri, you pinhead. The laughter died quickly. She cut her way through the line and handed a twenty to the bouncer to watch her bike. He nodded without saying a word. She idly wondered how he managed to nod without a neck. His glare was enough to silence the voices that shouted in protest at her immediate entry. O'Malley made her way to the bar and nearly had to shout to ask for Terri. One of the bartenders pointed toward the manager's office. She ignored the music, dancers, and customers as she moved quickly. Her knock was answered almost immediately. Hank Stillman pulled open the door and let her into the cramped space. Terri sat in front of his desk, tension lines on her face.

"You okay, Terri?" O'Malley asked quietly.

Terri nodded and clutched her purse. "Let's go home."

Hank chose to pipe up. "I can't let you leave that piece of junk in the parking lot."

"It's taken care of," O'Malley answered. "And Terri is taking a week or two off, starting right now," she added almost as an afterthought.

"No way. Her schedule's set."

"Do yourself a huge favor, Hank. Just give her the time off." O'Malley's gaze was level.

"She don't show tomorrow, she's fired," he threatened.

"Then she's fired," O'Malley said flatly. "You need anything from here?" she asked Terri in a tone that discouraged any argument.

Terri slowly shook her head, her eyes wide.

"Fine. We're outta here. C'mon."

Hank put a restraining hand on O'Malley's right arm, only to have his thumb trapped and wrenched painfully in a direction that it was not designed to go.

O'Malley's left hand wrapped itself around his throat. Strong fingers squeezed enough to get his attention. "She's fired, we're leaving, and you never touch me again. Got it?"

Hank managed a squeak that Terri assumed was a yes. She rose from her seat and stepped carefully over to O'Malley. She knew better than to startle the volatile woman, but Hank was beginning to turn purple from the pressure constricting his throat.

"He gets the message, O'Malley. C'mon. He's not going to try anything or sic anyone on us. Are you, Hank?" The not-so-subtle message sank into his brain. "See, we can go," Terri said. When O'Malley did not seem to hear, she added, "Please."

Finally, after a long tense moment, O'Malley released Hank to his pain. Pulling Terri along with her, she edged out of the room sideways. She knew better than to turn her back on a viper.

Terri closed the office door and O'Malley's hand wrapped around hers. An odd sensation of safety flooded through her despite the potentially dangerous situation. She followed as O'Malley led the way through the club and outside. She waved to the bouncer as she stopped short in front of the bike, took the helmet that was handed to her, and secured it in place as O'Malley started the engine.

"You gonna be okay for the ride back or do you need the jacket?" O'Malley's words were soft.

"I'll be okay. I just want to be out of here."

O'Malley held out her hand and Terri held on to it while she settled herself onto the bike. With a quick look to make sure the coast was clear, O'Malley pulled onto the asphalt and made her way to the exit of the parking lot. Two sets of hearts beat rapidly, for different reasons. O'Malley was mentally berating herself for losing control in the office; Terri was trying to figure out the enigma that was Callan O'Malley. One minute the woman was an open book, and the next, she was explosive.

Terri's head hurt from trying to figure the whole situation and from the stress of walking out to the truck on her break and finding the slashed tires. She knew that it had to have been Trey or one of his own little yes-men. She sighed and wished for the first time that she wasn't a cop, wasn't undercover, and that she could have her normal life back.

When the bike took a turn a little too fast for her comfort, her arms tightened automatically around O'Malley's waist. She felt

O'Malley's hand touch hers in reassurance, then the hand was gone. She rested her head against O'Malley's back. It had been one very long, trying day, and she was tired. She let her mind drift for the rest of the ride back to O'Malley's house and waited until the bike was turned off before she moved.

Terri unbuckled the helmet and handed it to O'Malley before getting off the bike. Without waiting for the biker, she pushed open the door and made her way into the house, where she pulled two beers out of the refrigerator and twisted off the caps. She looked up when she heard O'Malley's boots on the hardwood floor and the keys hit the counter. Not missing the tired and unsure expression in O'Malley's eyes, she held out one of the beers.

"Thanks." O'Malley took the bottle and sipped from it. "I was an asshole earlier. I want you to know I'm sorry."

"You did warn me about that," Terri said. "I just didn't know where it came from and I don't really know you, so I didn't know how to act."

"If you can't tell, Hank isn't one of my favorite people. He just pushes some button in me. You got the fallout."

"Well, maybe I got the fallout, but I think he got exploded on tonight." Terri took her beer, walked over to the couch, and sat down. After a moment, she started to chuckle. "Did you see his face?"

"When his eyes bugged out or when he turned funny colors?" O'Malley asked wryly, as she sat down in her favorite overstuffed chair.

"In general. I think I owe you some money. I've always said that I would pay to watch someone kick his ass."

O'Malley held out her hand. "Hand it over."

Terri managed not to spill her beer as she doubled over with laughter. She hadn't expected the biker to play so easily. After a minute, she was able to compose herself. "Can I pay you after I get another job?"

O'Malley set her beer on the floor. "You don't have to get another job," she said quietly. "I can take care of us both. I had a talk with Spyder today, and there's no help there. I'm guessing Spyder had a talk with Trey and it set him off. I didn't figure him to do something like this. You'll be safer if I'm around."

Terri stared at the biker. "You're gonna protect me?" she asked with a tinge of regret.

"It's sorta my fault that you're in this mess, so yeah, I'm gonna try." O'Malley picked up her beer. "I don't know you that well either, you know," she said after a long silence.

Terri looked at her, surprise written on her face. "What do you want to know?"

"Haven't thought about it yet. When I think of something, I'll ask."

"Okay. Does that work both ways?" Terri pulled off her shoes and tucked her feet under her.

O'Malley ran the question through her head and nodded when she came to her decision. She knew what some of the questions would be, and she would just have to deal with them when they came. She would answer as honestly as she could and deal with the aftermath later. She watched Terri struggle with the unexpected permission and guessed that questions and free thought hadn't been real high priorities in a relationship with Trey.

They spent the rest of the evening making small talk, avoiding asking questions. O'Malley was curious about Terri's life before she had hooked up with Trey, but something held her back from asking about it. She recognized it for what it was: she didn't want to get too close. Curiosity had a way of making one care, and she didn't want to care when she was so close to seeing her plan come to fruition.

Terri wanted to ask a million questions, but didn't know where to start, and after such a roller-coaster day, she didn't want to ask anything that might set the biker off on another round of silent treatment or possibly worse. There were few things that truly scared her, but one of them was the type of barely restrained beast that had shown itself in Hank's office. That sort of person was too close to home.

Chapter 4

O'Malley let the stuffed overnight bag fall to the floor with a thud and a heavy exhalation. Not knowing where they were going and what the weather would be like, Terri had packed for a variety of situations, which unfortunately meant a backbreaking carry. She peeled out of her blue shirt and let it fall to the floor.

Terri drew up short as it dropped. The white tank top O'Malley had on was well worn and tight over defined muscle. In that instant, Terri knew why she'd been able to drop Trey with one punch. The strength of the woman was hidden beneath the clothes that she chose. She also saw the tattoos on both shoulder blades that disappeared beneath the cloth. Two ridges of scar tissue bisected the air assault tattoo on the right—a helicopter with whirling blades. The material of the tank top obscured most of the image of a baby dragon on the left.

"Nice tats," Terri commented. "Bet those hurt."

"Nope. I think I was too loaded to notice." O'Malley smiled and fell onto the bed.

Terri let the second, lighter bag settle on the floor by the bathroom. Nine hours of driving and talking had worn her out. "I'm gonna hit the shower, unless you want it first."

Pale blue eyes turned in her direction. "Are you saying I stink?"

Terri nodded, comfortable that the biker wouldn't bite her head off. "But I would also have to say I do too." Bending, she pulled a pair of jeans from the bag and rummaged for a shirt and bra.

O'Malley laughed. "Well, in that case, I'll go second. You hungry?" She reached for the remote and managed to turn on the TV.

"Starving," Terri said as she stepped into the bathroom. She blinked against the bright lights and set her things on the counter next to the sink.

"You want Chinese or Italian?" O'Malley shouted from the

front room.

"You pick, but if it's Chinese, I like mine spicy." Terri started the water. She didn't hear O'Malley's reply as she shut the door and wasted no time undressing and getting into the shower.

The water on her body felt like paradise, even if it did nothing to quell the nervousness in her stomach. She didn't like going to El Paso. There were still enough members from the drug gang not in jail that could recognize her from her last assignment. *It's only one night. What could go wrong?* her mind asked. The events of the last few days replayed in her memory. *I'm not going anywhere tonight.* Terri ducked her head under the spray and closed her eyes.

* ~ * ~ * ~ *

O'Malley hung up the receiver, then reached into her wallet for the money to cover dinner. Placing the cash on the nightstand, she let her eyes linger on the photograph that smiled up at her. With a sigh, she closed her wallet and tossed it onto the nightstand, where it came to rest on top of the money. She took cold comfort in the fact that very soon she would be able to settle old scores. Maybe then she could move forward and let some things go. She might even be able to regain a sense of herself, reconnect with the person she had once been.

She listened to the shower and wondered why she was rescuing some woman in distress yet again. O'Malley wouldn't dare call Terri a damsel; she had too much fire in her to be helpless. A small smile found its way to her face. She had to admit to having a thing for women with fire. There was something alluring about being drawn to the flame. The trick was to avoid being consumed by the heat, a lesson she had learned too late with Ellen.

O'Malley pushed the past into the little space deep inside as she rolled off the bed and peered out the window, catching a glimpse of a vehicle she'd seen many times during the day. She searched her mind for the reason that the car looked familiar. She came up blank, but considering how long they'd driven during the day, she wasn't surprised. She also didn't believe in coincidence. If she had to put money on it, she would have bet that Trey or Spyder was having her tailed. She would put the same money down that her tail was watching at that very moment. *Nothing like honor among thieves.*

She smiled coldly and turned away from the window without

closing the curtains. Tugging off her tank top and letting it fall to the floor, she heard the shower water stop running. Taking a deep breath, she realized that she would have to disclose the fact that they were being followed, which was going to move up the timing of their relationship. She had no idea how her newfound girlfriend was going to react to public displays of affection and intimacy. Hell, she didn't even know if the woman was a good kisser. She was still mulling over the prospects and doubts when the door opened and Terri stepped out dressed in dangerously tight jeans and a T-shirt. O'Malley's brain experienced a momentary short circuit. She took a moment to remind herself of where she was and what she was supposed to be doing.

"That is so not nice," she muttered as she let her O'Malley persona fall into place.

"I heard that," Terri shot back with a smile. She dropped her dirty clothes in a small pile by the bed and sat down. Picking up her brush, she started the process of untangling her hair.

O'Malley chuckled, but sobered instantly as she carefully selected her words. "I really hate to tell you this, but we seem to have company—dark-colored sedan in the parking lot. It's been on our tail since we left."

Terri's brush halted instantly. "And you're just telling me this now?"

O'Malley could see the fire rising in those eyes. "I wasn't sure until they pulled into the parking lot. It's a highway, Ter, lots of people use 'em. Sometimes they even use them at the same time," she answered tightly.

"I'm sorry. Did you get a look at who's driving?"

"Yeah, but I don't know the face. Since I stink, I'm gonna jump in the shower. The food should be here soon. Leave the curtains open, act natural, and if you can, get a look at the driver. Maybe you'll recognize him." She grabbed her clean clothes. "Money's on the nightstand. Give 'im a good tip."

Terri could only nod as O'Malley crossed the room and disappeared into the bathroom, finally letting out a breath when she heard the water turn on. Since she was supposed to be acting normal, she resumed brushing her hair. *How do you act normal when you have someone watching you and you know it, but you leave the curtains open on purpose? Our training courses seem to have skipped over that part of the instruction.*

Driven by curiosity, she finished brushing her hair as quickly as possible and rolled over the bed to the nightstand. As quietly as she could, she picked up the wallet and opened it.

She had to laugh at the mug shot on the driver's license. *So that's how you spell "Callan".* She did not miss the photo of the striking woman. Though it was in a protective plastic holder, the picture was worn around the edges, as though it had been handled a lot. *Whoever she is, she's important enough to take center stage.* Terri filed the thought away for future reference as she closed the wallet and put the money in her jeans pocket, just in case she needed an explanation for why the wallet had been moved.

Taking a chance, she glanced out the window toward the parking lot. Even at a distance, she recognized the face. It took a great deal of discipline to keep her expression neutral. The driver was one of Trey's kiss-ass flunkies, who was obviously trying to curry favor by handling this assignment. She lay back on the bed and stared at the ceiling, her brain churning.

* ~ * ~ * ~ *

Ellen Rivers quietly opened the door to the exam room and stifled a chuckle. Callan O'Malley lay on the table, her face mostly covered by the standard blue ice pack. Ellen closed the door and walked over to the soldier. She let out a slow breath.

"Helloooo, nurse," Callan said from beneath the ice pack. "Does my face have freezer burn yet?"

Ellen lifted the ice pack and winced. "Nope, no freezer burn, but damn, that's going to be one hell of a shiner." She let the ice pack rest on the table. "Why is it every time I see you, you're hurt?"

"Shh, this is just a play for sympathy." Callan tried to smile. "Okay, maybe not. Damn, what did he hit me with?"

"His fist," Ellen answered. "You really should have asked him if he was afraid of needles." She couldn't help the smile that quirked her lips.

"I wish I'd thought of it," Callan said. "It just didn't come up in the conversation. Actually, he just grunted at most of our questions. How's Sean?"

"He's feeling better, I think. He's flirting with Joan at the nurse's station. The x-rays came back negative, so nothing's broken."

"Someone please tell my face." She groaned. "What time is it?"

Ellen checked her watch. "Jeez, it's one in the morning. No wonder I'm tired."

"Great, I went off duty half an hour ago." Callan sat up slowly. "Care

for a cup of coffee with an old friend? Unless you're too tired."

"What about your gear?" Ellen asked.

"I'll get Sean to take it in for me. We do it all the time. Just tell me you have wheels here. My car is on post, and I'd rather not have to go back there and take all the shit I'm gonna get when they see my face."

Ellen laughed softly. "We can take my car."

* ~ * ~ * ~ *

Callan led the way into her rental. It was a modest, one-bedroom house with a big backyard and a much shorter front lawn. Ellen slowly followed Callan into the living room, closing the front door behind her. All around the room were family photos and framed recognitions of achievement, the progression of Callan's life.

"Don't pay too much attention to all of that," Callan said over her shoulder as she made for the kitchen. "My mom did that last time she visited." There was an odd twist of love and regret to her voices.

"Looks like she's proud of you," Ellen observed.

Callan shook her head. "She wasn't until after I got hit in the desert." Callan hit the start button on the coffeemaker and pulled down two mugs. "You want to jump out of that uniform? I have several sets of sweats that you can use. 'Course, they all say Army on them."

Ellen's face was a mask of undisguised shock. "You're going to make me wear Army clothes? The shame of it all."

Callan smiled. "Them's the breaks, baby," she teased. "You watch the coffee, I'll get you the sweats."

Ellen waited until Callan was out of the room and then drew in a shaky breath. They had already played superficial catch-up on their lives. Callan had returned to active duty and several final hectic months at Fort Hood. Her assignment to Fort Bliss in the desert city of El Paso had come as a surprise, but she seemed to enjoy the odd change of pace. Callan had looked absolutely smug when she mentioned that field duty was a thing of the past, at least until she was posted somewhere else. Ellen had only glossed over her own life after Ramstein Air Base. Callan plopped herself on the couch and without a word unlaced her combat boots and let them fall to the floor. Wriggling her toes, she let out a sigh of pleasure. "I've been waiting all day to do that. Make yourself comfortable. My house, such as it is, is yours." Callan's smile was tired. "Bathroom is down the hall to the left. I'll make sure the coffee machine doesn't explode."

After the nurse took the offered sweats, Callan poured coffee into two mugs and blew on the contents before she gingerly took a sip. It didn't help; she still scalded her tongue. That served only to remind her of the pain from the fist connecting with her face, which in turn reminded her of the shock of seeing Lieutenant Ellen Rivers again. She set her coffee cup on the counter. A part of her was still in shock. She had resigned herself to never seeing the woman again, and now her world was off kilter. Despite it all, she smiled.

"What are you smiling at?" Ellen's voice was tinged with curiosity.

Callan turned to see her placing her folded clothes on the lamp table.

"Just smiling about seeing you again," Callan answered honestly. She picked up both coffee mugs and carefully carried them over to the coffee table.

"It was a surprise," Ellen said, sitting on the couch.

Callan sat in her favorite chair. "Last postcard I got, you were in San Antonio."

"I was, then I was transferred to Utah."

"I was in the field when your postcard came, and it took me a while to get a letter sent off. It came back."

"Mail forwarding is only in effect for so long, O'Malley. Since I wasn't living on base..." Her voice trailed off.

"I know, I suck at letters," Callan admitted with a knowing smile. "So, what the hell are you doing here? I mean, has the Army been invaded by the Air Force?"

Ellen laughed aloud and leaned further into the couch. "You guys aren't that dysfunctional yet. The Army and the Air Force have a sort of exchange program. We swap personnel sometimes, a sort of 'find out how the other guy lives.' I happened to be available when a rotation came up, so here I am."

Callan grinned. "So, how do you like the Army?"

"You people go into the field way too much. I've been here two months and have been in the field three times. Why do you do that? The Army has a perfectly good, solid, nonmovable hospital."

"We only do that when we have other services around. It makes you think we earn our pay or something," Callan teased. "It is nice to see you. I can honestly say I missed you." She had been dying to say those words for the last hour or so, but in an Army town, one had to be careful.

Ellen sipped her coffee thoughtfully, her eyes locked on Callan's. "I missed you, too."

"So why did you really take the temporary duty station?" Callan asked. Ellen's eyes widened. "Can't fool a cop, Ellen."

Ellen let out a small breath. "I was in a relationship that I didn't want to be in anymore. I broke it off and came here to hide," she finally said. "I wasn't in love anymore."

Callan nodded. "I can understand that. What about the other person?"

"She took it better than I expected," she answered, and held her breath. She did not meet Callan's eyes.

"Her loss," Callan said quietly.

Ellen lifted her eyes. "You're not shocked?"

Callan chuckled. "No. You don't have to worry about the Air Force finding out from me. If I outed you, I would have to out myself as well."

Ellen set the coffee cup down on the table with a dull thud. "You?"

"Like you couldn't tell." Callan tried to smile but could only manage a grimace. "Damn, face still hurts."

"I couldn't tell, honestly," Ellen managed.

"Well, it's not like I was at my best. I was a little mangled at the time. Not at my most charming."

"Charming enough. I respected the hell out of you when you woke up. Not too many women get shot up in combat. I fell in love with you the day you saw Barnes and cried because you couldn't keep him from getting hurt," she said. "I kept telling myself that it was hero worship, that I was infatuated with the way you dealt with things, your irrepressible humor. Then you went back to Fort Hood and I was lonely. Even with my girlfriend there, I was lonely."

Callan was confused. "Why? Lonely, I mean."

"She was and is totally dedicated to what she does. Sometimes I think she loved her research and test tubes more than she loved me. You made me feel like I was special. It was hard to accept that feeling, but harder to lose it once I'd had it." Ellen couldn't stop the tears. "When we got to Utah, I discovered that I didn't want to live that way."

"I don't know what to say to that, Ellen. Except that you shouldn't live that way. You deserve someone who is going to love you for being you, despite anything else that is going on. You deserve someone who will treat you like you are someone special, someone who won't ignore you or forget you're there. She was a fool."

Ellen nodded. "Yes, sometimes I think she was. What I want to know is what are you?"

"Well, I can tell you that I'm not a fool," Callan said softly, her eyes searching Ellen's face. "You've had my heart since you put my glasses on my face." She let out a slow breath and jumped in with both feet. "Where do we go from here?"

"That depends," Ellen answered with a small smile.

"On?"

"On what you're doing tomorrow night."

"I'm doing whatever you want to do."

"Then we're going skydiving," Ellen deadpanned.

Callan paled. "You're kidding, right? I mean, why would anyone jump out of a perfectly functional airplane on purpose?"

Ellen laughed as she rose from her spot on the couch. Closing the distance between the two of them, she placed a gentle kiss on Callan's undamaged cheek. "I'm kidding. How about you show me the city? All I've done for two months is work, sleep, and watch movies."

Callan smiled. "Instant tour guide—just add kisses."

O'Malley opened her eyes and ignored the sting of water. She hadn't planned on taking a trip down memory lane. The memories seemed to be coming more and more frequently lately as she got closer to finishing what she had started. She let out a harsh, frustrated breath, willing herself not to shed the tears she could feel under the surface where she locked down her feelings. Even that was getting harder to do. She had to shake off her fear and laugh at the irony. Ellen had worked her butt off to get O'Malley to open up and share her feelings. Now that she needed to be able to distance herself from those feelings, she almost couldn't do it.

"Damn it, Nurse, you ruined me," she rasped in a harsh whisper as she looked up. She would have given almost anything to have Ellen right there, claiming that she had not ruined her, she had only improved her.

O'Malley shook her head again and took a deep breath. Her brain knew she needed to suck it up and keep going. Her heart had other ideas. It seemed determined to keep her at least nominally human.

To distract herself, O'Malley recited the most tasteless, politically incorrect cadences she could remember as she continued her shower. Four raunchy songs later, she was clean and her mind was back to where it needed to be in order for her to move forward. She shut off the water and stepped out of the shower. She avoided looking in the mirror as she dried off; nothing good would be looking back at her.

O'Malley dressed quickly and pulled open the door to the bathroom. The scent of Chinese food hit her, making her mouth water. She hadn't realized how hungry she was. She had lost her appetite during her time in jail. She had thought that Army food was bad, but compared to jail food, Army meals were gourmet. If she could keep in shape, she wouldn't mind packing on a few pounds to make up some of the weight she'd lost.

She stepped out of the bathroom and watched as Terri set dinner on the bed. It was almost a picnic. Terri looked up, smiled, and placed the plasticware next to the containers of food before settling on the bed.

"I see dinner's ready." O'Malley smirked as she let her clothes fall on top of Terri's.

"Yeah. It got here a couple of minutes ago. I took a look out the window. The driver is one of Trey's boys. I think his name is Thumper."

"Thumper?" O'Malley couldn't keep the look of disbelief off her face. She started to laugh. "He calls himself Thumper?" She laughed harder, almost falling off the bed. For some reason, she kept getting the movie rabbit as a visual.

Terri could only stare at O'Malley as if she'd lost her mind and wait until O'Malley regained some control over her laughter. "Yeah, he's got one hell of a right hook. He's broken more jaws than I care to think about."

O'Malley sobered. "Well, ain't that just grand," she muttered as she lay back on the bed.

"If it makes you feel any better, he's not too bright. Normally he just does what Trey tells him to," Terri explained as she picked up her fork and dug into her dinner.

O'Malley knew that there was nothing she could do about the situation other than to keep an eye out for her new watcher. Reaching out and grabbing her own fork, she decided that she was going to have dinner and think about the rest later. For tonight, she was going to just hang out and relax.

They ate in a semicomfortable silence. O'Malley had to laugh when Terri nearly bolted off the bed and slugged back two quick glasses of water when the food proved to be spicy.

Once their meal was over, they settled back on the bed and turned on the television. Together they watched an Austin Powers movie, each one acutely aware that she was not alone. At one point, they noticed that Thumper had finally gotten something to eat. They burst into laughter again when Terri wondered out loud if they should send breakfast out to his car in the morning.

* ~ * ~ * ~ *

As the sun set, Terri decided to take O'Malley up on her offer to answer questions. She rolled over and pillowed her head on her hand. She decided to start with something simple. "How old are you?"

O'Malley cast a sidelong glance, an interesting expression on her face. "I'm thirty-four."

"Really? You look older."

"Okay, how old do you want me to be?"

Terri blushed as she realized what she'd said. "I'm way busted, huh?"

"Nah. I've heard it before," O'Malley said. "What else do you want to know?"

Terri tested the waters as diplomatically as possible. "What do you want to tell me? I mean, I don't know anything about you."

"Hmm, let's see. I have a mom who isn't all that crazy about me but she puts up with me when I decide to show up. I'm not much for staying in one place for very long if I don't like the place. If I like it, I'll stay for a while. I guess the Army did that to me. I moved every couple of years."

"How long were you in the Army?" Terri interrupted.

"Seven very long years." She sighed. "I went to the desert, and when I got back, they sent me to one more post and I got kicked. I've really just been kicking around since then."

"What does 'kicking around' mean?" Terri tried to sound casual.

O'Malley shook her head. "Ask what you really want. I can see it in your eyes." Her words were even, with nothing harsh in them.

Terri decided to take a chance. "What do you really do? For a living, I mean."

"I sell guns to Spyder," O'Malley answered after a moment's reflection. She watched as Terri stiffened for a moment and then relaxed.

"That's it? Just guns and nothing else?"

"Just the guns. Of course, they are stolen."

"O'Malley, who are they stolen from?" Terri's voice had a tremor in it.

"You know if I tell you, then you're an accessory after the fact."

Terri nodded slowly and let her eyes lock on O'Malley's. "It's not like they'd believe me if I said you never told me," she reasoned.

"I have some old contacts who steal weapons from different military armories. It's a sweet little setup. We make some money, Spyder is happy, and no one's the wiser."

"It's dangerous, isn't it?"

O'Malley laughed. "Hell, Terri, life is dangerous. You can get killed riding a bus or driving your car." There was a bitterness in her voice that Terri could not have missed if she were deaf. It didn't seep through, it poured.

O'Malley shifted on the bed. "The dome light in the car just went on. I want you to go to the window and start to close the drapes. When I come up to you, just go with it, and whatever you do, don't hit me in the head."

Terri couldn't tell if O'Malley was joking with the last part of her statement, but she nodded anyway. Right now, her life was in the hands of the woman on the bed next to her. If she had been ordered into a tub full of Jell-O and whipped cream, she would have jumped in with a smile plastered on her face. To her surprise, she wasn't trembling or showing fear as she stepped in front of the window and raised her arm to catch hold of the plastic guide rod.

Without warning, a pair of warm hands slid around her waist and then O'Malley's body pressed against her back. She could feel the woman's breath on her neck. She let her arm down slowly and her hand came to rest on O'Malley's shoulder. O'Malley's left hand moved to her stomach and pulled her in closer. Warm lips came into contact with her neck, making her gasp as O'Malley sucked on a very sensitive section of flesh. Without meaning to, she moaned out loud.

O'Malley lifted her mouth for just a moment. "Close the drapes," she ordered softly, and then let her mouth fall back to its pleasant pursuit.

Terri needed three tries before her hand found the rod again, enabling her to pull the drapes closed. When they were closed, she took in a deep breath to steady herself. "They're closed," she whispered, then was tugged backward toward the bed.

When O'Malley sat, she pulled Terri down next to her. Terri let out a surprised squeal as she landed. She was pressed down against the bed when O'Malley rolled over her. She had a fleeting moment of uncertainty as the biker reached out and turned off the light, then she squealed again when strong fingers tickled her sides. She rolled around the bed trying to get away, but O'Malley's weight kept her from escaping.

After a few moments of torture, O'Malley abandoned her assault and fell against the mattress. She snuggled in close so that she could whisper in Terri's ear. "Sorry about that, but you are supposed to be having fun in my bed," she explained.

Terri tried not to think about how good the breath on her ear felt. "So you tickled me?"

"It was either that or..." O'Malley let her voice trail off. "Well, you know." She sounded almost embarrassed.

Terri got the idea. "Oh. Good thing for you I'm ticklish," she whispered, her eyes stealing to the window. The dark curtains showed no shadows from the outside. "You think he's out there?"

"I would have to guess so," O'Malley answered.

"How thick do you think the windows are?"

"I have no idea."

"Oh God, that feels so..." Terri moaned out loud. "Don't...stop...right there."

She moved in close to O'Malley's ear. "That should give him something to tell Trey," she whispered, stifling a laugh. "He's gonna pop a vein or something when Thumper tells him. I wish I could be a fly on the wall when it happens."

"You are full of surprises, aren't you, Terri." It was a statement of fact, and O'Malley obviously meant it as such.

Terri was saved from answering when O'Malley's cell phone rang. Both women froze for a moment.

"Don't you dare answer that." Terri put as much frustration as she could into her voice even as she smiled in the dark. If asked, she would have admitted that she was having fun for the first time in months. O'Malley flipped on the light and both women would have sworn that they heard the scrape of footsteps retreating quickly. The cell phone rang again. "The Ride of the Valkyries" was becoming annoying.

"Yeah." O'Malley sounded as though she was trying to catch her breath. "No, I'm not there yet. Jesus, Spyder, I said a couple of days. That would be tomorrow. ... Yeah, well, you would be pissed too—"

"Spyder," Terri breathed into the phone, "call her back tomorrow. After lunch." O'Malley lay back on the bed, laughing silently. It took a few moments for her to regain her composure. When she looked at Terri's face, she broke out in laughter all over again.

Terri just knew the woman next to her had lost her mind.

"Oh, God, I wish I could have seen his face. What on earth possessed you to do that?" O'Malley asked when she could breathe again.

Terri smiled shyly. "Well, if you were in the middle of having sex and someone called, wouldn't you ask them to call back? Much later."

O'Malley thought about the question for a second. "Yeah, it's exactly what I would do. I gotta give you credit, Ter, you're playing this game very well."

"With the proper motivation, I can play any game well," Terri said as she shifted on the bed to get comfortable.

O'Malley's curiosity showed as she looked down at Terri. "So, what's your motivation this time?"

"Trey treated me like crap. I'm just beginning to see how bad it was. My motivation is to give his male ego a monster kick in the balls."

O'Malley smiled and nodded. "I think that is a definite possibility." She chuckled.

"Can I ask you a question?"

"Go ahead." O'Malley stretched back and let her head hit the pillow.

"What's with the hickey thing?"

O'Malley clearly knew what Terri was talking about. "Just call it marking my territory. Around these guys, you gotta mark what's yours or they'll try to take it, and to tell you the truth, I get real tired of getting hit in the head. If you hadn't noticed, these guys are way bigger than me."

"I can see your point. Did you leave a hickey on my neck?" She was amused when O'Malley peered at the side of her neck and a smug grin appeared. "I'll take that as a yes," she said dryly.

"Does that bother you?"

Terri thought about the question for a moment. "No, it doesn't."

Chapter 5

Callan juggled the drinks as she struggled to close the patio door. After a moment of indecision, she decided to just leave the door open. She padded to the hot tub in her bare feet, handed off the four beers, then slid quickly into the tub and took one bottle back. She leaned against the rim of the tub and gazed at Ellen.

"You're staring," Ellen commented.

"Yep. I am. Sometimes I can't help it; you are beautiful." She took a sip of beer.

"And you have got to be the most handsome woman I've ever met. Even more so since that shiner is almost gone," Ellen said shyly.

"I don't think I've ever been called handsome."

"Well, you're too androgynous to be called beautiful. That really didn't sound like a compliment, did it?" Ellen asked without needing an answer. "You've got this really strong jawline, those high cheekbones, and I don't know how else to explain."

Callan smiled. "It's the O'Malley curse. I'm just too damn cute for my own good," she teased. "Hey, you never did tell me how you managed to get four whole days off to match mine."

"I'll remind you around Thanksgiving." Ellen groaned. "I did some wheeling and dealing."

Callan put her beer down on the deck floor and slid close to the woman she loved. "Thank you." She leaned in and pressed her lips gently against Ellen's. "Thank you." She kissed her again, this time teasing her warm lips with the tip of her tongue. She was almost surprised when Ellen's lips parted and their kisses turned into something passionate. Two stolen weeks of sharing precious moments away from the prying eyes of the military had drawn them closer in the slow pursuit of what they both admitted they wanted. She felt Ellen's arms snake around her neck as she nibbled lightly on the nurse's lower lip.

Ellen pressed her body closer to Callan's and let her actions speak for her. She sucked gently on Callan's tongue and slowly released it, causing Callan to moan softly. Ellen trailed kisses along the Callan's jaw up to her ear. "I want you," she breathed. "I want all of you."

Callan let her hands roam down Ellen's back, stopping only when she reached her shapely butt. She pulled Ellen forward until there was no space between them. "Are you sure?" she asked gently.

Ellen slowly pulled away and managed to get out of the hot tub with her gaze still locked on Callan. Instead of answering with words, she reached behind her neck and undid the ties of her swimsuit, then let the material fall to the ground. Her nipples grew harder in response to the chill night air. Turning, she then walked into the house.

Callan smiled and shook her head. Sometimes she wondered who was the bolder of the two. She followed quickly, not bothering to dry off or caring about the water being tracked into the house. She found her heart's desire lying on the bed, waiting for her. At the edge of the bed, she slowly peeled off her own suit. She had a momentary flash of fear that Ellen would be repulsed by the many scars on her body, but then remembered that the nurse had already seen them.

Easing herself onto the bed, Callan began a slow, torturous journey of kisses up Ellen's body. Her hands glided over smooth skin, and she was lost in the sensation of loving Ellen. She could not get enough.

Ellen laughed when Callan's tongue dipped into her navel and back out again. She shivered in anticipation as lips and tongue traveled closer to her breasts. She moaned when the warm mouth closed over a rigid nipple and sucked gently. She tangled her hands in Callan's short hair and pulled her closer. Her back arched as the edges of Callan's teeth closed around her nipple. Callan pulled back, only to renew the loving assault on her other breast.

"Oh, God, you keep that up and you'll make me come," she gasped into Callan's ear.

Callan's lips left Ellen's nipple. "I think that's the point." She smiled as she kissed the hollow between Ellen's breasts, then trailed a wet path with her tongue to Ellen's neck, kissing and gently nipping at tender skin along the way. "What would you like?" she asked in a ragged whisper, wanting only to please the woman in her bed.

Waiting for an answer, Callan sucked at the pulse point of Ellen's neck, pleased when she felt the goose bumps rise. Ellen's hand closed around Callan's and guided her fingers to the slick treasure between long legs. Callan let Ellen lead, let her set the pace, ready to go as fast or as slow as she wanted.

"I want you inside," Ellen rasped. "And I want you to taste what you do to me." Ellen parted her legs wider, giving Callan free access.

Callan teased with her fingers, drawing slick moisture to Ellen's clitoris, circling a time or two, then pulling back. Ellen's hips bucked upward, trying to reach Callan's fingers. "Please, don't tease."

Callan slipped one finger inside her lover and watched Ellen's eyes close in ecstasy. She moaned when the snug walls closed around her finger. Leaning forward she kissed Ellen, trying to convey all of her emotions, trying to let her know exactly how she felt about her. Falling easily into the rhythm her lover wanted, Callan was kissing her way down Ellen's body when hands pushed down on her shoulders. She knew in that moment that she would give her anything she wanted.

Callan took a moment to savor the scent of her lover before she let her tongue trace swollen flesh. She did not still the movements of her hand as she feasted on Ellen's clitoris. Feeling the tremors begin around her finger, she waited until the last possible second to suck the swollen nub of flesh into her mouth.

"God, yes...please...it's been so long," Ellen gasped. She moved her hips faster with want and need. It wouldn't be long before she reached orgasm.

Callan wrapped her free arm around Ellen's hips to keep her from breaking contact. She sucked and licked even as Ellen came, wanting to give her as much pleasure as possible for as long as possible. She felt Ellen's fingers tighten painfully in her hair and smiled inwardly when the spasms renewed themselves, tearing a soft cry from Ellen's throat. Callan thrust her finger in time with her tongue, until finally Ellen had to push her away with a quiet plea to stop. Gently withdrawing her finger, Callan kissed her way back up Ellen's body.

Ellen pulled her close and wrapped her arms and legs around Callan's body. Her heart raced, trying to beat its way out of her chest. "Proud of yourself, aren't you?" she murmured, and kissed Callan.

"Oh, yeah," Callan said with a grin. "God, you're amazing." She kissed Ellen again. "So beautiful and sexy." She felt Ellen's hand slide between her legs, but stopped her. "If you touch me right now, I'll come in a second. I want to hold you for a while."

"I think I could be talked into cuddling for a little while," Ellen mumbled. She shifted with Callan so that her head was pillowed on a strong shoulder and smiled as Callan's arms closed around her. Gentle fingers traced small circles on her cooling skin. She kissed the point of Callan's chin. "Thank you for making me feel special."

"I hate to break it to you, Nurse, but you are *special."*

"Nurse?"

"Yeah. That's what I call you in my head. You're my nurse."

"I can live with that...Irish." She felt Callan's laughter before she heard it. "Hey, if I get a nickname, so do you. Deal with it."

"Yes, ma'am," Callan answered with all the love she could convey with her voice, and tightened her embrace.

O'Malley woke without the usual startled reaction. Rolling to her left, she watched the red numbers on the alarm clock. 5:15. She felt the lump in her throat and silently damned her memory. The things that had at one time brought her joy now brought her sadness, and she found she could not lock them away. She sighed in the dark.

Movement from the other side of the bed caught her by surprise, and it took a second for her to realize that it was Terri sleeping beside her and not Ellen. She stopped herself from calling out Ellen's name just in time. That would lead to questioning she was not yet ready to face. There would be time to answer those questions later.

Terri rolled over in her sleep, and her arm snaked around O'Malley's stomach as she snuggled close. The biker could hear her mumbling in her sleep. She couldn't make out the words, but the sound was not a good one. The mumble turned into whimpering, and without thinking, O'Malley let her hand trace a soothing pattern on Terri's arm. After a few moments, the whimpering ceased and Terri's breathing evened out.

I guess I'm not the only one fighting demons. O'Malley wished for a cigarette. She hadn't wanted one in a long time. She'd given them up on the advice of the respiratory tech who'd tortured her so long ago in an Air Force hospital. She had tried every dirty trick she knew of to get back at the woman. It was just her luck to have been given a tech whose father was a retired sergeant major. The tech had not been impressed or intimidated by O'Malley's attempts at retribution. She had merely laughed.

Terri's mumbling resumed and turned into a low-pitched keening. O'Malley felt the smaller woman's body coil and tense. For the first time in quite a while, O'Malley felt helpless.

"I'm sorry, Daddy. I'll be good. I promise." Terri sounded like a frightened child, and it broke into the ice around O'Malley's heart. "I'm sorry, I'm sorry." Terri's voice trailed off.

O'Malley rubbed Terri's back gently in small circles. She wasn't prepared when Terri sat straight up in bed, the blankets falling from her body. Moving slowly so that she didn't startle her, O'Malley turned to face Terri.

"You okay?" she asked in a whisper. When she did not receive an answer, she said, "I'm going to turn on the light. Close your eyes."

Without turning her head, she managed to find the lamp switch with her hand. She blinked against the brightness. Terri looked a mess. Her hair was tossed in all directions, and her cheeks were tracked with tearstains. Terri's eyes slowly opened, and after a minute, her whole body sagged. When O'Malley tugged her gently to her chest and wrapped her arms around Terri, the smaller woman did not fight it; she merely let her body rest against the biker.

"I'm sorry for waking you up," she said in a hoarse voice.

"I wasn't asleep. You okay?"

Instead of answering the question, Terri asked, "O'Malley, do you ever wish you were a kid again?"

"Yeah, when being a grown-up gets to be hard," O'Malley said as she stroked Terri's arm in comfort.

"I don't. I try not to think about being a kid." A new rush of tears rolled down Terri's cheeks. "I ran away the first time when I was five. I got to the end of the block. I sat on the curb for hours 'cause I didn't have permission to cross the street by myself." She sniffled and stared at the wall. "Pretty pathetic, huh?"

"Why were you running away?" O'Malley asked, sincerely wanting to know what would drive a five-year-old to such an extreme. She had some ideas, but she wanted to hear it from Terri.

"My dad. He talked with his fists a lot. It lasted a long time. It got worse after my mom filed for divorce and the judge gave him custody."

O'Malley wondered what kind of idiot would give him custody. "Why?"

"The judge was a woman. My dad was a cop." Terri shrugged her shoulders. "I read the transcript once. He made up a whole bunch of lies about my mom, and his buddies backed him up. The judge said she was an unfit mother, and he got custody of me. I ran away for good when I was eighteen." Terri sounded broken and drained. "He was always very cool and charming in front of other people, but as soon as we were behind closed doors, I was his punching bag for every lousy thing that happened during his day. He didn't even need to be drunk."

"What were you dreaming?"

Terri sighed. "I was six. I broke a glass." She turned and looked into O'Malley's eyes. "I wanted some milk." She turned away again. "He hit me hard enough to crack my jaw." She fell silent again for a long time. "Sometimes I just want to hide away from it all."

Knowing Terri needed some kind of gentle contact, O'Malley hugged her close. "You can hide with me. Is your dad still around?"

"Sometimes I feel like he's everywhere, but I know what you're really asking. He's still alive, and he always seems to be able to find me. I guess he's still got contacts around. He calls from time to time."

"Would you let me know the next time he calls you?"

"Would it do any good to say no?" Terri sounded defeated.

"Not really. I have some old contacts that I can use for good this time." There was humor in her voice.

Terri smiled. "Why do I think I'm gonna regret watching that good-guy-saves-the-world movie with you?"

"Count on it. I'm sure I can convince him to leave you alone," O'Malley promised with an evil smile.

Terri sighed. "I'll let you know the next time he calls." She settled deeper against O'Malley's body.

When she started to move away, apparently realizing how close they were, O'Malley held her fast. "Stay where you are. You get some sleep. I'll keep you safe," she promised quietly.

"What about you?"

"I've slept all I need to for now. I'll crash after we get to Sean's."

Terri didn't seem completely convinced, but nodded after a jaw-popping yawn. She closed her eyes.

O'Malley watched her fall back to sleep and vowed that this time she would not fail. She would keep her safe. Without moving her body, she turned off the light and stared into the darkness.

* ~ * ~ * ~ *

"Thank goodness," Terri said when O'Malley pulled into the driveway at their destination. She exited the truck and made a run for the open door of the house, with only a quick glance at the blond man who passed her as she flew through the door.

O'Malley was having a hard time getting out of the truck; she was nearly lying on her seat. Her laughter boomed out at Sean Barnes, and he smiled. Yanking the truck door all the way open, he grabbed hold of a belt loop on her jeans and pulled her out of the vehicle.

O'Malley found herself in a bear hug and lifted off the ground. "Lemme down, you dumb-ass." She tried to sound intimidating, but couldn't pull it off while laughing.

"Say it," he demanded in a playful tone.

"No fucking way." O'Malley was defiant even if she couldn't touch the ground.

"Say it or I'll zerb you," he threatened with a growl.

"Oh man, not the zerb." She groaned. "Okay, okay. I missed you. There, I said it, now lemme down."

Sean Barnes let his friend's feet touch the ground and pulled her into another hug, this one a heartfelt demonstration of his affection. "So, who's the stranger who just ran into my house and, I'm guessing, my bathroom?" he asked with a grin when they both pulled back from the hug.

"That's Terri. I'll tell you about it over dinner. Joan did cook, right?"

"Yeah, she's putting on the finishing touches now. You know, I'm beginning to think you come here for her and not for me."

"Yeah, well, I'm a slave to my stomach, and let's face it, buddy boy, you can't cook to save anyone's life." O'Malley grinned as she pulled the overnight bag out of the truck.

"Sometimes I hate the truth." Sean's voice was almost a whine.

O'Malley looked at him for a moment. "You got the stuff?" She watched him nod and brush his hand over his almost nonexistent hair. "Cool."

"I'll give you the tour later. You know Joan—business after dinner. Does Terri know?" he asked, his voice taking on a serious tone.

"She knows I run guns for Spyder, and that's pretty much all she knows. I wanna keep it that way, got it?"

"Roger that one." He took the bag from O'Malley and stopped in his tracks. "What the hell did you bring?"

"Talk to Ter about that, she packed. Come on, I'm starving." O'Malley turned and walked backward toward the house as she watched her friend. She flashed an evil grin at him. "Welcome to my world, buddy boy."

"Jesus," he gasped, and struggled up the path with the bag.

O'Malley stomped through the house to get Joan's attention, knowing just how much the woman hated it when she did that. She found her blocking the entrance to the kitchen, and O'Malley knew she was in for it. She smiled anyway. It had been way too long since she'd visited her friends. They knew it, and so did she.

O'Malley did the very thing Joan would have expected. She rushed her and pulled her into a very close hug. Her eyes took in the raven-colored hair, chocolate brown eyes, and proud cheekbones of her Indian heritage. She grinned widely. "Hi, gorgeous. Gimme a kiss." O'Malley wiggled her eyebrows and was extremely surprised when Joan complied. Her best friend's wife planted a kiss full on her lips.

"Okay, someone tell me if I should be jealous of what I just saw." Terri's voice pulled both women out of their silence. O'Malley let go of Joan and faced Terri, not quite sure she could explain what had just happened.

"Hi, I'm Joan Barnes. The silent, no-hair guy is Sean, and you already know the dumb-ass trying to decide what to say," Joan bubbled. After years of being teased by O'Malley, she'd finally gotten her. "That'll teach her to demand a kiss every time I see her." Joan turned back to O'Malley. Sean chose that moment to drop the back-breaking overnight bag.

Terri decided that she liked the other woman a lot. "Hi, I'm Terri. O'Malley, you're off the hook, for now." She flashed a grin at her newfound friend. "Got any good, embarrassing O'Malley stories you might care to share?"

"Only about a million." Joan smiled sweetly at O'Malley. "Callan, how long are you two staying?"

"Ten minutes," O'Malley mumbled, knowing when she was beat.

"Bullshit," Joan shot right back. "Callan, you and Sean go put your stuff away while Terri and I get to know one another."

Sean looked at O'Malley with something close to sympathy. "You are so screwed. Come on, we'll put this away, and I'll show you something totally sweet."

He led the way to his work shed. "I want you to know this was a bitch for me to do. That being said, I want your first three children," he demanded as he reached into the cooler.

"Hell, Sean, why not just ask for the Sportster. That would be easier to arrange." O'Malley took the dripping beer he offered.

"Well, I'd take the bike if I thought you were serious. C'mon." He went further into the work area and halted at a tarp-covered form. "Take it off."

O'Malley let her hands take up a fold of material. "Is this what I think it is?" she asked as she pulled off the tarp and revealed her dream bike. "Oh, man, I owe you big time for this." She walked around the rebuilt 1974 Harley, just looking, taking in each detail. It was her dream machine, the one she and Ellen had drooled over and planned for. O'Malley felt her legs go weak, and the lump in her throat suddenly made words difficult.

Sean watched as she battled her emotions and memories. "She'd want you to go on, my friend. Just hear me out. I know how you two felt about each other, and what happened sucks, big time. At least you had each other for a little while, and you know what? You were both happy. When things get hard, save that and roll around in it. Once you take care of unfinished business, you're going to have to decide what you're gonna do. But, Callan, whatever you decide, don't forget that she would not want you to live in some dark shadow. She saw that once, and I know she wouldn't want you there again."

"Are you done?" O'Malley asked gruffly. Sean nodded. "I know all that in my head, but in my heart, I can't let go."

"I know. No one says you have to let go completely, you just have to go on. I loved her too, Callan, in my own way. So did Joan. So did everyone who met her and got to know her," he said softly. He gave O'Malley a moment to get herself together, then tipped his beer bottle in her direction. "So, what are you gonna name her?"

O'Malley tapped her beer bottle against his. "Hell, Sean, you know what I'm gonna call this bike. *Nurse.*"

Sean smiled and reached into the cooler again. Taking out an unopened beer, he shook it up and without warning, slammed it against the gas tank. Glass flew and beer foam shot all over the area.

"I christen thee *Nurse.*" He looked at O'Malley. "Did I mention that I played with her motor a little?" There was an evil little grin on his face that almost scared Callan O'Malley.

* ~ * ~ * ~ *

Terri pushed away from the table, protesting that she'd had more than enough. She couldn't remember the last home-cooked meal she'd eaten. Diner and microwave food did not qualify. She had worried for a while that O'Malley's friends would look down on her when they found out how they'd met, but both Sean and Joan accepted what had happened with little fanfare. Terri felt guilty about having to lie about her true circumstances, but she couldn't come out and admit who she really was. There was too much at stake.

She brushed off the protests as she picked up the dishes on the table. With a shy smile, she went into the kitchen, her arms feeling the load of plates and silverware. She was aware of how domestic the whole thing seemed, but she was supposed to belong to O'Malley. This was just one more of those things that she was expected to do, and she would carry the role as far as she needed to. She could hear bits and pieces of their conversation. As she was loading the dishwasher she sighed when she heard the voices drift off. She jumped when a hand touched her shoulder and she turned quickly to find Joan standing there with an amused smile.

"That was so not nice. Did you take lessons from O'Malley?" Terri snapped as she recovered her breath. She chose to ignore Joan's chuckle.

"God no. I learned it a very long time ago, and then when I met those two, I got better. Those two were terrors way back when." Joan took a place next to Terri so that she could pitch in to clean up. "Of course, they're terrors now, too. Look, I might be out of line here, but lemme say it. I love Callan, and sometimes I hate that she's chosen to live her life like this. I have some idea of what your life in the club is like, but when you're here, you are not required to wait on her hand and foot." Joan held up a dripping hand when Terri opened her mouth to protest. "My house, my rules. Besides, she likes a challenge." Joan smiled an evil grin. "Sometimes it's better when you make her work for it."

"Is it too soon for me to say I like you?" Terri asked with a small laugh.

"Nah, not too soon at all," Joan answered, then turned to a serious subject. "They're outside, and it might not be a good idea to interrupt right now."

Terri nodded and settled another plate in the dishwasher. "O'Malley told me how she makes her money. I know better than to go poking my nose where it really shouldn't be."

"I just had to make sure, you know?" Joan said as she wiped down the counter. "There, all done. C'mon, I'll show you some really embarrassing photos of those two."

Terri agreed without a moment's hesitation. There was something appealing about getting to see O'Malley in her younger days and in compromising positions. She followed Joan into the living room and spent the next hour and a half laughing hard enough to bring tears. The photos were one thing, but it was great to hear the stories that went along with the visuals. The two women hardly noticed when their respective partners came back into the house.

"Okay, now this one is when we went to Alaska, and someone decided it would be a good idea if we all went skinny—" Joan was interrupted when the photo album was pulled from her grasp. She protested loudly, trying to get the book back as O'Malley held her at bay.

"Nope, I've been embarrassed enough for one night," O'Malley said firmly as she closed the book. "Besides, I'm really wiped out. If y'all don't mind, it's time for a shower and sleep. We have an entire four days more; I'll make it up to you, sweets," she promised her longtime friend.

"Jeesh, she never lets me call her sweets." Sean assumed a pout as he took the album from her.

"That's 'cause she loves me," O'Malley teased as she pulled them both into a hug. "You, she only married for respectability."

Terri watched with something close to envy. These three obviously shared a bond that she could not begin to fathom. She knew it had a lot to do with how they had all met. The photos she'd seen that night gave validation to the stories she'd heard about soldiers finding a family within the military. She knew that some families were temporary things and others, like the one she was looking at, were permanent. A part of her wished that this family were hers.

Chapter 6

Sean looked over his shoulder at the expanse of pastureland that lay beyond his backyard. One of the reasons he liked living in the country was that he and Joan could have all the privacy they wanted. He couldn't shake the feeling that they were being watched, and for the moment, that was all right with him. It was one of the few times that being watched was important. He had listened to O'Malley describe the events at the motel and her suspicions, and had agreed that they needed to step up appearances while the two women were visiting. The four had discussed the problem and had come up with something that would make it look good.

He took a long time to study his friend and inadvertent savior. She had been, as they used to say, all bad boy with an attitude for the three days since she'd arrived. The days were spent reminiscing and renewing their old habit of competing. When they weren't tearing up the roads on the bikes, they were trying to outdrink each other. *The fight at the bar was not entirely our fault,* he mused. *When three rednecks hit on your women, you just have to stand up for what is yours.* It was fortunate for them that the county sheriff thought so as well.

Of course Sean, O'Malley, and Joan had been surprised when Terri took out one of the rednecks with a pitcher of beer. She'd shrugged and muttered something about sneaking bastards. He had to smile at that one and silently observed that she fit in quite well. He knew she was a bit on the quiet side and never gave out too much information about her life, but then he understood having secrets that couldn't be shared.

He looked again at O'Malley. In her riding leathers and cut-off T-shirt, she *looked* like a badass. He knew from experience that she didn't just have the look, she really was one. There was something in his friend that was harder, grittier, and far more dangerous than most people could ever imagine. Those were memories he could not forget, nor would he have traded them. If he had a brother, he would have imagined no one better than Callan O'Malley in that role. Chuckling at the oddity of the thought, he wished on the stars that someone would melt his "brother's" heart.

"You gonna stay there all night, or do you wanna see what we got Terri today?" Joan asked in a mischievous tone, bumping him with her hip. Sean opened his eyes only when he'd completed his wish, and he smiled at his wife.

"In a minute. I was just—"

"Thinking. Hoping. Wishing," Joan finished for him with a soft smile. "Trust me, white boy, I'm working on it my own way."

Sean had to smile. The first time she had called him that, he had been shocked, but then so had her parents when she'd brought a white man home. Stepping onto the Lakota reservation had been an eye-opening experience. Almost ten years later, he was an adopted member of the Nation, and welcome.

"I can't wait to see O'Malley's eyes pop out of her head when she sees Terri," Joan said with childlike glee.

"You, my love, are evil. And thank you for not making us stay at the mall all day long," he said dryly. His wife could live at the mall if he'd let her.

"Hey, I had fun. You are going to thank me later for all the hell I didn't put you through today." She laughed. "Besides, after the fight, I figured we owed you two."

They had spent the day shopping and riding their bikes. It had been hard to see someone other than Ellen on the Harley with O'Malley, but Joan had to admit that Terri looked good sitting on the back of the bike, holding on tight. She had seen flashes of the old Callan O'Malley and recognized the look of hunger on her face. Joan was sure that O'Malley was interested in Terri, and unless she was blind, Terri was interested as well.

In her own sly way, she was hell-bent on helping the two of them get closer. Their last stop had been at her favorite leather store, and she was sure that O'Malley was going to love the outfit they'd chosen for Terri. She pushed Sean toward O'Malley and walked past him.

"I'm going to make sure she's all set. Get me a beer, would you?"

"One beer, ice cold, coming up. Don't take too long." He leered. She was a vision in her riding leathers, tight, lace-up pants and a fringe-edged halter, the tribal symbols of her Lakota heritage making her that much more alluring. When she felt like riding, her eyes took on the mysterious quality that ran in a family laced with shamans and seers. It was almost as if she knew what was going on before anyone else, as if she had some special insight that was reserved just for her.

Joan walked through the house, a familiar warm feeling spreading through her body. She just knew tonight was going to be one of those really good nights. She sighed contentedly and knocked on the guest room door.

"Just me," she announced, and waited for Terri to invite her in. When she did, Joan entered and stopped dead in her tracks. In the tight tan leather hip-huggers and short leather vest, Terri looked amazing. The difference in her appearance was like going from librarian to junior goddess. "Oh my God."

Terri's face fell. "That bad, huh? Maybe I should change."

Joan reached out and stopped her. "No. That was a good 'oh my God'. You are going to give Callan and O'Malley a heart attack."

"Huh? What is she, twins?"

Joan had to sit down on the bed for a minute. "Okay, lemme see if I can make some sense of that last one. Look outside at Callan and tell me what you see."

"I see O'Malley playing with Sean."

"Yep, that's who you see. Sometimes my friend down there can be like two people. She has two very different sides. The side that everyone sees most is the O'Malley side, but the side of her that's kinda quiet and gentle, now that's Callan. And you are going to give both of them a heart attack." Joan grinned like a fool.

"Joan, can I ask you a question?"

"Sure."

"Which one of those two women would try and dump Sean into the pool headfirst?"

* ~ * ~ * ~ *

"Let go of my boy before you get hurt, O'Malley." Joan rumbled with laughter. "Not in the water, you dolt." She grinned when O'Malley let him off the proverbial hook. "Now the two of you sit down and enjoy the unveiling," she ordered as she took her seat. "Okay, Terri," she shouted.

O'Malley sat down in her lounger. She was curious to see what Joan and Terri had cooked up, but she wasn't going to give her friend the idea that she was curious. She casually took a sip of her beer, and when Terri walked out of the house, she almost choked. She knew Terri was good looking, but in tight leather that hugged all the right places, she was simply stunning. Her tight hold on her hormones slipped and she knew it was going to be one very long evening.

Sean let out a whistle that earned him a slap on the stomach from his wife. "What? Baby, she's damn hot in that. You did good."

Joan chuckled. "You got that right, big boy, but if you don't want O'Malley to shake your eyeballs out of your head, I'd behave." Joan went over to Terri and hugged her while handing her a beer. "Sean says someone's out there. You two are gonna have to play it very cozy," she whispered, and felt Terri's small nod of acknowledgment. She let Terri out of the embrace. "I propose a toast," Joan said loudly, lifting her beer. "To bikes, shopping, and leather."

"Definitely leather," O'Malley agreed, and took a healthy drink of her beer. She swallowed hard as she watched Terri drink to the two parts of the toast. The last three nights of having Terri sleep next to her had been difficult enough, but this was sheer torture.

Sean reached over and grabbed the stereo remote. With a push of a button, the music started and he pulled his wife close. "Hey, O'Malley. What do you say to a night ride?" he asked as he ran his hands over Joan's arms.

O'Malley took her eyes off Terri for a moment to look at him. She recognized his question for what it was. Joan leaning into him with an expression of wanting did not help. She turned back to Terri, who looked confused. She grinned. "What do you say, Ter? Feel like tempting the powers that be?"

"How would we do that?"

"Well, sometimes we just like to prove what badasses we are." O'Malley had a sly grin on her face as she walked to Terri, who stood like a deer caught in the headlights. She halted just outside of Terri's personal space. "Sean and me, we've seen inside the belly of the beast, and we lived. Sometimes we like to remind the beast that we're still here," she said. "It's like we need to prove there's a reason we're still here."

"I'll make you a deal. I go with you three and tempt your powers that be, and you tell me what beast you two survived."

"You got a deal. And, Terri, just so you know, I'm not drunk, and I won't risk your life or limb," O'Malley promised. "Hey, Sean, we're on. Let's get the bikes."

* ~ * ~ * ~ *

Terri lay on the pool deck, her body still humming from the bike ride. Taking the winding roads in the dark with no headlights had been an incredible experience. For the first ten minutes, her heart had been in her throat, but once she'd felt the adrenaline pump through her, she was hooked. It was like nothing she'd ever felt before. There had been times when she'd felt a thrill while making an arrest, but this was so much more intense. Every nerve ending was on fire. Now she understood what tempting the Fates meant. She had put her life in O'Malley's hands and found the biker more than capable. She felt like she'd drunk an entire brewery, but without the fuzzy feeling. She was alive, and very happy about it. It was a new high for her, and she wanted to experience the feeling again sometime in the near future.

O'Malley dropped down next to her with a satisfied grin. "How ya doing?"

"That was just incredible." Terri sighed. "Why haven't we done that before?" she asked before she could stop herself.

"Didn't feel like it before. Sometimes when I hook up with Sean, I just feel like it," O'Malley said.

"I think Sean's in for a long night." Terri laughed. Joan had literally attacked her husband upon their return.

"I think they both are," O'Malley answered with a matching laugh. She pillowed her head with her hands and stared up at the sky full of stars. "When Sean and I went to war in the Gulf, the morning the ground action started, we kind of ran over a land mine. Our vehicle was ripped open like a tin can. We had to get back on foot. Those two and a half miles to our lines seemed like forever. We spent most of those miles under small arms fire. Everybody in the group was hurt in some way or another, but somehow we made it back. Sean was probably hit the worst. That's the beast we faced," O'Malley explained quietly.

Turning her head, Terri gazed at the woman next to her. She reached out a hand and let her fingers trace the fine scars on O'Malley's face. She felt O'Malley tense for a moment, then relax. "That's where these came from, isn't it?" She took a closer look.

"Yeah. Mortar fire. I took some shrapnel. The scars on my back are from then, and the ones on my legs. Those stitches itched like hell for the longest time," O'Malley recalled with something close to a smile. "But those docs and nurses did one hell of a job putting us back together."

Terri noticed the wistful, almost sad expression on the biker's face. Instinctively, she knew there was more to the story, but she also knew that O'Malley wouldn't speak about it until she was ready. She would not push. She had no idea what the ordeal was, but she knew that it had to be one of the most frightening things a human being could go through. She was glad that O'Malley had not gone through it alone, and then wondered where the thought had come from.

O'Malley rolled over, reaching for her beer. The bottle was empty and she set the bottle down, surprising Terri when the clunk was louder than she had expected.

"I'll get it." Terri got up quickly, grateful for a distraction. As she walked to the cooler, she suddenly remembered that they were most likely being watched. An evil grin crossed her face. If Trey and his cronies were expecting a show, she would give them one.

She fished two bottles out of the cooler and twisted off the caps, then walked back to O'Malley, a bottle in each hand. Instead of going to O'Malley's side, Terri straddled her.

O'Malley looked up. Reaching out, she took the offered bottle, set it down within reach, then took Terri's hand and pulled her down. She smiled when the smaller woman readily sat on her stomach. "Finally remembered we have company, huh?" she teased as she reached for her bottle and took a sip.

"Yeah. Don't know how I could have forgotten that," Terri answered dryly. "I figured it was time we got cozy."

O'Malley finally put words to the question. "I can do cozy, but can you kiss?"

Instead of answering with words, Terri leaned in and pressed her lips to O'Malley's. It wasn't the usual shy type of kiss but an intimate kiss like lovers are supposed to share, and it left Terri breathless. For several long moments, she found herself lost in it. Without thinking, she used her mouth to trace a wet pattern over O'Malley's chin and then roved back to her lips.

O'Malley returned the kisses with equal enthusiasm, pulling Terri closer. Finally, when breathing became critical, they slowly pulled apart. "Well, that's one hell of a good answer," O'Malley mused. She kept her hands on Terri's hips. "I can see you like the adrenaline."

"Mmm-hmm," Terri purred and leaned in close to O'Malley's ear. "Every nerve in my body feels like it's in overdrive."

"Then we'll have to do it again sometime," O'Malley teased with a smile, then ducked her head to run her lips over the sensitive skin of Terri's neck.

Terri's hands roamed through O'Malley's hair and down her arms and back. She let out an unrestrained moan when O'Malley sucked on her pulse point.

"I think we should take cozy inside." Without waiting for an answer, O'Malley rolled Terri from her perch and managed to get them both standing. With Terri's mouth latched on to hers, O'Malley stumbled back toward the door. Tugging her lips away after a moment, she took a deep breath. "You are playing with fire," she warned with a throaty growl.

"I know. Just once in my life, O'Malley, I don't want to think," Terri said. At the moment she was not thinking about being a badge or that she was working. She thought only about how she felt, and how much she was enjoying being alive and how vivid that was.

"You do this now and there will be no playing, no faking, with others around. You think you can deal with that, live with that on a twenty-four/seven basis?" O'Malley didn't sound cruel, just blunt.

Terri was forced to think, and she shut her eyes tight against her dilemma. She was confused, her logical side at war with her sensual self. She wanted everything she knew she couldn't have. Opening her eyes, she felt the tears start. She wanted, and yet a part of her didn't want. She felt O'Malley ease away, her silence having been enough of an answer.

"We have a long day tomorrow." O'Malley's voice was husky. "Guess it's time to turn in."

Her vision blurred, Terri watched O'Malley make her way down the dark hallway to the bedroom. She weakly wiped away the tears as she tried to figure out what to do. She stood in the living room for a very long time, thinking and not thinking. Finally, she let her feet take her to the threshold of the bedroom door. Peering inside, she could just barely make out the form of O'Malley under the blankets.

Quietly, Terri peeled off her clothes and crawled into bed naked. She lay in the dark and tried to will herself to sleep. Not even O'Malley's deep breathing could lull her into slumber.

Terri tried to recall the last time she had spent so much time sleeping next to someone other than Trey. Her brain supplied the name, and she flinched against the memory. Barbara had been all bluster and charm, and Terri had fallen hard. Terri rolled over in bed and wished she hadn't started that particular trip down memory lane. Barbara had looked every bit the Nordic goddess, seemingly everything that Terri wasn't. It had been a whirlwind romance during specialized training, courtesy of the FBI.

The days had been filled with learning all she could about deep undercover work, and her nights had been filled with Barbara and a notion of romance that normally ended up in a very different type of undercover work. The sex had been almost like a force of nature. Terri thought everything was perfect until she had come back to their shared apartment and found Barbara in the arms of another person.

That it had been Barbara's husband was a hard blow. Somehow she had forgotten to mention the fact that she was married, or that her husband had been out of the country on assignment. Terri still didn't know how she had kept herself from pulling her sidearm and shooting both of them. Instead, she quietly closed the door and sat on the couch until they finished and came out of the bedroom. She would always remember the momentary look of panic on Barbara's face when they both stepped out.

Terri couldn't recall his name, but she did remember being calmly civil as he ran around the apartment gathering his things, explaining that he had to catch an airplane to another part of the world. When he finally left, she had looked at Barbara and surprised herself by not crying or betraying her crushed heart. Without speaking, she gathered her things and placed her key on the counter.

She tossed her bags into the car and left without looking back, moved back into her assigned room at the FBI Academy visitor's dorm, and never acknowledged Barbara's attempts at an apology. The rest of her time was spent learning to lose herself in her undercover work. She had never counted on meeting someone like O'Malley.

Terri rolled over in bed, her gaze coming to rest on the lean lines of the biker's face. Even in sleep, she was stoic. Terri had watched as O'Malley experienced nightmares. The tone of her voice, never her face, gave away her distress. Sometimes Terri wondered if she was even aware of it. O'Malley shifted in bed, and Terri sighed. She could not figure O'Malley out. There was something she could not pinpoint that lurked just under the surface, something she thought she had caught a glimpse of during the night ride, and that something was dangerous and alluring.

Terri sighed again and quietly rose from the bed. She pulled one of O'Malley's long-sleeved shirts from the dresser and slipped into it, the soft material soothing her. After stepping into a pair of boxer shorts, she made her way out into the living room. Sitting on the couch, she reached for one of the photo albums on the coffee table, one that Joan had never opened during the "let's embarrass O'Malley" photo show. She opened it to the first page and was surprised to find a photo of O'Malley in a formal best-man tux standing next to a green-looking Sean. The next photo was of Joan, the happy bride, standing next to the woman whose snapshot lived in O'Malley's wallet.

The first three pages were typical wedding photos of the happy couple at the altar with the priest presiding over the ceremony, and then there was the kiss photo. Terri had to admit that Sean and Joan looked absolutely adorable together. Their photos, however, paled in comparison to those of O'Malley and the woman on her arm. The look on O'Malley's face could only be described as worship.

Terri flipped through the entire album and found, on the back cover, a listing of the wedding party: *Ellen Rivers, Maid of Honor, and Best Man and best friend, Callan O'Malley.* She closed the album, finally having a name to put to the face.

Chapter 7

O'Malley let her truck door close and hefted the case in her hand, getting a better grip as she walked along the sidewalk that bordered the clubhouse. Checking out the bikes in the parking lot, she was relieved not to see Trey's. She was in a lousy mood, and she knew from experience that she would not be able to control herself if he started in on her. The visual that passed through her head was almost enough to make her smile. She needed some stress relief, and beating the crap out of him just might do it.

She shook her head, paused for a moment to take a deep breath, then pushed open the front door of the clubhouse. She nodded a greeting to Boomer when he looked up from his bike magazine.

"Hey, O'Malley. You carrying anything I need to know about?" He was all business, and watched as she carefully opened her jacket with one hand, lifting it slightly then doing a complete turn before letting the jacket down.

"I got some samples for Spyder in the case," she said, laying the case on the countertop in front of him. She pushed open the latches and turned it toward him.

He opened it and shifted the three Berettas inside, then closed the case. "Those things suck, you know," he muttered as she snapped the latches closed.

"Tell me about it. He's waiting for me," she answered, taking the case in hand.

"In the back." Boomer went back to his magazine.

O'Malley turned and walked through the large main room. The walls were essentially bare, except for the Harley flags and posters of mostly naked women draped over bikes. Two pool tables took up one section of the room, and the bar on the opposite side was, as always, well stocked. The eight tables were half full of bikers. She let her gaze travel to the booth in the back of the room. As expected, Spyder was there holding court. The beer bottles in front of him were not all his. Two of his three favorite boys were in attendance, as was his girlfriend.

O'Malley grabbed a chair and dragged it over. After turning it backward, she laid the case on the table and sat down without a word. She didn't bother to take off her sunglasses, knowing that leaving them on would bug the club leader and today was all about pushing his buttons.

"O'Malley." Eyes guarded, Spyder leaned back in his seat. She was early, and he hated being surprised.

"Samples. There're fifteen more on the way if you like 'em. Price is not negotiable," she said with a hard edge.

Spyder pushed the empty bottles out of the way and opened the case. He took his time with the weapons, breaking each one down and checking it over. She did not miss the fleeting, satisfied smile on his face. He placed the last weapon back in the case, then set the case down by his feet.

"You got a deal. These are better than the last batch. Half now and half on delivery."

"Cool. I'll make shipping arrangements." She moved to get up.

"Stay for a minute," he ordered. "Why don't you three go do something else?" It was not a request, and everyone at the table knew it. Spyder's face remained impassive as the other occupants left the booth. Once they were out of earshot, he said, I need a special order."

"What kind of special order?"

"Something with a little more firepower. The boys in Washington are having some competition problems. Seems the other side got their hands on some AKs. I was thinking along the lines of a couple of SAWs."

O'Malley was glad she'd left her sunglasses on. She was sure her surprise would have shown. The Squad Automatic Weapon was the military's answer to upgrading the M60. Slightly lighter than the mainstay machine gun, it had the added advantage of being fed by magazine or belt ammo. It was a meat grinder that worked well in any environment.

"That one might be a little rough. They're still pretty new, and they haven't kicked too many out for recycle. I'll see what I can do. It's gonna take me a while. What's your time line?" she asked without giving anything away.

"A month. If you can do it sooner, that would be good." He took up his beer bottle.

"If I can do it at all, it's gonna cost," she warned.

"Hell, O'Malley, I figured that. Two would be good, more would be better."

His voice was tinged with laughter, but she heard the threat behind the laugh. "No promises, Spyder, but I'll give it a try. I think I might know someone who can pull it off."

He leaned forward with an expression she couldn't identify. "What's the problem?"

"Oh, the potential supplier hates my guts. I might have to use a go-between. If I do that, it'll jack the price. I gotta cover all the bases, if you know what I mean." She leaned back.

"I get your drift. It'll be worth it if it keeps my competition out of my business."

O'Malley forced herself to shrug. "Like I said, no promises."

He quickly changed the subject. "So, how was your trip?"

O'Malley tried to keep up with the shift in conversation. She let a sly smile slide over her lips. "What do you really want to know, Spyder? I'm not good with dancing around the subject."

"Is she any good?" The tone in his voice left no doubt what he was asking.

O'Malley forced a laugh. "My mama taught me not to kiss and tell, but between you and me...very good and very tasty. I'm gonna need a vacation to rest up from my vacation."

"That's good to hear. I guess we won't have to take care of her then."

O'Malley leaned forward just a bit, her leather jacket creaking. "Anyone touches her and they lose a body part, Spyder, you included. Get my drift?" There was nothing teasing or friendly in her voice.

"Getting soft on some chick, O'Malley?" he challenged, then took a drink from his bottle.

"Just making sure that what's mine stays mine." O'Malley stood and pushed away from the chair. "The rest of the shipment will be here in a couple of weeks."

"I'll have Boomer bring the first half over to you tomorrow. Hey, O'Malley," he called as she turned away. "Trey's probably gonna be a problem."

"He already is. Just so he stays clear, all will be cool," she said quietly before she walked away.

* ~ * ~ * ~ *

Terri sank into her usual seat across from George and listened to him grunt into the phone. *This is getting to be a habit,* she thought to herself, biting back a smile as her boss rolled his eyes in exasperation. He finally hung up the phone after she propped her feet up on his desk. She was tired and wrung out.

"Your feet are not on my desk, right?" George asked, not expecting an answer.

When his eyes locked on hers, she moved her feet to the floor. "Nope. Did you miss me?" It was an attempt to lighten the mood and judging from his expression, she had failed.

"Very funny." He pushed a thick file folder toward Terri. "Callan O'Malley. You sure know how to pick them."

Terri reached across the desk and picked up the folder. "Hey, Trey did this, not me. Kick his ass for a change, would you?" She opened the folder and was faced with O'Malley's mug shot. The double bruising around her eyes was definitely not attractive. She could only describe the expression frozen on film as rabid raccoon. The woman was definitely angry. Terri moved past the photo and skimmed the highlights, her eyes widening at the charges.

"Three counts of assault on a police officer?" she read. "She took on three cops for..." She skimmed back over the file. "Half a dime bag?"

George nodded. "Yeah. The bag was on a table at the clubhouse. She copped to the possession and, according to the report, resisted arrest."

"Before or after Bates cuffed her?" Terri asked, not bothering to cover her sarcasm. She knew the arresting officer for what he was.

"Officially, she resisted when they took her into custody. I asked some of the other officers not listed on the report. According to them, Bates threw the first punch. Seems she took offense to his comments toward her companion, so she questioned his parentage. Richards and Henderson are so up Bates's ass, they just followed his lead. They ended up in the same emergency room. You might want to look a little deeper in there. She's dangerous, Terri. According to her military record, she got kicked out for theft and breaking her hand on an officer's face. I want you away from her."

Terri closed the file. "And how am I supposed to do that, George? Trey got me into this fucking mess, and now you want me to just walk away." Her eyes pleaded with him to give her an answer. When none was forthcoming, she sighed and slapped the file on the desk. "Pull him and I'll walk away."

"I can't." He sounded defeated. "I can't do that any more than I can pull you." He sank into his chair and stared out the window for a moment. "Nice hickey." His voice was flat.

Terri nodded absently. "It's not what you think. I didn't sleep with her," she said in a low tone. "Trey sent one of his boys to follow us. We had to make it look like she was having her way with me. If she hadn't marked me, they'd know."

George nodded. Terri was good, with a natural ability for undercover work. Her last two assignments had resulted in high profile busts with a large amount of money and drugs confiscated. Several out-of-state departments had requested her based on her reputation alone.

"I'm sorry, Terri. I'm at a loss."

"Don't be, George. I learned some good stuff this week, so it's not a total loss. You can add buying stolen weapons to Spyder's list." She almost laughed at George's expression. "It seems my girl-friend sells him stolen military weapons."

"Holy shit," he muttered. "This is deeper than I thought. I might have to call in the feds on this one, or at the very least, the military."

"You do that and they'll yank us for sure. I've never been yanked from a case, and I'm not gonna start now. Just give me some time on this one, George." Her voice wasn't desperate, but it was close.

It took him a long time to reach a decision. She knew that he desperately wanted the club behind bars. The police chief and the mayor were breathing down his neck, and she knew they were getting heat from several other agencies.

"I'll give you all the time I can. Now what do you know about these weapons?"

Terri outlined what little she knew and what she'd been able to piece together from the photos. She gave him dates and places that she could recall from the conversations with Sean and Joan. There was a small part of her that felt guilty about it, but the bigger part of her knew that they were profiting from illegal activities.

George scribbled furiously as he took notes. He would have a great deal to research before their next meeting.

"Oh, and she knows Maria Cortez from somewhere in the past." Terri couldn't keep the curiosity from her voice.

"The owner of Traders out on I-10?" he asked to clarify. "Do you think she's involved with any of this?"

Terri thought the question over for a moment. "I don't think so. The bikers like to hang out at Traders when the club isn't open. I'm sure they make some deals there, but I've seen her toss 'em out if she catches any of them dealing in her bar. I think she's a bar owner with a lousy customer base."

The relief on his face showed, and Terri smiled sympathetically. She knew he had a soft spot for the bar. At the end of her life, just about the only joy Helen, his wife, had experienced was her Baileys on the rocks and listening to the oldies that played on the jukebox at Traders.

"I think we're done here. Two weeks from now, unless something else comes up," he said in a low tone.

Terri recognized the loneliness. She knew he would probably go home, pour himself a drink, and stare at photo albums most of the night. "Hey, George, when this is all over, let's you and me go to Traders and get plastered," she suggested.

"Plastered, yes; Traders, no. We'll both be marked. Would you settle for a barbecue in the backyard?" He attempted a smile.

"You have a deal." Terri picked up her bag, shouldered the strap, and looked at him for a long time. "I think O'Malley is the key, George. Trust me." She signed her paperwork and walked out of the room. It wasn't until she was at the bus stop waiting for O'Malley that she realized that he had not answered her.

~~*~*

"You're going where?" Ellen asked as she blinked against what she'd just been told.

"Bosnia," Callan repeated patiently. When her platoon leader had explained the assignment, Callan knew that Ellen would pitch one hell of a fit. She swallowed the groan that wanted to escape as she watched her girlfriend's posture turn rigid.

"When you give me information like that, you really shouldn't look so

damned pleased." Ellen's words were clipped and short.

"I'm not pleased, Nurse. I don't really want to go, but I don't have a choice. I'm on the short list. MPs are going to be a huge part of the peacekeeping mission." Even as she tried to explain, she knew that her words weren't going to matter.

"It's not fair. We finally have time together and now you're going again. You even went Airborne so that we could be in the same city. You fucking hate jumping out of airplanes."

Callan smiled gently. When her posting at Fort Bliss had come to an end, Ellen had been assigned to Pope Air Force Base. Without telling her, Callan had asked for airborne training and assignment to Fort Bragg. She would always remember the surprised look on Ellen's face when she showed up at the flight clinic and just stood there until the nurse looked up.

Without thinking about it, Callan wrapped her arms around Ellen and let her chin rest on the top of her head. She closed her eyes and put everything she felt in the embrace.

"I don't want you to go. I know it's selfish and probably childish, but I want you here with me. I want us to be together and at least pretend to be a normal couple," Ellen said into Callan's shoulder as she wrapped her arms around her.

"I want that too, baby. You have no idea how much I want that. But I have to go."

Ellen nodded. "I know. You're a good soldier." She didn't bother disguising the sarcasm.

Callan sighed. "Yes, I am. That's how you met me, remember?"

"How could I forget that one, Irish? You looked like hell when they brought you in. I don't want that to happen again. I don't think I could deal with it twice."

Callan tried to lighten the mood. "It won't happen again. Sean won't be driving, so no land mines."

"You're going into a potential war zone, O'Malley. Joking about it won't change the fact that you could come home in a box." Ellen's voice trembled as she pulled out of the hug.

"Ellen, I could go up in a plane and pile drive into the ground on a chute failure tomorrow. Damn it, baby, I'm in a dangerous profession. You know that. Hell, you're in the Air Force. You should know it better than anyone." Callan stood her ground. If Ellen was going to fight logic, she wasn't going to chase her.

"Thanks, O'Malley. That makes me feel so much better."

"What do you want me to do? Go to my CO and say 'Gee, sorry, sir,

can't go. My girlfriend won't let me.' That would go over real well." Callan
sank into her favorite recliner.

*"I don't know what I want you to do. I just know that I want to wake up
next to you for the rest of my life." The tears finally escaped.*

*"Ellen, look at me." She waited until the woman of her dreams complied.
"This is who I am. I don't know any other way to be. I love being a soldier,
and I'm damn good at being an MP. If this were a different assignment, I
would be worried. This is a peacekeeping mission, not Iraq. I can't promise I
won't get hurt, but baby, I will come home to you. I will always be there to
keep you warm."*

"And if you die there?"

*Callan sighed. "Then we'll both be pissed." There wasn't much more she
could say.*

*The rest of the evening was spent in strained silence. That night when
Ellen slipped under the sheets, she pulled Callan close and kissed her gently.
"I know you have to go. Come back home to me when it's time, Irish, and if
you're not in one piece, just know that I'm going to kick your butt."*

*Callan shifted and wrapped her arm around her lover, pulling her close
and feeling Ellen lay her head on her shoulder. "I promise with everything I
am, Nurse."*

O'Malley blinked when she felt a tap on her shoulder. She
smiled softly when Maria handed over a bottle of ice water. Looking
up at the night sky, she shook off feeling sorry for herself.

"What were you thinking about?" Maria asked as she closed the
door to the back patio.

"Oh, just irony." O'Malley took a sip from the bottle. The cold
water felt good on the back of her throat. "So, what's up?"

"Nice marking of your new territory." She smiled.

O'Malley tried not to blush and failed miserably. "Yeah, well,
we had eyes on us...had to make it look good. Besides, you're the
one who pointed out that I have a tendency to mark my women."

"That I did. Don't you think you should be inside paying her all
kinds of attention instead of being out here sulking?" Maria leaned
against the wall and stared out at the dark beyond the few stree-
tlights.

"I'm not sulking. The smoke inside was starting to get to me. I
came out here for some air."

"For half an hour?"

"Damn. I lost track of time," O'Malley said.

"Well, come on in and lose track of more time, only lose it with her, okay?" Maria ordered in her soft voice. "Rednecks are starting to come in, and we really don't want her to get caught up in the middle of all of that."

O'Malley smiled and nodded. "You sure you weren't a drill sergeant in a past life?" she teased.

"Nope, never that. I would have had to have been a Marine or something."

"Such language from a lady." O'Malley chuckled as she pushed away from the railing. Together they walked through the door and danced around the crowd to get to their spots at the bar. O'Malley tensed as she noticed a redneck bothering Terri. She started toward her, only to have Maria hold her back with a hand on her shoulder.

"Let her fight her battles until she needs the help. She's no fluff. You have to learn that she's tougher than you give her credit for," Maria said before O'Malley could argue. "Besides, he's new and doesn't know any better."

O'Malley watched Terri deflect the redneck's every advance until he rested his hand on her thigh and leaned in to whisper something in her ear. As soon as she saw Terri's shoulders bunch up slightly and the red rise on her ears, she felt sorry for the young man. She was almost proud when she noticed his face screw up in pain as Terri dug her nails into the top of his hand. O'Malley and Maria moved closer, just in case they were needed.

* ~ * ~ * ~ *

"I already said no. I'll spell it out for you. I'm with someone and even if I weren't, I still wouldn't be interested. Do I make myself clear?" Terri never raised her voice, but nevertheless it held an edge.

He persisted, even though her nails were about to draw blood. "I don't see anyone."

"Then turn around," Terri ordered. She could see O'Malley in the mirror. In leather and denim, she looked like an angel. *A really pissed-off angel*, her brain amended.

The redneck managed to turn around, obviously expecting to see some guy, but instead he saw the bartender and a woman in a leather jacket. He turned back to Terri.

"I don't see nobody," he repeated flatly. "Now, why don't you let go of my hand and we'll get outta here and have us some fun."

Terri let out a frustrated sigh. She let go of his hand with a final painful dig and quickly slid off her bar stool, avoiding his hand as she walked up to O'Malley. She reached up and rested her hand on the back of O'Malley's neck. With a quick smile, she tiptoed closer and planted a kiss on her lips. Feeling O'Malley kiss back, she couldn't help herself as she let her tongue dart over the biker's warm lips.

O'Malley wrapped her leather-clad arms around Terri and pulled her closer. Terri knew they were drawing attention to themselves, and for a split second wondered if it was a good idea. Another moment of kissing O'Malley, and she knew she didn't care.

The redneck almost fell off his stool in shock and anger. He stood quickly, his fists clenched, as the two women finally pulled slowly away from each other.

"Hi, baby, miss me?" O'Malley's hands roamed possessively over Terri's back. None of the bikers watching mistook the action. O'Malley was making sure everyone knew Terri was hers. Most of the rednecks got the idea, even if they didn't like it. The bikers outnumbered them by at least a two-to-one margin.

"Oh yeah. Where have you been?" Terri asked with a mischievous smile.

"Lost track of time outside. You ready to go, or do you want to stay for a while?"

"We can stay. I'm not ready to leave yet." Terri leaned closer into O'Malley's body. "I don't want that asshole to think I'm going to run every time he's in here."

O'Malley smiled an evil smile. "You want me to scare him a little?"

Terri chuckled. "How about a lot?" she teased. "No, I think he gets the picture now." She flashed a smile and took hold of O'Malley's hand, then led the way back to the bar. A couple of bikers grinned at the women and vacated their seats. One of the men winked at Terri and exaggerated a bow.

O'Malley ordered the men a round of drinks as she settled in, shifting her stool closer to Terri. Wrapping her arm around Terri's shoulders, she pulled her in close. "Nice move with that guy, by the way."

"Yeah, well, my mom once told me that long nails could be a girl's best friend," Terri answered with a half-smile.

"Good for Mom." O'Malley chuckled and turned to watch the activity in the bar. At a nearby table, Terri's would-be suitor complained to his buddies. She shook her head.

Terri nudged her and smiled. "You any good at pool?"

"Maybe." O'Malley grinned as she looked down at Terri. "Are you?"

Terri licked her lips and leaned in close. "Maybe. Wanna find out?"

"Lead the way," O'Malley challenged, and dug in her pocket for quarters.

Together they wound their way to the pool table and waited for a few minutes while the players finished their game. They claimed an emptying table, and O'Malley slid out of her jacket. Terri took the time to spy on the crowd. Aside from the usual barflies and associate club members, there were only rednecks. She was relieved not to see any of Trey's shadows. She hadn't realized how tense she had become in the last week.

Terri vowed to let herself relax. Letting out a slow steadying breath, she turned back to O'Malley to find she was being watched. O'Malley's face was impassive and Terri could not tell what she was thinking.

O'Malley dragged her eyes away and set her cue against the pool table. With sure, confident movements, she racked the balls into their triangle.

Terri knew she was staring, but she found that she didn't care. Years of riding bikes and who knew what else had given O'Malley strong, toned arms. Shoulder muscles danced beneath her black T-shirt.

"You gonna grab a stick or do you wanna share?" O'Malley asked as she rolled the cue ball to Terri.

"Sharing is good," Terri answered as she flagged down one of Maria's waitresses. She ordered two beers and rubbed her hands on the white block of chalk. "My break or yours?"

"By all means, ladies first," O'Malley answered with a grin.

Terri's lithe figure bent to take the break, and O'Malley had to shake her head. Two balls found pockets, and Terri stood up with an evil grin.

O'Malley groaned as the waitress brought their beers. "You actually play well, right?" She paid the tab and waited for Terri to answer.

The woman in question merely smiled and surveyed the layout of the balls. She took her time, called her shot, and smiled sweetly as she struck the cue ball. She laughed as O'Malley's head sank at the same time the ball did.

"I'm screwed," O'Malley moaned.

Chapter 8

Boomer coasted his Harley to a stop at the curb in front of O'Malley's overgrown lawn. He rubbed his hand over his mustache and goatee in an attempt to scrub some feeling back into his face. The morning had dawned unseasonably chilly, and the one thing he hated about owning only the bike was that his face stayed cold in the winter, despite all efforts to protect it. Dismounting, he flipped open the closest leather saddlebag and pulled out the pouch that Spyder had given him. He didn't need to look inside to know what it held. He shook his head with a wry smile. With each deal and each payment, his boss reeled O'Malley deeper into the club. He knew that Spyder would prefer to have the quiet, dangerous woman in his back pocket. Spyder did not like loose ends.

He slipped the pouch under his leather jacket and tucked it securely into the back waistband of his jeans, then walked casually up the concrete path to the front door. Instead of knocking, he peered in the front window. Beer bottles littered the coffee table and clothing was strewn across the floor. His inspection shifted to the outside of the house, and he was surprised to see that the curtains over the side window weren't quite closed. Having been to her place enough times to have memorized the layout of the house, Boomer knew the window was in O'Malley's bedroom.

Guessing that the occupants of the house were still asleep, he moved stealthily to the window, avoiding the stray neighborhood cat that stared at him intently. He looked in, and froze. O'Malley's naked back was toward him. Her head was deep in her pillow and her arm was wrapped tightly around a mostly covered figure. There was no mistaking the familiar light brown hair, and Boomer watched as Terri turned slightly and snuggled closer to O'Malley, who tightened her embrace. The movement drew his attention to the tattoos on the strong shoulders, and to the scars. He winced at the obvious damage that had been done, knowing that it would have caused O'Malley a world of hurt.

He'd heard the other bikers taunt her by calling her a war hero. He didn't know the whole story behind the goading, but he figured those scars had to be a part of it. For a moment, he wondered if anyone knew the whole story, or if anyone really knew O'Malley. He filed the thought away for a later time. Backing away from the window, he returned to the porch and punched the doorbell, then heard the chimes sound in the house. After a minute, he tried again.

* ~ * ~ * ~ *

O'Malley opened her eyes when the doorbell rang the first time, instantly awake. She slipped quietly out of bed, grabbed a pair of discarded jeans, and pulled them on. After hastily fastening the buttons, she retrieved her Sig 9mm from beneath her pillow and slipped it into the back of the jeans. She didn't bother with a bra, just pulled on a T-shirt, then glanced at Terri to make sure she was still asleep. The doorbell rang again. She padded to the side door, eased it open, and stepped out into the chilly morning. The grass was cold on her feet as she wrapped her hand around the weapon and pulled it free. She brought it up as she turned the corner of the house and aimed it at the figure on her front porch.

"Turn nice and slow," she ordered, not sounding at all like she'd been deeply asleep minutes before.

Boomer slowly lifted his hands away from his body before he followed the order, and an instant of fear flickered across his expression as he came face to face with O'Malley and her 9mm.

She lowered her weapon and slid it back into her waistband. "Next time, call first." She yawned loudly and stretched. "Come on, back this way." She turned and walked around the corner, not bothering to look back. She knew he would follow; they always did. As she became more aware of how chilly it was, she walked quickly to the side door, pushed it open, and stepped into the house. O'Malley's lips quirked into a small smile at Terri standing in the doorway of the bedroom, a short robe that barely covered the essentials wrapped around her body and sleepy confusion on her face.

"We have company," O'Malley announced needlessly. "Coffee."

Terri nodded and went to the kitchen to start the coffee.

Boomer stepped into the kitchen. "Hey, Terri." He stopped

short and blinked a couple of times. He pulled himself together just as O'Malley came back from the bedroom, her cold feet now covered in thick socks.

She walked into the kitchen and pulled down three coffee mugs from the cupboard. "Baby, go put something on before Boomer has a heart attack," she directed.

Terri finished pouring the water into the coffee machine, then turned and snuggled into O'Malley's arms. "Can't we just go back to bed?" Still tired, she burrowed her head against O'Malley's shoulder.

O'Malley became very aware of how thin the robe was; she could feel Terri's warmth. Her arms automatically went around Terri's body in an embrace. "You go ahead. Boomer and I have some stuff to do."

"Mmmkay," Terri mumbled, remaining where she was. O'Malley sighed, and Terri took the hint. "I'm going." She pulled away from O'Malley and walked toward the bedroom, waving to Boomer as she passed him.

O'Malley waited until she heard the bedroom door close, then met the biker's gaze. He was almost smiling. She shrugged her shoulders in response to his amusement and sent a mental "hurry up" to the coffeemaker. She wanted coffee and an aspirin or fifty for the headache that was beginning. The previous evening was mostly a fog in her brain, and she wondered how much they'd had to drink and, more importantly, what had happened between her and Terri.

"Looks pretty damn domestic, O'Malley."

She quirked an eyebrow and wondered if the pain showed on her face. "Yeah, it does," she finally answered. "What time is it?"

Boomer chuckled and had the decency to look a little sheepish. "Eight thirty."

"When I wake up, I'm gonna kick your ass," O'Malley muttered. Rising early was not one of her virtues.

Boomer laughed and slipped the pouch from his waistband. "I thought you might want this. For some reason, Spyder doesn't like to keep you waiting." He sat down without an invitation, waiting for a cup of coffee.

"What's that supposed to mean?" She grabbed a coffee mug and took her time pouring.

"It means just that. You're the only one I get morning duty with; everyone else gets to wait. You got any idea why he might do that?"

"It's self-service here, Boomer. You want a cup, you gotta get off your butt and get it." O'Malley set the pot back on the warmer plate and sat on a stool before responding to his question. "I have an idea that he doesn't like me being freelance, but hey, it's my life. I like my freedom."

Boomer appeared to think about that as he crossed to the coffeemaker, his boots sounding loud on the floor. He grabbed the mug and poured some coffee. "I get that. I don't think he likes it. You could be a problem later."

O'Malley laughed, and had to ignore the resulting shooting pain in her head. "Like I'm gonna, what? Run to call the cops? Fuck, Boomer, I do that and I'd be cutting my own throat. Can you imagine that conversation? 'Gee, officer, see, I sold guns to this biker and now I wanna turn him in.' Do you have any fucking clue what the Army would do to me?"

The bitterness was evident in her voice. "No, I don't. Why don't you tell me?" he said.

"In their eyes, I'd be worse than a traitor. Ex-soldier stealing weapons and selling 'em to a bike club, that'd go over real well." She didn't bother to mask her sarcasm. "Think of the worst pain you've ever been through." She watched him mentally do just that. "Now multiply it by a thousand. That's what they'd do to me," she finished grimly.

"That sucks."

"Welcome to my world," O'Malley muttered as she rubbed her face.

"So why do it?" Boomer sounded sincere in his confusion.

"Because I was the perfect fucking tin soldier and I did every little thing they asked of me, and when it was my turn to need and ask, they said no. Never fuck with a pissed-off, very well-trained tin soldier. It will always come back to bite you in the ass," she answered bluntly. Her head throbbed with a vengeance, and anger and betrayal oozed from her.

"I can see that," he offered weakly. He gulped his coffee. "You want to count the cash?"

She almost smiled. "You really think I can do math right now?"

After a second, Boomer laughed. "Nope." He stood and drained the coffee mug. "Tell Ter she makes a killer coffee; I'll be awake for days." He started for the front door, then stopped just as he was about to open it and turned back. "Hey, O'Malley, watch out for Trey. He's sniffing, and that little weasel is out for your ass."

O'Malley looked at the biker for a moment, trying to figure him out. She'd been around the club long enough to know that only loyalty garnered warnings. She had no idea what would bring out that sort of thing in Boomer, since his only loyalty seemed to lie with Spyder. After nearly two and a half years, she still had no idea what Spyder had on him.

"Thanks, Boomer," she answered with quiet sincerity, and then listened for the shutting of the front door behind him.

O'Malley closed her eyes in an attempt to push out unwanted thoughts and memories. She didn't want to revisit the old feelings and silently damned Boomer for inadvertently raising them and herself for answering honestly. It still burned inside: the betrayal from the one organization to which she had pledged life and loyalty. All those years, and the one time she had needed something, she had been turned down cold. Her request for emergency leave had been denied—denied because it didn't concern a member of her immediate family. She choked on the sob that threatened to escape.

O'Malley knew that the only thing she could do to exorcise the anger that coursed through her was to physically drain it off. She peeled off her clothes, pulled on dirty shorts and a tank top from the laundry room, and stalked out to the garage. She eyed the heavy bag hanging from the chain. After a moment, it was not stitched canvas, but the faceless enemies who had cost her her dreams.

With even, practiced movements, she tugged and tightened the fasteners of her workout gloves. In her need to bleed off the dark energy, she didn't bother with the hand wraps. She faced off against the bag and began with a spinning roundhouse kick that would have hurt if her body had been aware of such things. She watched the bag react, and in her mind she had just broken the jaw of the enemy. She finished him off with a crushing blow to the windpipe, then circled and advanced on the next faceless form.

* ~ * ~ * ~ *

Terri woke to the sound of a strange yet familiar rhythmic sound. She reached across the bed for O'Malley and was surprised to find she was not there. She vaguely remembered Boomer coming over earlier and that she had asked to go back to bed. Her eyes stole to the digital readout on the alarm clock. It was ten o'clock. She reached for her robe and slipped it on, then stole out of bed. The rhythm was still there, and now that she was more awake, she knew it was close.

In the living room, Terri saw the clothes she had worn to the bar the night before strewn all over the living room floor and wondered why. As she moved through the house in the direction of the sound, she spotted a set of O'Malley's clothes on the floor of the laundry room. That didn't make sense, either. Terri shook her head at the puzzle and continued to follow her ears.

She shivered as her bare feet touched the cold concrete of the garage floor, then stopped dead in her tracks. O'Malley was drenched in sweat from head to toe. Terri could see, even from a distance, the blood seeping through the top of the socks on O'Malley's feet and the trail of blood that trickled from glove-covered hands down bulging forearms. At any other time, she might have been aroused by seeing O'Malley in tight workout shorts and her trademark tank top, muscles playing as she moved. This time, she was worried. O'Malley seemed oblivious to the damage she was inflicting on her body as the bag shuddered from blow after blow.

Terri moved to O'Malley's side. The biker didn't seem to know she was there, and Terri had to duck suddenly when she touched O'Malley's shoulder.

O'Malley pulled up short when she realized whom she had almost punched. Her breathing was ragged as she turned and planted her gloved fist into the canvas of the bag, rocking it violently.

Terri straightened, and for the first time, she was afraid. She had never seen this side of O'Malley. Even when she had pinned Hank to the wall she had seemed to be controlling herself. There was no control in O'Malley's eyes this time. "O'Malley," she whispered, desperately trying to mask her fear.

"Go away," came the muttered, terse reply.

She touched the sweaty shoulder gently. "I can't." She watched O'Malley sag for just a second. "You're bleeding."

"I don't give a fuck. Just go, Terri. Let me work this out." O'Malley's words were clipped and short.

Terri moved in closer and let her hands rest on the gloves. "No." She pulled the fasteners open before O'Malley could object. Terri yanked at the gloves, and when they came free, she let them fall to the ground. She lifted O'Malley's hands and winced at the raw cuts she found.

"Damn it, O'Malley. Look at what you've done to yourself." She groaned in empathy, knowing it had to hurt. A second later, she realized that O'Malley wasn't feeling a thing.

O'Malley pulled her hands away. "Go away." Her teeth were clenched.

Terri stood her ground. "Fuck you. I will not stand by while you do this." She touched O'Malley's face. "I'm not going away. You are stuck with me."

O'Malley tried to push Terri away, but instead let her body sag for a moment and then, without a word, turned and walked slowly back into the house.

Terri took a deep breath before she followed. She didn't see O'Malley in the laundry area, so she followed the trail of blood droplets on the floor and found her in the bathroom, sitting on the toilet, a lost expression etched on her face.

Terri opened the linen cupboard and pulled out a couple of hand towels. Working quickly, she ran the water until it was warm and soaked one of the towels, then poured on some gel soap. Sitting on the edge of the bathtub, she silently took O'Malley's right hand and gently cleaned it.

O'Malley didn't even seem to notice, even when Terri gently removed her bloody socks. She merely sat there and let Terri work on her hands and scraped feet.

Terri glanced at the scars on O'Malley's legs. Somewhere inside, she knew they came from that night in the Iraqi desert. O'Malley barely flinched when Terri dabbed alcohol on her broken skin. "I'm going to have to cover these. Do you have anything larger than Band-Aids?"

O'Malley shook her head. "No. Just leave 'em. They'll need air to heal." Her voice was flat and devoid of emotion.

"Come on. You need something to eat," Terri said as she put the towels in the hamper. She watched O'Malley shake her head. "Well, I'm hungry, and I hate to eat alone. I'll make breakfast."

Her tone was meant to give O'Malley the idea that she wasn't going to win this one, and Terri knew O'Malley had no energy to fight. Obediently, she stood on shaky legs.

She sat at the counter and watched as Terri moved around the kitchen. Terri kept a subtle eye on her, watching as she went through a series of emotions, able to tell when she shifted thoughts. Terri fought the urge to just hold the obviously tortured woman in her arms, unsure as to whether she would accept the comfort. She poured the mixed eggs into the pan, then watched as the omelet cooked. It wasn't going to be her best breakfast effort, but O'Malley needed something to eat—fast. Terri could see her hands trembling slightly and wasn't sure if it was from hunger or fatigue, but she was determined to remedy both.

When the eggs were done, she filled both waiting plates and carried them to the counter. She handed O'Malley a fork and stared pointedly at her until she ducked her head sheepishly and began to eat. Terri turned her attention to her own breakfast, and they ate in silence.

~~*~*

When O'Malley was finished, she eased her body off the stool and carried her plate to the sink. Without uttering a word, she began cleaning up the kitchen. She was about to start the dishwater when Terri's hand touched her forearm. She hadn't even heard her move.

"Leave them," Terri ordered softly and carefully took O'Malley's hand. She led them out of the kitchen and through the living room.

"Where are we going?" O'Malley asked as it occurred to her to wonder once again what had happened between them the night before.

"We're going back to bed. You need to crash, and I'm feeling really lazy today." Terri gently tugged on O'Malley's hand to get her moving again.

O'Malley let herself be led into the bedroom and tucked into bed. With her head deep in the pillow, she avoided watching as Terri shed her robe and crawled under the blankets. It wasn't the nudity that bothered her—she liked looking at naked women—but she felt like a slug for putting Terri in the position of seeing the uncontrolled side that she lived with. It had been a long time since she'd had feelings of shame.

Terri slid closer to O'Malley and wrapped an arm over her chest. She propped her head on her hand as she looked at O'Malley. "Better now?" she asked quietly.

"Yeah." O'Malley's voice was rough. "Sometimes I just lose it.

I guess today was one of those times."

"Is it always that bad?"

O'Malley shook her head. "No, most of the time it's worse. Today all I beat up was the bag." She frowned and tried to roll over.

Terri's arm kept her in place. "You don't get to run from me, O'Malley. I don't understand what happened today, but I'd like to." Terri took a deep breath. "You've been good to me, and I'd like to return the favor. I like you, O'Malley, and I don't like watching you hurt yourself like that."

"Terri, sometimes the choice is between me working it out on the bag or taking it out on whoever's close. From what you told me about how you grew up, I doubt you'd like me if I took it out on you," O'Malley answered bluntly. "I did that once upon a time, and the woman I was with damn near left me. If I get like this again, just let me take it out on the bag."

"Even if you rip up your hands and feet like this again?" There was a hard edge to Terri's voice.

O'Malley chuckled. "Next time I'll try to remember to wear shoes and wrap my hands." She fell silent. "Thank you," she said after a moment.

"You're welcome." Terri smiled as she looked down at O'Malley.

"I'm kinda used to being alone, but I want you to know that I appreciate you doing all of this. It's been a very long time since anyone took care of me."

"Why are you used to being alone? I know it's not for a lack of offers." Terri held O'Malley's gaze. "When they found out about Trey losing me in a bet, some of the dancers told me about you. They had mostly good things to say about you and the condition your girlfriends seemed to be in." There was teasing in her voice.

"I lived with someone once," O'Malley admitted, her voice thick with regret. "We were together three years. She had an accident and she died. God, I loved her like crazy."

"So you don't want anyone in your life because you think they might die on you?"

"No. I don't want anyone in my life 'cause my life is entirely fucked up. Who in their right mind would want me? And besides, have you seen some of the women I'd have to chose from?" O'Malley asked with a wry smile.

"So it's one-night stands," Terri said without judgment.

"And the occasional casual girlfriend thing that lasts a week or two." O'Malley let the smile drop from her face. "God, I sound like a total worm."

"Did you lie to any of them? Promise them something you couldn't deliver on?"

"No. I was up-front. I don't like complications."

"Then you aren't a complete worm. You're human, O'Malley, just like the rest of us."

"Sometimes I wish I weren't. You ever just wanna turn the feelings off and leave 'em off?" O'Malley asked softly, not really expecting an answer.

"Yeah. When I was seventeen, I did that. I don't think I felt anything again until I ran away. I knew I had to change something the night he beat me up so badly I almost couldn't walk."

O'Malley turned toward Terri. "What happened?"

"I'm really not sure what started it, but he hit me and I went down. Usually he'd stop when I went down. That night, something inside me wouldn't let me stay down. I got back up, and he hit me again. I don't know how many times I got up. I remember at one point asking him if he was done yet. He hit me again and I didn't go down. I told him to make the next one a good one, 'cause he wasn't going to ever get another chance." Terri seemed to be unaware of the tears that streaked down her cheeks.

O'Malley wrapped her strong arms around her and held her as she cried. "We're a pair, ain't we?" she said when Terri finally composed herself.

"I feel really pathetic. You're hurting, and I start bawling my head off."

"Shh. Maybe somehow we needed this," O'Malley observed as she watched the ceiling. "Hey, Terri?" she asked after a long while.

"Hmm?"

O'Malley finally had the courage to ask the question that had been bothering her. "Why are our clothes out in the living room, and what exactly happened last night?"

Terri groaned and closed her eyes. "I was kinda hoping you might be able to tell me. The last thing I remember was kicking your butt at pool last night."

"I let you." O'Malley smiled.

"Sure you did." Terri snuggled close and relaxed against O'Malley. A moment later her eyes widened and she gasped. "O'Malley, you don't happen to remember licking your way up my spine, do you?"

O'Malley thought about the question, then her eyes opened in a flash. It sounded too familiar. "I'm not sure," she admitted. She groaned. "God, please don't tell me I took advantage of you."

"Well, if these visuals are what happened last night, I don't think you did. I'm pretty sure I was a willing participant."

O'Malley felt a rush of relief. "So, was I any good?"

Terri smacked O'Malley's chest. "I'll tell you if I remember it all. Go to sleep." She closed her eyes. The bed dipped a couple of times as O'Malley moved around. "What are you doing?"

"I'm looking for hickeys," O'Malley explained with a grin.

Chapter 9

Terri felt something brushing against her cheek and tried to swat it away. The sensation disappeared, only to return a second later. She slapped at it again, then her eyes flew open when her hand came into contact with something solid. Pale blue eyes watched her with a hint of amusement. She pulled her hand quickly away from its place on O'Malley's chest. "Very funny," she croaked out. She yawned as the sleepy fog started to lift from her brain.

O'Malley was still laughing. "Come on. I'm taking you out for dinner," she said as she got out of bed.

"What time is it?" Terri asked.

O'Malley turned her head to see the clock. "It's seven thirty, and I'm hungry." She walked out of the bedroom. "I'm gonna take a shower and then you are, and then we're going to dinner." Her voice trailed away as she disappeared into the bathroom.

Terri stretched and realized that despite the turmoil earlier, she felt surprisingly relaxed. She let her mind drift over the day's events. She had learned more about O'Malley in one morning than she had in two weeks, and she was beginning to understand how O'Malley's mind worked. In some ways, O'Malley was an honorable woman, and in others, she was a criminal. She was tough and hard, yet still had moments of weakness. The woman Terri was living with was a walking contradiction, and Terri was determined to figure her out. She heard the shower start and groaned aloud when the visual of O'Malley in workout clothes jumped into her brain. She also had a fuzzy recollection of them making out on the couch in the living room.

She shook off the memory and slid out of bed. Moving quickly, she picked out her clothes for the evening. Since she didn't know where they were going, she decided to wear her nearly new black skirt and a gray sweater. It was the best outfit she had with her. A probie wasn't supposed to have nice clothes, and for a moment she longed for her life before undercover work. She missed her nicer things, including a tight red dress she was sure O'Malley would drool over. Her inner voice chose that moment to wake up and sound off. *Earth to Terri...She's a criminal.* Terri felt like killing her inner voice.

* ~ * ~ * ~ *

O'Malley closed her eyes as she worked the shampoo into her hair. The sudden visual of Terri leaning in and sucking gently on her neck almost forced her to open her eyes, but she caught herself in the nick of time. She groaned silently at the feeling that the previous night's activities had gone further than she might have intended. She wished she could remember it all and mentally cursed herself. She wasn't sure how she was going to control herself. Terri had every quality that was a turn-on for her. She was obviously smart, good looking, stronger than she appeared, with just the right amount of soft to go with it...and a damn good kisser. O'Malley let her head rest against the shower wall as the water beat down on her.

The last several nights of sleeping next to the desirable woman had been an exercise in self-control for O'Malley. She realized that she'd wanted Terri since the morning after they had arrived at Sean's. Every morning since then, she woke up wet and wanting Terri, and every morning she forced herself to walk away. They still had some things to talk about first, and she found herself avoiding the conversation. O'Malley ducked her head under the water to rinse away the shampoo and tried to shut off her flow of thought, but her mind was having none of that. It chattered on as she washed up and rinsed off. If it wouldn't shut up, she reasoned, she would just ignore it. She shut off the water and shivered for the moment it took her to find the towel. She dried off, then quickly dressed, hissing softly when her left foot protested the sock she tried to pull over it.

O'Malley sighed and stepped out of the bathroom with her socks in hand. She padded into the bedroom and tossed them onto the bed, sitting down on the mattress with something close to a pout on her face.

Terri noticed the expression. "What's wrong?" she asked.

"Can't get my socks on."

"Your feet aren't happy, I take it?"

"Not one bit." O'Malley sighed and lay back on the bed.

"Well, no wonder. It's okay, O'Malley, we don't have to go out. Let me take a shower and you can order dinner in. We can do movie night or something," Terri suggested.

"Yeah. I just don't like that we haven't seen anything from Trey. I was hoping to go by the club house and the bar...just to keep tabs on him."

"He won't be there," Terri said as she put her clothes away and chose some sweats and a sweatshirt to wear instead. "On Wednesdays he likes to have his own little get-together with his boys. They sit around bitching about Spyder and plotting some sort of takeover. It's pretty pathetic, really."

"Really?" O'Malley tried to keep the interest out of her voice. "And where does Trey have his little get-togethers?"

"Over at Miller Park. Usually in the barbecue area 'cause it's the only place in the city they can do the open flame thing." Terri looked up at O'Malley. "Why?"

"Well, if he's always there on Wednesdays, we can have at least one night a week where I don't have to worry about having my head handed to me," O'Malley lied easily. "What do you want for dinner?"

"Um, surprise me. I'm just gonna be a few minutes." She grabbed up her clothes and retreated to the bathroom.

O'Malley waited until she heard the water going in the shower; then, moving as quickly as she could, she grabbed up her cell phone and dialed a number. She grew impatient waiting for the call to be answered. Her excitement was hard to contain; she finally had something she could work with.

"Yeah?" the voice on the other end answered curtly.

"O'Malley. Lemme talk to Cage," she ordered just as curtly. There were some people she just didn't like, and the voice on the other end belonged to one of those people. She waited for what seemed like forever, half listening to the shower.

"O'Malley, what can I do for you?" the new voice asked with a silky purr.

"Be here before next Wednesday. I need your help."

"We gonna kick some ass?"

"This first one is strictly recon. I'm gonna need my kit bag. It's gotta be a late night show-up. I don't want anyone knowing you're here until at least Thursday. Kick ass might come later."

"Cool, I love it. I'll be there. You better have steak in the freezer; recon always makes me hungry." There was a teasing quality to the woman's voice.

"Thanks, Cage. I'll owe ya."

"Nope. I've been bored lately. See you in few days," the woman promised.

O'Malley cut the connection with something close to enthusiasm. A rough plan was forming in her mind. As she plotted, she rummaged through the kitchen junk drawer trying to find the delivery menus. Sifting through them, she made a quick decision and called the Italian restaurant not far from the house.

Just as O'Malley hung up the phone, Terri emerged from the shower. She looked adorable in sweats, and O'Malley quickly looked away, quashing the rush of desire that hit her.

Terri didn't seem to notice as she passed the biker and wandered into the bedroom. She found her brush and started to work the tangles out of her hair, still working on it as she walked back into the living room.

O'Malley was browsing through the *TV Guide* and shaking her head as she flipped through several pages of listings before admitting to herself that there was nothing worth watching. She didn't feel like seeing a sappy movie and was sure she didn't want to watch one of the plethora of war movies. Since the desert, she couldn't watch them anymore. The nightmares that usually followed weren't worth it.

"Eight million channels and nothing on?" Terri asked with evident irony.

O'Malley looked up and arched an eyebrow. "Anyone ever tell you you're a smart-ass?"

"Just about everyone who's ever met me," Terri confirmed with a wicked smile. "If there's nothing on, we could just play cards or something."

"I guess. Wish I hadn't tin-canned my feet. I really did want to do something nice for you." O'Malley had a moment of panic. She hadn't meant to confess that last sentence out loud.

"Then talk to me. Tell me something about you I don't know," Terri answered as she sat down on the couch.

O'Malley blinked in surprise. She thought about it for a moment and wondered if she wanted to walk down that path. Knowing Terri, she would ask more questions about everything, and sometimes O'Malley found herself answering with complete honesty.

That alone made her nervous. She was sure she didn't want Terri to know everything; it would be too risky for them both. "Okay," her mouth answered before her brain could say no. Shaking her head in self-surprise, she walked to her recliner and settled in. "I'm afraid of heights."

Terri's eyes went wide. "You're actually afraid of something?" This time there was no sarcasm.

"Hey, you're the one who pointed out that I'm human. I just don't like being real far off the ground." O'Malley couldn't keep the indignation out of her voice.

"Okay. Hey, no pouting." Terri smiled softly.

O'Malley nestled deeper into the recliner. "So, tell me something about you now."

"Um..."

"Fair's fair. I told you mine, now you have to tell me yours." O'Malley couldn't help the flirting tone in her voice.

"You know, that's totally unnerving," Terri said before she could stop herself.

O'Malley was confused at the change in Terri's voice. "What is?"

Terri blew out a breath. "You walked away from me when we were at Sean's, but you flirt with me every chance you get. When you think I'm not watching, you look at me like I'm on the menu. I've been getting some very interesting visuals about last night, and I have the funny feeling that it was you that stopped us. I'm not used to being this damn confused," she said, looking down. "I feel like I made a mistake, but I don't know how I'm supposed to act around you. I know that we're playing a game to keep them from thinking I'm a cop, but damn, you make it hard not to like you." Terri wouldn't meet O'Malley's gaze.

"You act like you, Terri. I'm not asking you to be anyone other than yourself when it's just us. When they have eyes on us, it's a different story and I have to act like an asshole. If I hurt you by pulling away and stopping us the other night, I'm sorry, but it's 'cause I really didn't want you to wake up in the morning and regret what we did, or were about to do," O'Malley said softly.

Terri wiped the tears from her eyes. Sinking deeper into her seat, she closed her eyes. "And last night?"

"I don't know. What I do know is that I don't think I've ever taken a woman to bed when we were both too lit to do anything. I guess it goes back to not wanting regrets."

Terri sighed and set her hairbrush on the coffee table. "I'm sorry if I said too much."

O'Malley let a gentle smile to cross her face. "Don't be. It's kinda nice knowing what's going on in your mind."

Terri was about to answer when her cell phone rang. She picked it up, checked the caller ID, and answered with a smile. "Okay, what do you want?" she teased, as she stretched out on the couch. "What do you mean, open the door?"

O'Malley got up from her chair and walked to the front door, wishing she had her 9mm close, but she figured there was no threat if the expression on Terri's face was any indication. Looking through the peephole, she saw the distorted figures of two familiar women. As she pulled the door open, the shorter of the two disconnected the cell phone. O'Malley felt Terri come up behind her.

"What are you two doing here?" Terri asked. "And why do you have our dinner in your hands?"

Rhea held up the bag, teasing both women with it. "The price of entry is twenty-two fifty-eight. I tipped the delivery kid. I hope that was okay?" she said to O'Malley with an uncertain smile.

"O'Malley, I'd like you to meet a couple of my friends. The one holding dinner hostage is Rhea, and the scaredy-cat behind her is Candace."

O'Malley decided to play nice and let Terri's friends off the hook. The hopeful looks on their faces let her know how much Terri had been missed. "Come on in." Stepping back, she let the women into her house. Watching Terri transform from momentarily insecure to bubbly happy, she closed the door and wondered if there was going to be enough dinner for all four of them.

~~*~*

Terri groaned and let her head rest against O'Malley's chest.

"Come on, cutie, you have to answer or pay the consequences," Rhea teased with a leer. "You chose truth."

"O'Malley, kill her." Terri tried to sound serious, but it came out in a squeak.

She felt O'Malley chuckle. "Nope, I want to hear this answer."

"Argh. Okay." She held her hands a short distance apart. She tried not to blush and quickly dropped her hands.

"You're kidding?" O'Malley couldn't help her laughter. She slid sideways, leaving Terri sitting alone.

"I was fifteen. What the hell did I know?" Terri asked indignantly.

"Point well taken." Candace sided with her. "Okay, Little T, your turn."

Terri let her gaze fall squarely on Rhea. She hoped revenge was going to be sweet. "Rhea, have you ever had sex with a woman?" She didn't bother asking "truth or dare"; there was no way she was going to give the dancer an easy out.

"Um...I...you...don't I get a truth or dare with that?"

Candace smirked with pure evil. "Oh no. You opened your mouth and sounds came out before the question. You have to answer."

"Bitch." Rhea glared at Candace. "Yes, I have. Now, Candace, truth or dare?" she asked quickly.

"Oh, not so fast, details required," Candace insisted. She grinned and took a long drink of her wine.

Rhea's head dropped. "I hate you and I'm going to shrink your thongs."

"Stalling has serious consequences," Terri reminded her.

"Yes, I've had sex with a woman. And yes, it was a totally mind-blowing experience." The gleam in Terri's eyes told Rhea it wouldn't be enough.

"Who was it?"

Rhea stood her shaky ground. "I'm not telling."

"Oh, come on. Was she a troll or something?" Candace teased as she bumped her friend with her shoulder.

O'Malley decided to take pity on Rhea. "You two can let her off the hook. She slept with me." Three sets of eyes turned to the biker. Two were surprised, and one looked slightly upset. O'Malley looked at Terri. "It was almost two years ago, Ter," she explained without apology.

"Oh." There wasn't much more that Terri could say. Her brain understood that O'Malley had a past with other women; she just hadn't expected the past to be so close.

With that startling information on the table, it didn't take long for the impromptu party to break up. Rhea hung back with Terri for a moment, while Candace and O'Malley walked to the door. Rhea looked awkward and uncomfortable.

"I'm sorry, Terri, I should have said something earlier, but...I didn't know how to say it. It was a long time ago and as nice as it was, I'm still mostly into guys."

"How? How did it happen?" Terri asked, not really sure if she wanted the answer.

"I was at the bar, I saw her, and something inside told me that I wanted her. I mean, look at her—she's a walking wet dream. I flirted with her and made her an offer. She basically told me it would be one night, maybe two, but she wasn't into getting serious or tied down. I was okay with that."

Terri watched the fear and insecurity in her friend's eyes and wrapped her in a tight hug. "It's okay. Believe me, I understand. It's just a little weird to hear that you and O'Malley have a history."

"That's what it is, Little T, history. You're hers now and she's yours, so to speak. You have nothing to worry about from me."

Terri nodded. "I know. I just wish I had heard it earlier. It's okay, Rhea, honestly. Now you and Candace go out and have fun. And Rhea?" Terri waited until her friend turned to face her. "Don't you dare drive." She smiled.

Rhea waved at O'Malley and joined Candace at the sidewalk. The two women climbed into the car, Candace behind the wheel, and drove away.

After O'Malley closed the door, Terri couldn't help staring at her. The biker looked up, and Terri looked away, unable to meet her eyes.

"You're driving me crazy, Ter. Just ask what you want to ask and let's get it over with," she grumbled.

"You never said anything," Terri said, trying not to sound accusatory.

"I didn't even know you two were friends," O'Malley reminded her with a sigh. "I can't take it back, and I don't want to."

"It just feels a little weird."

"Knowing that I had sex with a friend of yours?" O'Malley didn't make the connection.

"Yeah. I mean, what if she wants to compare notes or something. If I don't say the right thing, it won't take long for the word to get around that I'm not sleeping with you," Terri explained.

O'Malley released a soft breath. "Oh, I hadn't thought of that. I'll figure it out in the morning. This has been one roller coaster of a day and I want off. I'm going to bed."

Terri shook her head at the sudden change in O'Malley. "You okay?"

"No. Don't worry about it. I'm just a little off balance right now and I don't think I can think anymore for today. I'm wiped out." Terri's expression reflected her disbelief. "What? Even the great O'Malley comes up empty sometimes."

Terri watched O'Malley walk into the dark bedroom. There were times when the biker took her by surprise, and this was one of them. She hadn't expected O'Malley to shove her head in the sand, but as she ran the day through her mind, she decided that the biker had every right to be tired. She looked at the mess from dinner, then pushed herself off the couch and started to clean up. Trying hard not to make any noise, she managed to clean up the living room then started on the kitchen. Moving the day's paper from the kitchen table, she noticed the tan pouch. What was inside made her felt light-headed; the bundle of money was not what she had expected to see. She quickly covered it back up and decided to forget the dishes. O'Malley had certainly been right when she had called the day a roller coaster.

The evidence Terri needed to connect O'Malley to Spyder sat silently on the table. Her stomach twisted uncomfortably; she knew she wouldn't be able to sleep. Right at that moment, she didn't want to be a cop. She stared off into space and tried to decide what to do. She had two choices: she could go to bed and forget about what she'd found, or she could wait until O'Malley was asleep, then go through the cash and write down all the serial numbers. She listened as the clock ticked away her decision-making time.

Chapter 10

O'Malley watched Terri walk into the mall, then pulled away from the curb and drove around the lot looking for a parking space. After a couple of minutes, she found one fairly close. As she turned off the truck's engine, she tried to think of a way to get rid of the uncomfortable tension between them. She was not at all happy with the moat of silence that had surrounded them since her confession that she had slept with Rhea. Unless either of them asked a direct question, they did not talk. O'Malley sighed. It was actually Terri who was not doing the talking, and initially the biker had not been willing to try and coax her out of her silence. That vow had lasted all of twenty-four extremely long hours.

She crossed the parking lot as quickly as she could. Guilt played a part in their going to the mall, but O'Malley also wanted to thank Terri for taking care of her and trying to comfort her. As her feet touched the curb, she was surprised to realize that she didn't like it when Terri wasn't talking to her. She enjoyed the sound of the younger woman's voice. Her step faltered, but she recovered quickly. With a deep breath, she pulled open the door and went inside.

Looking around, O'Malley spotted Terri sitting on a bench down the hall. As she just observed for a moment, her stomach clenched at Terri's lost expression. *I put that look on her face.* With renewed determination to make up for being an idiot, she managed to get down and across the hall without being run over by children or baby strollers, then plopped down next to her.

"That looked fairly traumatic," Terri said, trying not to laugh.

O'Malley couldn't contain her surprise. It was the longest sentence she'd heard in two days. "You have no idea. Come on, feel like running the gauntlet with me?"

For a second Terri didn't move, but then she looked up at O'Malley's hopeful face. "Sure. Where are we going first?"

"You tell me." O'Malley leaned in close. "Oh, that's right. I forgot to tell you that this is your trip. Anything you want is yours."

Terri's mouth fell open. "Excuse me?"

O'Malley reached over and gently closed Terri's mouth. "I've been acting like an idiot and I want to make it up to you. Remember when I said I wanted to do something nice for you? Well, I didn't get to take you out for a nice dinner, so this is choice number two."

"O'Malley, you don't need to buy me things."

"I know I don't need to. Believe me when I say I want to. I'm not usually good with words, Ter; all I really know is action. If I have to buy you the entire mall to put a smile back on your face, I'll do it."

"O'Malley, you remember when I said you make it hard not to like you?" The biker nodded uncertainly. "This is one of those times. I think what you just said has got to be the sweetest thing anyone has ever said to me."

The biker squirmed under Terri's steady gaze. "Well, hell, now I don't know what to say," she muttered, wondering when she was going to get her act together around Terri. She almost couldn't remember the last time she'd been such a goof around a woman. One minute she was completely in control of herself, and then at times like this, she found herself saying things she was sure came from her evil twin.

"Don't say anything, O'Malley. Let's just have a good day. Besides, you aren't the only one who's been acting like an idiot," Terri said. "The only way I can apologize is to say I'm sorry. I'll figure out a way to make up for it."

"You can do that by picking a store you want to go into and buying whatever you want." O'Malley gave Terri's thigh a gentle squeeze. "Please say yes. I'm losing butch points here. This is dangerously close to begging."

Terri had to laugh. She patted the biker's hand and nodded. "I warn you, this could get expensive."

O'Malley shrugged. "It's only money, Ter. Life's too short to worry about stuff like that."

For the next three hours, O'Malley carried the mounting number of bundles and bags. She remembered why she didn't like shopping, and it had very little to do with the usually noisy crowd, the rug rats underfoot, or the continuous walking. She simply hated being the one who ended up carrying the bags. No one ever carried *her* bags. She felt her stomach grumble. *If I'm hungry, my little eating machine must be starving.* For the second time that day, her steps faltered. She wondered when she had started thinking of Terri in terms of being hers.

Terri noticed O'Malley hanging back and returned. "You okay?"

"Hungry," O'Malley said as she looked around at the food court choices. "What do you think, you hungry?"

"I could eat. What do you want?"

"I was thinking the Mexican place. It's usually pretty good." O'Malley's mouth watered at the thought of food.

Terri shook her head. "I had Mexican for lunch yesterday. What else?"

O'Malley made a second choice. "Okay, the chicken place."

"Urgh. Chicken has unidentifiable parts. Pass on that one. Next?"

O'Malley was beginning to see a pattern. "No way. You choose."

"Me? Why me?"

"Each time I pick something, you don't want it. I'm starving here, Ter. You pick." O'Malley stopped short of stomping her foot.

"You are such a big baby sometimes," Terri noted as she looked over the offerings. "The sandwich place is always good. I'm sure we can find something there that will make us both happy." She led the way and pulled out a chair for O'Malley to set the bags on. "What do you want?"

O'Malley gratefully deposited the bags and started for the counter. Terri's hand on her arm stopped her.

"You've been doing all the pack work, I can go get lunch," she offered. "Besides, it would look funny if you were waiting on me." She smiled widely.

"If you insist." O'Malley couldn't help the smug look she knew had to be on her face. "I'll have the number three, no onions, and a Coke." She watched Terri look over the menu and frown. "What?"

"You might want the bread toasted," Terri answered.

"I don't want toast."

"It comes with tomato," Terri said, obviously expecting that to make sense to the biker.

"I like tomato," O'Malley countered, and stretched her legs out under the table, wincing when she shifted her foot in her boot and felt a twinge as the sock rubbed against the scabs just forming on her skin.

"Okay. I tried to tell you." Terri sighed and walked to the counter, shaking her head as she waited in line. When it was her turn, she ordered both lunches.

O'Malley wondered why the girl taking orders looked oddly at her, then shrugged her shoulders when Terri finished ordering and handed over the money. She couldn't make out their conversation and gave up. Just when she was sure that she would expire from hunger, Terri set the tray of food on the table. Having the decency to wait for her companion to sit down and drape a napkin over her lap, O'Malley hastily pulled her sandwich from its wrapper and took a big bite.

Terri bit into her own sandwich and chewed as she watched the disappointed look cross O'Malley's face.

O'Malley set her sandwich down. "It's soggy." Her voice sounded bewildered.

"I tried to tell you. Tomatoes always make a sandwich obscenely soggy, especially if you don't toast the bread."

Grumbling something under her breath, O'Malley tried to decide if she was hungry enough to finish her food. Finally, she huffed and took another bite of her sandwich. Terri suppressed a chuckle.

"Must be a girl thing," O'Malley mumbled after a sip of her drink.

"O'Malley, you are a girl," Terri pointed out with an amused smile.

"Well, yeah, but, oh hell, forget it." Her lower lip started its path to a pout.

"You lose butch points if you pout in the mall, honey," Terri said as she turned her attention to her lunch.

O'Malley didn't miss the endearment and was surprised to learn that it felt good be called something sweet. She knew how long it had been since she'd been referred to by such a word, and wrapped herself in the feeling. She went back to her food, the disappointment of soggy bread forgotten in her good mood.

After lunch, O'Malley picked up all the bags and packages and followed Terri through the last third of the mall. There was something satisfying about seeing a smile on Terri's face, and O'Malley was glad that she had thought of the outing. Terri was like a kid in a candy store. She looked at and touched just about everything. She only bought what she thought she needed, even though O'Malley kept insisting that she could have anything she wanted.

Terri stopped cold in front of the leather store and stared at the full-length black coat in the window. She pointed at the coat. "You would look great in this."

O'Malley glanced at the object in question and nodded. "Yeah, but this is your shopping trip."

"You said anything I wanted, right?" Terri asked with a little-kid smile.

O'Malley hated shopping for herself. "Yeah. Oh, come on, Ter. I've got, what...three leather jackets?"

"Four. And I think you would look incredibly hot in that."

"No pouting in the mall," O'Malley reminded her, then took a second look at the coat. It did look good. "I tell you what, I'll think about it, and when it gets closer to being cold, I'll let you know." It was the only compromise that crossed her mind. "You can come with me and remind me which one it was," she promised.

"You have a deal, and I'm going to hold you to it, O'Malley." Then Terri turned away as her attention was grabbed by another store. "Oh, I want to go in there."

She walked confidently into the store, and O'Malley felt her mouth go dry when she saw where Terri was headed. "I hope she only wants lotion," O'Malley muttered as she stopped in front of the Victoria's Secret sign on the storefront. Gathering her courage, she walked into the shop. It took a moment to find Terri, who was engaged in a conversation with an older saleswoman. She managed to keep her eyes off the more tantalizing garments as she walked over and stopped next to Terri. She noticed a subtle change in the saleswoman as she put the situation together in her head. The momentary expression of disgust was quickly covered up, but not quickly enough.

O'Malley saw the evil smile on Terri's face, the same evil look she'd had when they played pool. Terri turned to her and moved in close.

"Anything you want me to try on?" she purred seductively, running her hand up O'Malley's abdomen.

O'Malley's mind went blank for just an instant. Entirely too aware of the warm hand on her stomach, she managed not to stutter as she answered, "Whatever you want that will make you happy."

"I think I know what you'd like to see me in." Terri turned to the saleswoman, who was turning an unbecoming shade of red. "I'd like to try on a black teddy, please." She smiled an innocent smile as she gave her size, then watched as the saleswoman crossed to the rack full of the filmy garments and rapidly riffled through them.

O'Malley leaned in close to Terri's ear. "Ter, what are you doing?"

"I'm playing with a very closed mind. Did you see the look on her face when you joined me?" Terri whispered as she leaned in closer. "Come on, O'Malley, you wanna play?"

There was that purr again. O'Malley's brain short-circuited, and all she could do was nod. "I love playing."

Terri walked away from the biker toward the waiting saleswoman. She didn't bother looking back, but there was a playful smile on her lips as she took the teddy in hand and disappeared into the dressing room.

O'Malley looked away from the saleswoman's look of disapproval, and then her heart stopped when Terri stepped out.

"We'll take it. One in every color she wants," O'Malley said in a husky whisper. By design, the teddy covered all the strategic spots but still left a little to the imagination, and O'Malley had a very active imagination. She swallowed hard as she watched Terri slink forward.

"You like?" Terri asked needlessly.

"Yeah, you could say that." O'Malley briefly wondered what idiot was in charge of her mouth.

Terri leaned forward and planted a slow, deep kiss on the stunned biker's lips. "Good." She pulled back, ignoring the strangled noises coming from the saleswoman. "Anything else you want to see?" The playful gleam in her eyes was back.

"There's a lot I want to see, but that will have to wait until we're home," O'Malley answered, knowing full well that the saleswoman was listening to every word. "I can't wait to peel that off of you. We don't happen to have any whipped cream in the house, do we?" O'Malley teased, as she eased her arms around Terri's body.

"Oh, I love when you get like this." Terri tore her eyes off the biker and looked at the saleswoman. "I'll definitely take this one." She grinned and pulled slowly out of O'Malley's arms. "I'll be right back, baby."

The saleswoman silently picked out the other available colors in Terri's size and rushed them to the cash register. She was almost done when Terri brought the black teddy to the counter. The woman rang it up in record time, ran the credit card, and didn't bother to wish them a good day.

Terri and O'Malley kept their laughter in check until they were out of sight of the store. Terri almost doubled over with laughter, and O'Malley laughed right along with her. Each time they thought the worst of it was over, they would look at each other and it would start all over again.

"Oh, God, did you see her face. I thought she was going to swallow her tongue," Terri managed between fits of laughter.

"I think she did." O'Malley had to sit on the bench.

"Sometimes it's fun to mess with the straight people," Terri squeaked.

O'Malley looked at her with a strange expression. "Terri, you are one of the straight people," she pointed out.

"You don't know everything about me, O'Malley," Terri answered cryptically, and she winked before she walked toward the bookstore. "Come on, I want to check out that one."

O'Malley followed, her mind trying to catch up with Terri's statement. It was true that she didn't know everything about Terri, but she was sure she would have picked up on it if her companion had an interest in women. *Hello, Irish, you were pretty clueless about Ellen and her interest.*

The rest of the shopping trip was a whirlwind for O'Malley. Her brain was locked on Terri's statement and she couldn't get past it. As they walked to the truck and deposited the bags in the cab, she couldn't help wondering if she was going to be able to get the story out of Terri.

"You really should have stopped me. I think I went overboard," Terri said as she settled in the passenger seat and buckled her seat belt.

O'Malley grinned. "Nah. It was good to see you having fun. What do you feel like doing now?"

Terri thought about it for a moment. "Let's go back to the house and put this stuff away, and then we can go see Maria. I can't wait to show her that new outfit."

O'Malley nodded and put the truck into gear. She turned on the radio and started to sing along, ignoring the tortured expression on Terri's face. Not being able to sing had never stopped her. She was having fun with the woman sitting next to her.

* ~ * ~ * ~ *

Terri was sure she was going to have to kill O'Malley when the trip finally ended at the driveway. The singing, however, did stop. Finally, all she could do was laugh as they unloaded the truck and dumped everything on the bed.

The message light blinked on the answering machine and the caller ID indicated that there were three messages. One message was from a solicitor, one from Maria, and one from Rhea looking for Terri.

Terri called her friend on her cell phone, spoke for a few moments, and promised to call her back. She stuck her head into the living room to find O'Malley on the phone as well, and waved to catch her attention. "Rhea needs a ride after work. Would it be okay if I went to pick her up?"

"Hang on, Maria," O'Malley said, then moved the phone away from her ear. "Yeah, that's cool. You take the truck. Maria needs a hand at the bar for a little bit, so I'll take the bike and you can meet me there later." She returned to her call. "I'm back. We were gonna go by the bar later anyway, so this still works out. Just lemme take a shower and get changed, then I'm yours for a while." She finished the call, then entered the bedroom as Terri ended her call and set her cell phone on the dresser. She picked out her clothes for the evening—leather, since she was going to take the bike—and missed seeing the gleam return to Terri's eyes.

"I'm gonna hit the shower and head out," O'Malley announced, then went to the shower while Terri started sorting the bags on the bed. Terri listened for the sound of running water. The plan forming in her head made her smile, and she reached for the phone. She liked her plan; she just needed some words of encouragement. She dialed the number and waited.

"Barnes house," Joan's voice announced.

"Hey, Joan, it's Terri. I need to ask you something."

* ~ * ~ * ~ *

Rhea poked her head in and glanced around the bar as if she were looking for something or someone, then entered with Terri in tow. Maria almost dropped the bottle in her hand.

Mike rescued his beer just in time. "Maria, you okay?" She

pointed, and he turned and stopped short. "Oh, my God."

The two of them could only stare openmouthed. Terri was wearing a black vest with, as far as they could tell, nothing underneath, while her skintight hip-hugging leather pants looked like they had been painted on.

Rhea and Terri strutted through the bar and took possession of a couple of bar stools close to Maria. Rhea looked like a proud mama bear. She leaned over and whispered something in Terri's ear.

Terri nodded, then smiled at her stunned friends. "Hi, Maria. You like it?" she asked, setting her elbows on the bar.

"*Chica*, I love it. You look good," Maria answered with a grin. "O'Malley is gonna have a heart attack."

"Cool." Terri restrained a chuckle as she turned to Mike, someone Rhea had been interested in for quite a while. Now she saw that his eyes were moving from her to Rhea and back again. "Mike, I'd like you to meet my friend Rhea." She watched as Rhea extended her hand and Mike took it, nearly drooling. Her good deed for the night done, Terri turned away from them and ordered a beer, looking the crowd over while she waited. Her eyes narrowed when she caught sight of Trey.

He was sitting in a booth near the back of the room, and her instincts kicked in. She knew from experience that he hated being in the dark, loved being the center of attention. When she looked in the direction his gaze was tracking, her heart skipped a beat. O'Malley was just setting down a couple of cases of beer near Maria's office, and an attractive blonde was eyeing her hard. Terri wasn't sure what was up, but when she noticed the blonde cast an uncertain glance at Trey, she knew it couldn't be good. Bikers cheated on their women all the time, but even the perception of O'Malley cheating this early would be nothing but bad.

For a long moment, she sat very still. She had no idea what she could do to head this one off, then Joan's words from their earlier conversation rang in her head. *Callan's a sucker for leather, Terri. Toss in a kiss like you mean it, and O'Malley's along for the ride too.* Terri came to a fast decision: tonight she wasn't a cop; she was a woman intent on keeping what was hers, for better or worse.

She turned on her stool and tossed down a five. "Hey, Maria, can I have quarters? And what have you got on the jukebox that'll get O'Malley's attention?" she asked with an evil grin.

Maria leaned in close and returned the grin. "What kind of

attention are you trying to get?"

"I think you know what I'm talking about. What would get her moving in close with me?"

Maria shook her head as she pushed away from the bar and counted out the quarters. "Clapton's good, or some good old Southern slow rock. You'll find enough of that on the box." She smiled as she handed over the coins.

Terri took them with a renewed sense of self. She walked to the jukebox, avoiding several drunken bikers and rednecks on the way. She dropped in the quarters and punched in her selections, then stood by the jukebox, her eyes not leaving the blonde who was watching O'Malley. Terri could tell the blonde was waiting for just the right moment. When she finally made her approach, Terri held her ground, wanting to see what was going to happen. She watched the blonde in her tight jeans and crop top walk up to O'Malley and begin a conversation. From her vantage point, O'Malley didn't seem interested, just polite. It was killing Terri not to be able to hear the conversation. Her heart fell to her ankles when O'Malley walked the woman to the bar and ordered her a drink, and she noted the easy smile on the biker's face and the way she leaned against the bar close to the blonde.

* ~ * ~ * ~ *

O'Malley tried to ignore the woman talking at her. The blonde had one of those voices that grated on her nerves, and she had only barely been able to remain polite when the woman walked up to her and started a conversation. She had listened as the woman talked about being new in town and had told her that she should talk to Maria if she wanted to know what was going on. The blonde had pulled her shy act, asking if O'Malley would escort her to the bar, and O'Malley had complied. Now it seemed as if she was stuck. She shrugged her shoulders and leaned away.

The blonde turned to face the biker and inched closer, her interest apparent. She continued her stream of chatter, apparently oblivious to the fact that O'Malley didn't seem to be listening. When the sounds of a rock ballad came from the jukebox, she grabbed O'Malley's hand and tugged at her.

When the blonde clutched at O'Malley, Terri walked back to the bar, not waiting for the jukebox to finish its current song. Her eyes narrowed when the blonde brushed her fingers along O'Malley's arm, and Terri picked up her pace. She took up a position to O'Malley's left, leaning against the bar and saying nothing. She arrived just in time to hear the blonde's invitation.

"I love this song. Dance with me."

O'Malley shook her head. "Thanks for the offer, but no thanks."

"Come on, O'Malley. I won't bite, unless you ask me to." She brushed her breasts against the biker's body.

O'Malley wondered how the blonde knew her name. She hadn't introduced herself, and Maria hadn't said her name when she took their order. Little warning bells rang in the back of her head.

Terri leaned past O'Malley and addressed the blonde. "She said no, and she's already taken." She smiled sweetly when she caught O'Malley staring at her.

The blonde looked at Terri and blew her off as competition. She didn't move away from the biker. "Not for long." Her tone was confident, almost cocky.

"You think you can steal me away?" O'Malley asked, still looking at Terri. "How would you do that?"

"By doing or being anything you want," the blonde promised with a smile. "I can be your best fantasy. Can she do that for you?" She looked at Terri again. "It doesn't look like it to me."

O'Malley felt Terri stiffen, and she looked from one woman to the other. She saw smugness in the blonde's eyes and irritation in Terri's. If she wasn't the one in the dicey position, she might have laughed. She turned to the blonde and let her hand touch Terri at the same time.

"You should know that looks can be deceiving." O'Malley leaned closer to the blonde. "What she is to me and what she does to me is none of your business." She had a smile on her face, but her words were pure warning. She felt Terri's fingers squeeze her hand lightly.

"She can't be that good if you don't even kiss her hello," the blonde taunted, making sure that Terri heard her.

O'Malley chuckled and turned to face Terri, her eyes widening as she focused on what she was wearing. She couldn't help the low whistle that found its way past her lips. Terri looked spectacular in the leather outfit. It didn't hurt that O'Malley had been waking up next to that warm body and feeling the curves accentuated by the snug leather. She turned her gaze to Maria, who was watching and listening from behind the bar.

"Maria, watch my back."

"Always, O'Malley," Maria promised with a grin.

"Think I'm gonna hurt you?" the blonde asked.

"You? No. The rednecks might try," O'Malley answered without looking at her. She just wanted to look at Terri. She leaned her body close to Terri's and watched as Terri's eyes smiled at her. Dipping her head, she captured Terri's lips with her own and the rest of the world disappeared. All she knew was that Terri was returning her kiss without restraint or pretense. O'Malley let herself get lost in the sensation. She was dimly aware of Terri's arms wrapping around her neck. Their lips parted for a moment, and then the second kiss was better than the first.

She pulled back slowly. "Hi there," she breathed as she opened her eyes. "You look very nice." Her compliment sounded almost like a purr. "Did you get Rhea taken care of?"

"Hi," Terri returned. "Yeah. She's around here somewhere." Terri didn't move her arms from around O'Malley. "I introduced her to Mike." She pulled her gaze from O'Malley and stared at the blonde. "She doesn't need a fantasy when she has the real thing right here."

Terri's confident words apparently convinced the blonde that she had failed. With an exaggerated flip of her long hair, she grabbed her drink and walked away from the bar. As she passed Trey's table, she shrugged her shoulders. For a moment his face tightened, but then he relaxed.

Terri nuzzled O'Malley's neck, then worked her way up to an earlobe. "I think Trey sent what's-her-name, and from the look on his face, he's up to something," she whispered.

"Is he still sitting near the back?" O'Malley asked, her breath hitching. She was definitely enjoying what Terri was doing to her.

"Yeah, he is—" Her words cut off when O'Malley's hands slid slowly under the back of her vest. "Jesus, that feels good," she managed as her head rested on O'Malley's shoulder. She sighed her contentment.

"All right, you two, you really need to stop that." Maria's words cut into their little world. "You really ought to think about getting a room," she teased.

"We were just plotting," O'Malley said, but they both reclaimed control of themselves and leaned against the bar, unconsciously staying close to each other.

"So, that's what you're calling it now?" Maria asked as she fished a beer out of the cooler.

Terri batted her eyes innocently. "Calling what?"

Maria wasn't buying it. "Foreplay," she answered with a straight face. She had to laugh as Terri tried to think of a retort and couldn't come up with one. She twisted the cap off the beer and was still laughing as she walked down the bar to deliver it. She came back and flipped her towel over her shoulder. "You two interested in grilled steaks at our place tomorrow night?"

O'Malley reached across the bar and felt Maria's forehead. "No fever. Terri, check out her eyes. See if they glow red or anything."

"Me? No way. I'm not getting near her if she's possessed or something. You're tougher, you do it," Terri answered playfully.

"Jeesh, invite friends over for food and get abused," Maria griped without conviction.

"Well, damn, Maria, in the entire time I've known you, you've taken what, maybe five days off, and one of those was to get married. How long was your honeymoon?" O'Malley pulled over a stool to sit on. She turned in her seat and pulled Terri in close to her.

"Two days. It's not like we really needed one, if you know what I mean." Maria leered.

Terri covered her face with her hands. "Don't want that visual. No offense, Maria."

Maria rolled her eyes and snapped Terri lightly with the bar towel. "I'm in a good mood, so I'm not going to respond to that one. So come to dinner and have a good time with us. John and Mandy, us, and I invited Mike. Nothing fancy."

"So what's the big event? You taking the night off, it must be good." O'Malley took a sip of Terri's beer.

Maria's smile was huge. "We finally paid off the loan on the bar. Seven years is a long time, and we've been living on life's little edge to pay it off fast."

"Life's little edge? What's that?" Terri asked as she stole her beer back. "Please get her a beer or I'll never get any of this one," she pleaded.

"But I like stealing yours," O'Malley argued, then nuzzled Terri's hair.

Terri pouted. "Maria, she's being mean to me."

"I can see how mean she's being." Maria rolled her eyes. "The little edge is kinda like walking a tightrope without the net. One step in the wrong direction and you crater into the ground, or in our case, have to move in with Gato's mother." Maria's face wrinkled up in horror.

"She couldn't be that bad," Terri said, pulling her beer away from O'Malley.

"She cried for a week after we got married," Maria answered as she took pity on her small friend and opened the beer cooler.

"Well, that's 'cause it took you two so long to make it legal. You traumatized the woman by living in sin." O'Malley's left hand snaked up under Terri's vest to rest on her stomach.

"You're not getting my beer, O'Malley."

"Maybe I just want your body," O'Malley whispered.

"You can have my body," Terri whispered back, "but not my beer."

For a moment, they were both rendered speechless. O'Malley was glad that Maria was occupied and Terri couldn't see her face.

"A lecture on sin from you?" Maria asked with a teasing glare as she came back with the opened beer.

"Shutting up now." O'Malley smiled and took the bottle with her free hand. "You want to play with Maria tomorrow?" she asked.

"Do we get to tease her?"

"Yeah. It's required. Gato is optional." O'Malley ignored Maria's frown. "We like him better."

"Yeah, only 'cause he's the one who drives your sorry ass home after tequila night," Maria teased.

"I have to point out that your sorry ass is right next to mine on those nights, and we aren't doing tequila tomorrow no matter how much you whine." O'Malley hoped she had the willpower to follow through.

"Don't worry, O'Malley, I'll protect you," Terri promised, winking at Maria.

Maria laughed and shrugged, then someone called for a refill from the far end. "I really need to hire a waitress," she huffed before she went to take care of her customer.

"So, what did you mean earlier today when you said I don't know everything about you?" O'Malley asked as she played with the label on her beer bottle.

Terri blinked at the sudden change of subject. She turned in

O'Malley's arms and looked at her. "Just that. You don't know everything about me. My first time was with a guy, and he was sweet but not very good, now that I look back on it. My second time was with Kathy Zunetti. We had been friends all through school, and we liked each other. One night we ended up kissing, and that led to way more than kissing. I was so heartbroken when her dad took a transfer." Terri took a sip of her beer for courage. "When I was on the road, there were several women who helped me out. Some of them were interested in me and vice versa. I don't sleep with everyone, O'Malley, just the ones I want to."

"And Trey?" O'Malley asked without looking at Terri.

"Trey was a mistake. At the time, it seemed the easiest way, and he was okay until he hooked up with Spyder. What I guess I'm saying is that you assumed something maybe you shouldn't have," Terri said.

"I'm beginning to see that." O'Malley heard the jukebox change tunes. "I like this one," she said as she recognized the opening guitar riff.

"I know. Who do you think put in the music?" Terri shrugged her shoulders at the biker's questioning glance. "I had to do something to get your attention. That blonde with the megatits was trying to get into your pants."

O'Malley laughed. "The thought never crossed my mind. Did you get a good listen to her voice? She sounded like she'd been sucking week-old helium. Besides, she wasn't my type."

"And what's your type?"

"The type that can make me laugh, think, or come. I prefer all three," O'Malley answered bluntly. "If I was looking for someone, it wouldn't be a woman who would let me walk all over her or one who would play games with my head. I don't need that."

O'Malley watched as Terri battled something internally. When Terri chose not to respond, O'Malley figured that if she ever wanted to tell her what was going on she would do so in her own time.

Terri sighed and leaned into the biker. She took a deep breath, the scent of leather and O'Malley filling her. Gathering her courage, she let her lips trail over the exposed skin on O'Malley's neck and up to her ear.

O'Malley hummed in pleasure, goose bumps rising on her arms. She didn't know if she could control herself; Terri's little bombshell had her hoping that this time she wouldn't have to. O'Malley knew for certain that she didn't want to stop. Terri had become a constant ache inside her. She trailed her hands up Terri's sides and brought them up to cup her face, easing her lips away from the very happy ear. She lowered her mouth to Terri's, kissing her again, letting her lips convey her need and desire. She figured the message had been delivered when Terri returned the kiss with enthusiasm and ran her palms over O'Malley's breasts. O'Malley had to pull out of the kiss to suck in a deep breath. She took note of Terri's closed eyes and swollen lips.

"We should probably leave soon." Her voice was thick with desire.

Before Terri could answer, O'Malley felt a hand settle on her shoulder and tug at her. She tried to ignore it, but the tugging did not stop. Irritated, she turned her head and saw one man she had hoped she would never see again. Her desire was immediately quelled.

"Why are we not still kissing?" Terri asked, opening her eyes. There behind O'Malley, with his beefy paw on the biker's shoulder, was Officer Bates. She slid her hands out from under O'Malley's shirt and almost held her breath.

"I didn't know you were out and causing trouble again, O'Malley." There was a thin threat in his tone, and everyone within earshot heard it.

Several leather-clad bikers turned to watch. The tension level in the bar jumped. Suddenly the only sounds were from the jukebox and the group still playing at the pool table.

O'Malley managed to keep her body as relaxed as possible. She let her gaze travel up and down the policeman's form. He hadn't changed much since the last time she'd seen him, except that his gut seemed to stretch out his uniform around the middle just a bit more. She held back a smirk. "I'm just hanging out and having a beer, Officer."

He leaned in a little closer. "Not from what I hear. Seems you couldn't take no for an answer when the complainant didn't want your attention." His breath smelled of liver and onions.

"And when exactly was this supposed to be?" O'Malley asked.

"Got the call five minutes ago," he answered with a smile that lacked sincerity.

Terri did the math in her head. "Not possible. O'Malley was with me and has been for at least half an hour," she said in a firm voice. She watched Bates turn his gaze on her.

"I said I got the call five minutes ago, not that it happened then. The victim wants to swear out a complaint," he answered, and then his eyes narrowed at Terri. "I know you, don't I?"

She leaned against O'Malley. "I'm sure it'll come to you," she answered in a flat voice.

"Yeah." He turned back to O'Malley. "We can do this outside, or we can do it here. Personally, I'd love it if you would resist just a little." The last few words were soft enough that only O'Malley and Terri could hear him.

"And I would give you that satisfaction why?" O'Malley let her smirk widen. "This charge is bullshit; I'll be out by morning."

"Yeah, but you'll be our guest all night long, won't you?"

Chapter 11

O'Malley lay flat on the cold bench and restarted her counting of the dots on the ceiling. She was tired, hungry, and completely unfocused. The pattern of soft footfalls was also close to driving her nuts. At first she had tried ignoring the sound but discovered, after eight hundred dots, that ignoring it was an impossibility. She lifted her head up off the bench. "Could you quit that, please?" She managed to keep her tone civil.

Terri halted in her tracks, her expression guilty. "I'm sorry. God, where is Maria? I'm going nuts here."

"Yeah, I noticed." O'Malley chuckled and sat up slowly. "Come on, sit down here." She patted the spot next to her. "I warmed it up for you."

Terri hesitated for a moment, then sat down wearily. She looked up in surprise when her back pressed against the biker's warm chest instead of the cold cement wall. She closed her eyes and accepted the comfort. "Thank you." Her voice almost broke.

"You okay?"

"I hate small spaces," Terri said with a shiver. "Before my dad graduated to hitting me, he would lock me in his closet."

O'Malley tightened her embrace, trying to give warmth and comfort as well as she could. "How old were you?"

"Six, maybe. I remember my mom always telling me that there were no closet monsters, so that's not what scared me. It was the walls. I thought they would come together and squash me. It sounds silly now." She sighed and squirmed uncomfortably.

O'Malley loosened her hold and rested her chin on Terri's head. "It's not silly. Not now, and definitely not then. We all have something that scares us, Ter. You're just having to face one of your fears right now."

"So what are you scared of?"

"Gargoyles," O'Malley answered after a second. Terri shifted in her arms and stared up at her. "Really. I saw some TV movie once that had gargoyles in it, and they scared the hell out of me. My mom almost killed my uncle for letting me watch it before bed. I had nightmares for a week."

Terri laughed softly. "Gargoyles? I was expecting...I don't know...something more serious."

"Hey, those creatures were very serious."

The expression on O'Malley's face let Terri know that she was not kidding. "I'll protect you, then," Terri said softly.

"Yeah, I think I can count on that. You took on Bates, so what's a couple hundred living stone creatures?" O'Malley teased.

"A couple hundred? I think that's more than I could handle. Bates was easy." Terri sank back into O'Malley's arms.

"Thanks, by the way. You didn't have to do that."

"O'Malley, he was going to beat you to death on that car. I wasn't going to stand by and let it happen." Terri shivered at the memory of Bates repeatedly slamming a handcuffed O'Malley against the side of the squad car.

"Barclay."

The loud female voice boomed out and startled them both. They looked toward the source of the voice and saw the jail matron at the cell door. "You're sprung."

"Is Maria here?" Terri's voice conveyed her confusion.

"I don't know any Maria, but your probation officer is here. O'Malley, you gonna give me any trouble when I open the door?" The jailer arched an eyebrow. Given her size, she looked like she could give the biker a run for her money.

"Why does everyone think I'm gonna give 'em trouble?" O'Malley wondered aloud as she let go of Terri. "I'm the one who ate a squad car." She pointed at her cellmate and chuckled. "She's the one you have to watch out for."

"You just remember that, O'Malley," Terri teased as she stood up. "We'll get you out of here soon, okay? I'll hook up with Maria and see what the holdup is."

"Come on, Barclay. I don't have all morning." The uniformed woman unlocked the cell door and motioned Terri out.

* ~ * ~ * ~ *

Terri contained her emotions until they were down the steps and out of the building.

"Terri, what the hell were you thinking?" George growled when they were alone in his beat-up car.

"I was thinking that Bates was going to kill her," Terri snapped at her boss. "This was a total setup, and I'll just bet my last four paychecks that Trey had something to do with it." She recounted the events of the evening and the reasons for her suspicions.

George pulled out of the parking lot and onto the nearly deserted main road. "At this point, I'm going to have to agree with you," he said with a frustrated sigh. "I tried to find him and I can't. He missed his report drop, and the house is empty. The charges against you, by the way, are dropped. I talked to the assistant DA, and with all the witnesses there that backed up your statement, they're more worried about a lawsuit against the department."

"I'm not surprised." She didn't suppress the sarcasm. "So what was Bates doing there without backup to make an arrest, and who the hell was O'Malley supposed to have assaulted?"

"I couldn't get the ADA to give that up. The judge will see her in few hours for the arraignment. Where am I going?" he asked when he pulled up at a stoplight.

"Traders. I need to pick up the truck and then I have to find Maria. What are you going to do about Trey?"

George pulled forward when the light changed. "Other than calling his status in to the office, I don't know that there's anything I can do until I can get him pulled in on charges," he said. "I'll keep looking for him."

Terri nodded, and they fell into an uncomfortable silence for the drive to the bar. To his credit, George didn't question her any further, nor did he comment on the way she was dressed.

When she shivered a little, he turned the heater on full blast. Both cops' minds were a whirlwind of activity. There were far too many questions and not enough answers, and all trails ultimately led to Spyder. The lure of money and perceived power could corrupt almost anyone. They both knew from experience that cops were just as human as the rest of the population.

When George dropped her off at the truck, Terri offered him a small smile and a wave. He pulled out of the deserted parking lot to begin his search for his lost lamb.

* ~ * ~ * ~ *

The judge looked over his glasses, his eyes boring into the assistant district attorney. "What do you mean, you can't find the complaint statement?"

The ADA swallowed hard. "Your honor, the arresting officer doesn't seem to have included it in the file. I have officers looking for him as we speak."

"At least I don't have to do all the work this morning." There was no humor in the judge's statement. He shifted his eyes to the woman in leather standing next to the public defender. "I'm going to assume you're pleading not guilty."

"Yes, your honor," she answered for her client. "My client can attest to her whereabouts yesterday, and she can provide witnesses."

The judge looked down at O'Malley's record. "Considering Miss O'Malley's record and her known associations, I can't say that gives me the warm fuzzies."

"Your honor, the state asks bail be set at the highest possible amount. The defendant has a record. We consider her a flight risk."

He shifted his harsh glare to the ADA. "What law school did you go to, son?"

"Baylor, sir," he answered with pride.

The judge snorted. "Go back and look up what happens when you don't have a complaint statement. Suspension of charges until I have that statement. Miss O'Malley, I can't order you held, but I can tell you not to take any vacations. Do I make myself clear?"

"Yes, sir," she answered as respectfully as she could.

"Enter that into the court record. Next case." He slammed his gavel down and pulled the next file.

O'Malley followed the public defender into one of the tiny interview rooms and waited for her to speak. She didn't have to wait long.

"You got a break on this one."

"I didn't assault anyone. I don't need to."

"My office will be in touch with you when that statement is found. It would look better for you if you surrendered yourself instead of having to be arrested. Right now, that's the best I can do."

"Thanks. Can I go home now?" O'Malley was suddenly very tired.

"As soon as the paperwork is done." The lawyer pulled her next file out of her briefcase. "The bailiff will come get you. Don't say a word, and whatever you do, don't get arrested any time soon."

O'Malley nodded and sat down to wait as the lawyer tapped on the door and waited for it to open. She left without looking back or saying anything else. O'Malley closed her eyes and was surprised when someone shook her shoulder. Looking at the clock, she realized that she'd been asleep for half an hour. She followed the bailiff, read over the paperwork, and signed it. She gathered her things, then stepped out of the tiny courthouse, pulling on her jacket to take off the morning chill.

Maria's voice came from her right. "Hi, good looking, got a date?"

"Right now, that is so not funny," O'Malley muttered as she moved into Maria's arms for a hug.

"Yeah, but I couldn't resist. Come on. We're parked over here." Maria took O'Malley's hand and led her to the side parking lot.

O'Malley was relieved to see Terri and the truck. The expression of relief on Terri's face was clear. It was quickly replaced by an almost shy smile. As they got closer to the truck, Terri exploded into her arms.

"How are you?" she whispered.

"I'm okay," O'Malley assured her. "They suspended the charges until they can find the right paperwork. I'm not supposed to leave the city limits. How are you doing?"

"They dropped my charges before I was released." Terri pulled away slowly. "You guys hungry? I have enough money to buy breakfast at Gus's. I'll explain what my PO told me last night."

"I'll get breakfast," O'Malley offered. "But you have to drive. I'm wiped out."

They piled into the truck and drove in silence to the diner. Once coffee was provided and orders taken, Terri explained why her charges had been dropped. She sipped on her coffee and watched O'Malley carefully. The biker was obviously exhausted.

"We'll eat and then I'll get you home," she said quietly, gently squeezing O'Malley's hand.

"I gotta pick up the bike."

"Nope. I had Gato put it in the shed behind the bar," Maria supplied. "It'll be good until tonight. You two are still coming to dinner." It was not a question, more along the lines of an order.

Maria glared at both women until they nodded. "Now, what are we going to do about Bates?"

"I'm staying as far away from him as possible," O'Malley declared. "I have a feeling this ain't over. You know what I mean?"

"Yeah, it's starting to look that way. Any chance the blonde and Trey have something to do with this?" Terri asked.

"Well, anything is possible, but it looks like it's them. The timing is just a little too cozy for my liking." Maria frowned. "So, I guess what we do is keep you out of trouble, O'Malley. Terri, you're in charge of that one."

"Me? Are you sure?" Terri couldn't help but tease. "I mean, did she get into this much trouble before I came along? I could be a jinx, you know."

"Good point," O'Malley said. "But I think I'll be keeping myself out of trouble. Today I'm just gonna crawl into bed and sleep. At least until dinner."

Maria was about to remind her friend that trouble seemed to find her, when breakfast was delivered to the table. They dug in and ate quickly. It had been a long night, and they were all anxious to leave it behind. Maria arranged for Gato to pick her up at the diner, and they chatted over the last cup of coffee until he arrived.

O'Malley watched with envy the way her friend's face lit up when her husband walked through the door. It had taken Maria a long time to find the one man just crazy enough to deal with her and her wild moments. It helped that she was crazy enough to deal with his. They were a good match. O'Malley smiled as they greeted each other with a hug and a steamy kiss.

"There are children present, you know," she teased with a grin.

"You don't count," Gato grumbled as he sat down. "You look like shit, O'Malley."

"Thanks, Gato. I love you, too."

"He's right," Terri announced. "Come on, O'Malley, I'll drive home. Maria, we'll see you guys tonight."

"Hey, Terri, wear that outfit again tonight, okay?" Gato asked, letting out a huff of air when Maria's hand smacked him in the stomach.

"You are in so much trouble," Maria growled.

"I can look," Gato defended with a grin.

"Not if you know what's good for you," O'Malley said. She eased out of the booth and led Terri toward the exit. She let her arm fall around Terri's shoulder and they walked to the truck, ignoring the stares that followed them. As soon as they pulled out of the parking lot, O'Malley let out a monster yawn.

"Couldn't sleep, huh?" Terri asked as she drove carefully.

"Nope. After you left, they tossed in a hooker. She talked a mile a minute and never shut up. I've never been so glad to see a judge in my life. What's all this going to do to your probie status?"

"I don't know, my PO didn't say. I have another appointment next week, so I'm sure that I'm going to find out."

"How pissed was he?" O'Malley tried to stretch out.

"It was four in the morning, O'Malley, how pissed do you think he was?"

"So, why does a PO come get his probie outta jail?" the biker wondered aloud.

Terri sighed. "Because he knows that my original bust was bullshit and I got railroaded. I've never missed an appointment, and I don't give him a rash of shit like the others do. He's just a guy trying to do his job."

"You sure he's not something else?"

"Like what, O'Malley?" A hard edge sneaked into Terri's voice.

"You tell me. I've never seen a PO get his probie outta jail."

"I'm not fucking him, if that's what you mean," Terri snapped. "When we first got here, Bates busted me on prostitution charges. I was waiting for Trey and, like always, he was late. A car comes up and some sleaze asks me how much. I told him to fuck off, and before I know it, there's Bates reading my rights. I'm a new face, my boyfriend is nowhere to be seen, and since those upstanding officers certainly don't lie, the judge says I'm guilty. The PD got me probation because I didn't have a record. I don't know why my PO believed me, but he did. He's been an okay guy to me." Terri took the right turn a little faster than was necessary. "I don't know why he came to get me out of jail. I don't even know who called him. You want to know, you go ask him yourself."

O'Malley was stunned. She had certainly not expected Terri to go off on her, but she figured that she deserved the outburst. Suddenly, the whole situation struck her as funny. Maria kept telling her that Terri was no piece of fluff; now she was convinced. She chuckled out loud and leaned back.

"What the fuck is so funny?"

"Everything and nothing. This last month is like some bizarre bad dream. I think it's all just catching up to me."

"Now I'm a bad dream?" Terri's voice rose.

"Not you, damn it. It's this whole situation." O'Malley didn't raise her voice; she didn't need to. "Finding you is actually one of the better parts of this last month," she added with some hesitation.

Terri did not answer. Instead, she reached over and turned on the radio. The rest of the drive back to the house was an exercise in torture. When Terri pulled up into the driveway, she killed the engine and handed the keys to O'Malley.

O'Malley went straight inside to take a shower. Once she felt clean again, she turned off the water and took very little time to get dry and slip into a robe. She was too tired to think or feel anything except the dull ache in her left shoulder. Bates had done his job well. She'd hit the patrol car three times before Terri surprised him. She let out a sigh. She knew she would have to do something to make up for this one. Ellen had always cautioned her about speaking before she thought. Not that O'Malley ever listened. Sean's words came back to haunt her: *once a dumb-ass, always a dumb-ass.*

She stepped out of the bathroom and stopped short when she saw Terri out on the couch, a beer in hand and her head tilted back. Her eyes were closed, and from the rise and fall of her chest, O'Malley knew that she was asleep. O'Malley watched her for a long moment. The whole situation was a major screwup, and the only one getting the short end of the deal was the woman on the couch. She walked out to the couch, gently took the beer from Terri's hand, and set it on the coffee table. Sitting on the edge of the cushion, she reached out and shook Terri's shoulder, calling her name softly. It took a couple of tries but finally her eyes opened.

"Come on, sleepyhead. Let's go to bed. This couch ain't the most comfortable." O'Malley couldn't help smiling. Terri looked damned adorable half asleep. When she finally nodded, O'Malley led her to the bedroom, then turned down the covers for her. She busied herself with the hairbrush while Terri shed her clothes and slipped into bed. When she heard the contented, soft mumble, she knew she could turn around. Nudity didn't bother her and she was far from modest, but a naked Terri was damned difficult to resist.

She pulled off her robe and draped it over the foot of the bed, then got under the covers and pulled her share of the bedclothes close. As tired as she was, when she closed her eyes she discovered that she couldn't sleep. Her brain was revving into full gear. She opened her eyes again and almost laughed at the irony. In an effort to shut down her thoughts, she focused her hearing on the sounds of the house. The everyday noises that people seldom noticed were a comfort to her. Finally, her eyes started to droop and she didn't fight it.

* ~ * ~ * ~ *

Terri slowly floated out of her dream, wondering why her pillow was a blast furnace. She peeled open her eyes and came to several realizations at once. It was definitely late afternoon, she was wrapped around O'Malley's body, and if she moved one inch, they would both know just how wet she was. Her body was having an extremely happy reaction to being so close to the biker, and she had no idea how she was going to move without waking O'Malley. She sucked in a very slow breath and closed her eyes. It was torture, and a part of her was enjoying it immensely.

"Morning," O'Malley whispered, which caused Terri to jump. "Sorry, didn't mean to scare you."

Terri did not move. "I thought you were still asleep."

"Nope. I've been awake about half an hour. I would have gotten up, but I seem to be trapped here." O'Malley smiled and turned toward her captor. "Not that I'm complaining."

"Oh good. That you're not complaining, I mean." Terri stumbled over her words.

"Something wrong?"

"Um...no...I just...need to..." Terri couldn't think of any way to explain away the physical evidence.

"You just need what?" She shifted and let her thigh move between Terri's legs. "This, maybe?"

Terri gasped. "Yes." Her eyes drifted close as she let herself enjoy the sensations.

"Look at me," O'Malley requested gently. Terri's eyes found hers. "Is this what you want?"

Terri rocked her hips twice, very slowly, over O'Malley's strong thigh. "Does it feel like I want this?" She was having difficulty speaking. She shifted, placing her hands on O'Malley's shoulders in an effort to stay upright.

"Yeah, it does." O'Malley slid her hands up Terri's back, over her shoulders, and down to her breasts. The temptation of small, full breasts was too much for her. Tilting her head forward, she captured one nipple in her mouth and teased it unmercifully with her tongue while her fingertips played with the other.

Terri felt a surge of desire; it was like a tight string that went from her nipples straight to her clit.

O'Malley flicked the tip of her tongue over the nipple several times before shifting her attention to its twin sister. She was rewarded by Terri's growing even wetter. O'Malley kept up the sweet torture for quite a while, backing off each time Terri seemed close to going over the edge. Finally, she released Terri's breasts and pulled her body down on top of her. She moaned when Terri's breasts finally came into contact with her own. Her lips attached themselves to Terri's sensitive neck, and at the same time she slid her hand down her back and over her shapely butt until finally her fingers rested against Terri's flowing center, where they stroked gently.

Terri continued to thrust herself against O'Malley until she softly cried out, her words a jumble of what she wanted and needed. Each time she felt O'Malley's fingers graze her opening, she wanted them inside, but O'Malley kept denying her until she demanded them. Her growl turned into a satisfying groan when she felt two fingers slip inside. Together they set a maddening rhythm. As she moved forward, O'Malley's fingers slipped out, and as she moved back, those same fingers would slide back in. Her pace picked up when O'Malley sucked hard on her neck. Her orgasm came almost as a surprise, her breath catching in her throat as her back arched and her world was reduced to nothing but explosive pleasure.

O'Malley licked Terri's pulse point as she felt the pleasure tremors slow, then she gently eased her fingers from their snug nest. She trailed her soaked fingers up Terri's spine while she kissed the top of her head. She had enjoyed watching Terri move over her in such an erotic display of want and need.

"Oh, God, that was good," Terri finally said after she caught her breath and regained some composure. "I've wanted to do that for a while now," she said, stretching languidly against the body beneath hers.

O'Malley groaned at the full body contact. She felt Terri move and willingly accepted the kiss that Terri offered. Her fingers tightened in long hair as their tongues danced together. O'Malley was content to let Terri explore, and she let herself enjoy everything Terri was doing to her.

Terri grinned as she kissed her way down O'Malley's body, taking only a few moments to play with aroused nipples. She promised herself that she would come back to those later, but more than anything else, she wanted to taste O'Malley. She wanted to give her the same pleasurable release that she had been given. From the sounds reaching her ears, she knew it would not take long. She slid between the biker's strong legs and nuzzled gently before letting her tongue glide between swollen, wet lips.

O'Malley felt Terri's tongue enter and exit, stroke her clit, and begin the pattern all over again. Watching Terri as she came had pushed her close to the edge, and O'Malley knew she was not going to last very long. Her hips moved faster and her fingers curled tightly in the sheets.

Terri followed her lead and moved more rapidly, increasing the delicious pressure. Hearing the rough growl from O'Malley's throat as her thighs tightened around her head, Terri used her arms to hold the biker in place while she continued the pressure as O'Malley's orgasm washed over.

She released her hold on O'Malley and crawled her way up the heaving body, then collapsed in a happy heap on the biker's chest. She heard the contented purr from somewhere deep inside O'Malley. Weak arms wrapped around her, and fingertips danced lazy patterns on the back of her shoulders, making her shiver. She wondered how O'Malley knew that she loved that.

Terri smiled as she nuzzled her chin along overheated skin. "Hmm, thank you."

"You're welcome. Can you tell me what you were dreaming when you woke?"

"Don't laugh, but it was something along the lines of what we just did." Terri didn't mind admitting that now that they had stepped over the line. Oddly, she didn't feel the least bit guilty for having just had sex with the woman holding her.

"I like the way you dream." O'Malley chuckled as her hands slid down Terri's back to cup her butt. She pulled her closer and closed her eyes when she felt Terri respond by opening her legs wider.

"What time do we have to be at Maria's?" Terri asked as she nibbled on O'Malley's neck.

"Seven thirty." O'Malley groaned as she guided Terri slowly over her flesh.

"Oh good, we have time."

Chapter 12

Terri carried a stack of plates into Maria's kitchen and handed them off to her gracious hostess. She innocently returned Maria's pointed gaze, but couldn't repress the grin that had been creeping onto her face the entire evening. Maria took pity on her and said nothing, but her low chuckle spoke volumes.

They fell into a comfortable pattern as they rinsed off the plates and put them into the dishwasher. Eventually Maria couldn't stand it any longer. "Finally got her into bed, huh?"

Terri blushed and sighed. "Oh yeah." There was no mistaking the sound of satisfaction in her voice.

"Thought so. You have the look."

"The look?" Terri handed over a dripping glass.

"Yep. The completely satisfied, freshly fucked look. She has that effect on women."

After a moment, Terri said, "I can't tell if you're happy for me or if you're mad."

"I'm not mad. I just don't want to see her get hurt, or you," Maria said. "Sometimes she forgets that she's human, and when she does remember, it comes as a surprise. You have a handful in that one."

"Believe me, I honestly know that. Half the time I want to strangle her, and the other half I just want to hold her. I don't want either of us to get hurt, and with everything that's going on, I'm not sure that's possible," Terri said in a tight voice as she wiped down the counter.

"Then why do it?" Maria asked as she closed the dishwasher.

"I want to. Something about her just does it to me."

Maria nodded. She had heard a similar answer several years earlier. And now, hearing it from Terri was all the proof she needed to know that her troubled friend still had something of her old self tucked away, even if it was usually hidden from the rest of the world. Still, she wanted to be sure Terri was prepared for every eventuality.

"What if she turns into the kind of person most of us wouldn't want to know? She can and has done that." Maria held her hand up when Terri opened her mouth to answer. "Think about that for a while. At some point, all of the shit with Trey is going to spill over and you will find yourself treated like a trophy, not because that's how she wants to treat you but because that's how it is around here."

"I can't run, Maria. I don't have anywhere to go. And I know that she'll probably get tired of me and walk away, but right now, I can't think of a better place to be. For the first time in a long time, I feel like someone wants me."

Maria sighed and reached for a bottle of rum. "You don't look like a tequila drinker," she said as she poured out two drinks. "And if she walks away, what will you do then?"

"Deal with it as best I can," Terri answered as the glass was passed to her. "I'm not going to make the mistake of thinking this is permanent. I know that this will end." She shuddered at the taste of the rum.

Maria nodded and recapped the bottle. "If it does, you still have someplace to go. That's a promise."

Terri's eyes suddenly watered at Maria's words. She nodded in lieu of thanks and quickly brushed away the tears.

"Making my girl cry, Maria?" O'Malley growled playfully as she walked into the kitchen.

"Nah, just warning her that you can be a consummate asshole." Maria grinned as she took her glass and blew a kiss at O'Malley.

"Uh-huh, crying material." O'Malley shifted her gaze to Terri. "You okay, baby?"

"Yeah. Maria's just being nice to me; she still loves you more."

O'Malley smiled. "You two keep that between us. Gato finds out and I'm hamburger."

"Chicken?" Maria challenged, and laughed when both women nodded. She couldn't help but notice how much like night and day the two of them were. The few times she'd seen them together, they'd complemented each other well. If one had a moment of weakness, the other was there to offer strength. As much as she'd loved her Ellen, Maria knew that Terri was just as good for the often stoic, stubborn O'Malley. She managed to keep the knowing smile from her lips as she made a mental note to call Joan and give her an update. They had been working for what seemed like forever to get their mutual friend to move beyond the past.

Maria leaned her hip against the counter and just watched the two women interact. The soft smile that stole over Terri's face when O'Malley's eyes caught hers made the progression of their relationship quite apparent. What Maria saw in Terri did not appear to be just a result of the newly found intimacy that she and O'Malley shared; it was more as if Terri was emerging from some shadow that had kept her hidden. Maria could see the physical similarities that Terri shared with Ellen: the same slight frame that hid impressive strength; the shining eyes, though not the same color; and the obvious intelligence. The main difference was that Terri had lived a harder life and perhaps had her feet planted a little more firmly on the ground. Both women had found O'Malley at what would seem to have been a low point in O'Malley's life. *I just hope that Terri won't underestimate Callan O'Malley the way Ellen Rivers did.*

Maria pushed the thought aside and took a deep sip of her drink. She would not think ill of the departed. Joan would certainly hurt her for having such an uncharitable thought if she knew. As her friends were about to share yet another kiss, Maria pushed away from the counter and interrupted with an evil grin. "I say we take this out back. I still have to burn the deed."

"You really gonna dust the deed?" O'Malley's disbelief was evident in her voice.

Maria shook her head with a wry smile. "Nah. I went and got a copy of it. Just a symbolic thing, but hey, it will feel pretty damn good, ya know?"

O'Malley and Terri responded with twin laughs, then waited while Maria dashed into the back bedroom that served as a cramped office. When she returned, she found them locked together. The sight of their lips crushed together was almost too much, as they gave off a sexual energy that was infectious, and Maria wondered if throwing her guests out early would be in bad taste. She smacked O'Malley in the back of the head as she passed her and then tugged on the worn black T-shirt.

"Come on you, perv. Let's go burn some paper while Gato still has the grill lit. I cannot believe I finally own that rattrap."

Maria's enthusiasm was infectious, and it didn't take her guests long to get caught up in her excitement. Rhea, there with Mike, stopped her, then ran back into the house to extinguish every light that was not needed. When she returned to the flickering glow of the grill, the darkness provided a perfect backdrop for the deed-burning ceremony.

As Maria touched paper to flame, Gato's strong arms wrapped around her shoulders. "It was your dream, *cariña,* and you made it mine. You said we could do it in under ten. I shoulda known better than to tell you it couldn't be done. And I'm really glad you were right; I didn't want to live with Mom." The smile beneath his dark mustache was tender.

"Thank you, *mi amor,* for living on the edge so we could do this," Maria managed, despite the lump in her throat. "There was no way we were going to live with your mother," she announced.

"Hell, I'm just glad I have somewhere to drink beer." Mike grinned.

When the paper went up in a slow burn, Maria turned to her husband and kissed him with promise. "Now if I could just get some help behind the bar, I could spend more time with my wild man here." She laughed and tightened her hold.

"I could do that," Terri said. All eyes turned to her.

"You sure? I won't always be there to keep an eye out," O'Malley whispered quietly in her ear.

The warm breath made Terri shiver. "Yeah. Please. I'm going crazy not doing anything."

O'Malley lifted her head away from Terri's ear and nodded twice at her hostess. Maria did not miss the signal. She would take her at her word. If O'Malley said it was okay, then it would be okay.

"You better get used to having me around more," Maria teased Gato. His response was a kiss, followed by a leer.

* ~ * ~ * ~ *

The party broke up not long after a police cruiser rolled by the house. It didn't stop, but it did pass by slowly enough to draw notice. With the events of the previous twenty-four hours fresh in mind, everyone drifted into the house. Their offers to help clean up were waved off, so they said their good-byes. Mike and Rhea left first. John and his girlfriend Mandy left next, after he hid what he thought was their fair share of cash for dinner. O'Malley and Terri insisted on helping clear up the mess in the backyard, so she and Terri were the last to leave. It wasn't that O'Malley was being polite, she just loved torturing her friends by staying a little longer than they'd expected. She figured it was good for them to let the sexual tension build. Once they were finally finished with their tasks, O'Malley and Terri grabbed their jackets from their eager hosts and let the front door close behind them.

As O'Malley handed Terri a helmet, a thought skittered through Terri's mind and she watched the biker for a long moment. O'Malley looked up from putting on her own helmet and let her eyes ask the question.

"Would you do something for me?" Terri asked quietly in the darkness.

"Ask and I'll tell you," O'Malley answered with a wry grin.

"That's totally irritating. You're supposed to say yes."

"You're assuming I'm normal," O'Malley countered as she quirked her eyebrow.

Terri had to agree, but didn't do so aloud. "Take me on a night ride," she said. It was not a question and not a request.

"You sure you know what you're asking for?" O'Malley asked as she kicked her leg over the seat of her bike.

Terri settled in behind her and pulled close. "Yeah. If it's too much and I say so, you'll stop, right?"

She waited for O'Malley to look back and nod, then she pulled on her helmet without another word and straddled the bike, sliding close to the woman in leather. Terri waited until her pilot started the bike before she wrapped her arms around her.

The ride started like any other until they crested the steep hill a quarter mile from Maria's house. O'Malley let the bike idle for a long moment as though she was gathering either her thoughts or her courage. With deliberate movements, she reached over and flicked the switch for the headlights. Terri felt the deep intake of breath before the bike moved, and then they were flying. She pressed her body back away from O'Malley to give her room to maneuver. She resisted the normal human urge to close her eyes.

It was like flying in the dark. She knew her eyes were open when she looked up and saw the moon, full and bright in the sky. True, it looked like a blur and was somewhat surreal, but she felt alive. If she looked down on any turn, she knew that they were on asphalt and not sky, but it did not become solid unless she thought about it. It was like being and not being at the same time. She loved the feeling. Someone else was in control and oddly, she didn't seem to mind one bit. With each turn she just let her body touch O'Malley's, flowing in the direction of the body and the bike, the two of them almost one machine. It was a rush and it was dangerous and she loved it. After each turn, she would scoot back again. It was like the ultimate tease.

By the time O'Malley pulled into the garage, Terri was raw and wet and wanting. The garage door had barely closed when she pulled her helmet off and O'Malley's hands were on her. She let the helmet fall to the floor and winced when it sounded loud to her ears, but she didn't take much time to think about it. Terri leaned forward and attached her lips to the closest O'Malley flesh that she could find. The adrenaline rush alone was going to send her over the edge. She closed her eyes and sucked for all she was worth.

O'Malley's hand tugged her off the bike. "Inside, now."

Terri managed to slide off the bike, and for just a second, wondered when it was that O'Malley had managed to get off the bike and out of her helmet. Then it didn't matter as an insistent hand led her into the house. They didn't bother closing the door between the garage and the house.

"The Fates like us today," O'Malley breathed into Terri's ear as she leaned close.

Terri melted as she was pressed against the wall and her tight shirt was pushed up. Warm hands roamed at will, and she was powerless to stop them. She had asked for this, wanted this, and this time there would be no stopping.

Without warning, O'Malley's mouth was on her left breast. Terri moaned, wrapping her arms around the biker's neck. She could feel O'Malley's insistent tongue through the material of her bra, even as her skirt was tugged up to her waist. She let go of O'Malley's neck long enough to pull her bra out of the way. She was on fire, and with a hand full of her own flesh, she offered herself to O'Malley. Terri felt the raw edge of teeth close in on one nipple as two fingers entered her quickly.

"So wet...ready," O'Malley said around a hard, taut nipple. It was all that she could do to breathe, but she had to let Terri know what she was seeing and feeling.

Terri spread her legs farther. "Oh, God, please, don't stop," she begged, as she bucked against O'Malley and hoped that it would not end any time soon. It didn't. She was on the edge several times, only to have her lover back off. She whimpered her frustration and finally O'Malley trailed her mouth down Terri's body, never stopping in one spot for very long. Terri looked down as O'Malley's knees hit the floor, and suddenly she was on the receiving end of an incredibly talented tongue.

O'Malley groaned when she tasted Terri's essence. Her arms tightened around Terri's hips, and she pulled her impossibly close. She drove her fingers deeper and faster as her lips closed around Terri's clit. She heard Terri's head bump into the wall and felt the silky wet muscles around her fingers tighten and begin to spasm.

Terri opened her mouth as the wave of ecstasy slammed into her. She was beyond words and only vaguely aware of the noises she made as her entire body shook with the force of her orgasm. Her fingers tightened on O'Malley's shoulders. She finally realized that breathing would be good, and gasped in some air. Her body was still on sensation overload, and when O'Malley flicked her tongue over her clit, she came again almost immediately.

O'Malley cringed as Terri's fingernails found purchase in her shoulders. She didn't, however, stop what she was doing. The erotic rush was more important. She released the tantalizing flesh between her lips and eased her fingers out only when Terri begged her to stop. She stood and pressed her leather-clad legs around Terri's thigh. She quickly tugged off her own shirt so that Terri could cup her breasts. Fingers teased and pinched her nipples; her breath came in short, harsh gasps. Her mouth closed over Terri's lips and she eagerly received the warm tongue that invaded her mouth.

Her arms shot out to brace against the wall when Terri pressed hard with the thigh trapped between her legs. O'Malley groaned and welcomed the slick friction as she bucked her hips. She felt the fingernails of one hand slide down her back as the fingers of the other trapped one nipple, and it was all she needed to send her over the edge. She thrust herself against Terri twice more and came hard.

They collapsed against each other, barely able to stand on trembling legs, trying to catch their breath. After several moments, Terri leaned across the short distance and kissed O'Malley tenderly. Pulling away, she laced her fingers between O'Malley's and wordlessly led her into the bedroom.

* ~ * ~ * ~ *

Across the street, Trey watched from his perch in the shadows.

He had been so damn sure that the two women were only playing a game in public. When he had settled himself in to spy on them earlier in the evening, he had thought the naked window would provide him with the answer, one way or another. He flicked his cigarette away in anger. Now he had seen for himself that it was not an act, and the knowledge burned like bitter acid in his stomach.

Early on in the undercover assignment, he had become aware of the possibilities. He was sick of a cop's lousy hours and lousy paycheck, and he succumbed to the lure of easy cash and power in the circle of club members. He knew he could ultimately do as well as Spyder, if not better. After all, he had the valuable knowledge of how the authorities would react, how they would investigate. He loved the irony. Now all of his plans were in jeopardy because of that O'Malley bitch. No one had bothered to warn him about her or the odd respect that the older members gave her. It was the same respect they didn't give him.

He silently vowed that he would take her down several notches and gain that respect. He didn't bother to light another cigarette; he crept away from his spot and melted into the darkness.

Chapter 13

"GPS says we're here," Sean said quietly, knowing the mike would pick up the words and transmit them to the rest of the team.

"Roger that. Quinn, keep that gun ready. Hanson, keep the line open to base," Callan ordered calmly. Her eyes scanned the flat desert. The night vision goggles gave it a surreal green glow that made her slightly queasy. It was a feeling she never got used to. She shivered inside her coat and was grateful that they were in the vehicle and not out in the rain and fog. Scanning left and right, she tried to find some sign of the enemy that they were to locate. During the first two hours of the ground assault, headquarters had lost track of one of the Iraqi units. They could not afford to have any loose ends squirming out of the closing trap.

"Why are we here instead of the scouts?" Sean grumbled.

"None available, you dope. Scout means forward observation. This dump is not part of forward," Callan answered patiently.

Sean grinned without mirth. "I'm getting too old for this shit."

"Yeah, well, MP stands for multipurpose," Callan reminded him. "You want easy duty, you should have become a cook or something."

Quinn's voice sounded in their ears. "I've tasted his cooking, Sarge. You could be shot for treason for doing that to the Army."

"Blow me, Quinn," Sean muttered as he peered out the windshield.

Quinn chuckled. "You first."

Callan continued to scan as she got them back on task. "Boys, you can pick out furniture and rings when we get back. Right now, we got other things to think about." Her enhanced vision let her see what the human eye would have missed. It was a momentary flicker of some light source, and it was enough for her to move forward cautiously. "I've got something ahead at two o'clock. Sean, move us forward but be ready to get us the fuck outta Dodge," she ordered, her voice tight. Her fingers closed around her weapon as her training asserted itself.

Sean eased forward, being cautious because of the terrible driving condi-

tions.

"Oh, holy mother! We found 'em. Hanson, lock the GPS and send it back to base. Fire mission ASAP," Callan snapped out. She grinned slightly as she heard her radioman send the order in a calm tone. Nothing ever seemed to rattle the young soldier in the backseat. "Five—no, six APCs and one hell of a lot of ground pounders. I want high-explosive rounds at rapid fire."

"Roger that, Sarge," Hanson drawled out in his Kentucky accent. "Bravo two five confirms. Fire mission in ten mikes. Two five wants us out of the impact area," he relayed, even as he listened to the orders coming in over his headset. "Any idea how long they've been here?"

"I can see 'em enough to count, but not that well." Her words held a sarcastic, exasperated tone. She wasn't a miracle worker, just a soldier working in lousy weather. "With some luck, they won't be here much longer. Sean, get us outta Dodge. I want some distance."

"That I can do." He grinned and turned the wheel. He gave it a little gas and they lurched forward. In the middle of the turn, they hit a deep, muddy rut. Sean felt something solid under his right wheel. "Shit."

Callan was turning to look at her driver when the explosion ripped.

O'Malley lurched halfway up in bed, her arms supporting her, her mouth opened in a silent scream. It only took a moment for her to realize that she was not out in the desert. She sagged back and had to remind herself to breathe, then forced herself to relax her arms, which were tight cords of muscle holding her body up. She shook uncontrollably and kept her eyes closed until the tremors passed.

"Fuck," she spat, then tossed aside the blankets in disgust. Her eyes stole to the digital clock by the bed as she grabbed her jeans off the floor. Her movements were jerky, uncoordinated, and her fingers trembled as she worked the buttons of the fly. For the first time in days she was grateful that Terri was at work with Maria. She blew out a frustrated breath. She would be worthless for a while and she knew it. Pulling a clean shirt over her head, she went into the living room and then the kitchen. The restless feeling lingered, and although she didn't really want anything, she opened the door to the fridge, only to slam it shut.

She jumped when the cell phone rang and took a deep breath before answering. "O'Malley."

"I'm here." Cage's voice was on the edge of a purr.

"Where?" O'Malley asked.

"Thought I'd check the layout of the bar. Maria looks good, by the way," Cage answered.

"Yeah. Happy becomes her." O'Malley pulled down the can of coffee. "You get me the car?"

"I'm hurt. Black Camaro." Cage recited the license number. "Keys are in the tailpipe and the kit bag is on the passenger floor. You're set for sight and sound. It's almost like the old days, ya know."

"Cage, the old days sucked," O'Malley reminded her longtime friend.

"Says you. You got my steak ready?"

"Thawing as we speak." O'Malley turned on the tap and filled the carafe. "You know what we have to do?"

"Keep hurting my feelings, O'Malley, and I'm gonna have to kick your ass," Cage growled into the phone.

O'Malley chuckled as she poured the water into the coffeemaker. "Humor me. And you've never been able to kick my ass, you lightweight."

"We make the switch after you take the cut-through to the parking lot. I take your girl and you go play spook with this fuckhead. You might want to tell me what you're wearing so I can match it."

"Black jeans, black shirt, and my leather jacket."

"Oh, that's a surprise." The sarcasm was thick. "Your girl know anything about this?"

"Nope. I'll make the introductions later. You want me to bring you coffee?"

"That would be good. How long you gonna be in the bar?"

"At least an hour. I gotta make it look like I'm fucked up. You do remember how to do the stumble and bumble, right?" O'Malley asked. She didn't need the answer, she just liked to yank Cage's chain.

"I think I did it last night," Cage answered without hesitation or guilt. "It was well worth it."

O'Malley laughed and the restless feeling ebbed. "I'm sure it was. I'll leave here in an hour, then we're on."

"Roger that," Cage confirmed, then cut the connection.

O'Malley lowered the phone and closed her eyes. If she was going to pull off the recon that evening, she needed to be in the right frame of mind. The nightmare had thrown her off kilter. The last time she'd had that particular nightmare was during her visit to

Sean and Joan's on her return from Bosnia. She'd been a mess then, grief and guilt pushing her mind to places that she thought she had hidden away forever.

The gurgle of the coffeemaker pulled her back from those thoughts. Shaking her head, she rummaged for a thermos, needing a routine to keep her mind on track and away from the past. It was a trick one of her platoon leaders had taught her long ago. Methodically, she poured the coffee to a precise measurement, then screwed the lid tight. For the next hour, everything she did was thought out, planned, and executed by the numbers. Finally she was ready, and as she lowered the blinds to the front window, she lowered her human side. Tonight she was not a gunrunner; tonight she was a shadow.

~~*~*

Maria nudged Terri and leaned in close when she looked at her. "O'Malley's cut off right now."

Terri shifted her gaze to her lover at the bar. The biker, none too steady on her feet, was in Mike's face about something. She poked her finger in his chest and stumbled badly when he pushed her away.

"Maria, you think it would be okay if I took her home?" Terri asked as she looked around, assessing the crowd.

Maria nodded. "I think you'd better get going. I'd hate to see Mike get his ass kicked." She took the bar towel from Terri. "I'll distract her while you get your stuff."

Maria moved quickly around the end of the bar and stepped between Mike and her drunken friend. The hickory-sweet smell of Jack Daniel's was strong on O'Malley, and she was in no condition to be out. O'Malley only drank the hard stuff when the memories got to be too much. If Terri didn't get her out of there soon, O'Malley would be paying off the damages for years.

Maria wrapped her arms around her friend. "Hey there, O'Malley."

O'Malley's face lit up in a foolish grin. "Maria! Hey, baby. How 'bout you and me go get something to drink and have some fun?"

"You're already having too much fun." Maria chuckled. "It's a light night, why don't you take Terri home and have some private fun?"

O'Malley's eyes lit up at the suggestion. She slid to the side and bounced into the counter, banging her elbow. "Ow."

Terri brushed her hand over the back of O'Malley's neck and settled in close to her. "Hi, baby. Looks like you started early." She managed to keep her tone light despite her worry.

O'Malley grinned like a fool and rushed in for a sloppy kiss. "Yeah. Wanna go home and catch up?" she slurred.

Terri resisted the urge to roll her eyes. "Sure, baby. Let's go." With a fluid move, she ducked under O'Malley's leather-covered arm and stood up. The biker followed her without complaint. Terri was acutely aware of the eyes that followed them. She didn't dare look around to try and figure out what people were thinking or who might want to take advantage of the situation. She was sure O'Malley's friends would watch their backs. She cringed when O'Malley raised her voice to join in with the jukebox. *There are times that I hate the Doors.*

As they made their way out, Terri discovered that O'Malley's balance was shot. She lost count of the number of times they listed to one side or the other and banged into something. She heard a couple of bikers laugh as they parted to let the two women pass out the back door. Terri envisioned a number of tortures for O'Malley in the morning. She was sure that the hangover was going to be a major bitch. Outside, on the uneven pavement, O'Malley leaned toward the corner and Terri thought it was just another balance glitch.

She was surprised to find another person in the alley that led to the back parking lot. When O'Malley didn't react, Terri felt a flash of fear. O'Malley was in no condition to fight anyone off, so Terri pushed forward and stood in front of her as she halted. The figure that stood in front of them stepped into the light, and Terri was immediately struck by how much the woman looked like O'Malley. Their eyes were different colors and she could tell some other subtle differences, but the resemblance was almost eerie.

"Well, look at what we have here." The voice did not sound at all like O'Malley's; it was much smoother.

"Whoever the hell you are, you should leave." Terri hoped that the shaking inside her was not audible in her voice.

The woman laughed softly and relaxed her stance. "You've got a tiger on your hands there, O'Malley."

Terri felt the change in O'Malley's body tension and was suddenly confused.

"Yeah, I do, and you know what, it doesn't bother me one bit." O'Malley's voice was crisp, devoid of any slurring. She gently moved past Terri and offered her hand to the woman. They embraced for a moment, then pulled back from one another. "You gained some weight. Too much desk time?"

"Bite me," Cage shot back with a grin. "You gonna introduce us?"

O'Malley nodded sheepishly and turned back to her bewildered lover. Terri shot her a look saying she was going to have some serious explaining to do later. "Terri, I'd like you to meet an old friend of mine. Cage Quinn, meet my own tiger, Terri Barclay." Unexpected pride laced her voice as she unzipped her leather jacket and handed it over to Cage.

"Nice to meet you." Dark hazel eyes flicked to O'Malley. "She reminds me of your nurse. Same protective nature." She slipped into the jacket and flexed a couple of times to get comfortable.

The light blue turned arctic and O'Malley's voice was oddly flat as she responded. "You talk too much. I'll be there as soon as I can. Terri, just do what Cage says, within reason of course." There was no humor in her tone.

As Cage draped herself around Terri, O'Malley pushed down a momentary twinge of jealousy. With a reassuring smile, she squeezed her lover's hand, then drifted into the shadows and watched as Cage managed a creditable imitation of a drunk being led to the truck. She let out a low, easy breath when the headlights came on and the truck finally moved.

* ~ * ~ * ~ *

O'Malley waited until she was sure that no one was following. She didn't think there would be, but she didn't want to take the chance. She checked her watch and finally moved from her spot, giving thanks to whatever power above that Trey picked Wednesdays, a notoriously slow night at the bar, to have his little powwows.

She moved quickly across the parking lot and emitted a low whistle as she approached the car Cage had obtained for her. It was a thing of beauty. She loved muscle cars, and the engine on this one could outrun almost anything on the road. She extracted the keys from the tailpipe and let herself into the car. Settling into the leather bucket seat, she exhaled softly with pleasure. Closing her eyes, she turned the key, and melted as the engine roared to life. It was a rush, and she loved it.

Throttling back her desire to see what the engine could do, O'Malley drove cautiously to the neighborhood where the park was located. Getting stopped by a cop was not in her plan. She let her mind rove back into shadow space. She was nothing more and nothing less than the dark of the night. Usually the feeling led to someone dying, so it was a place she rarely let herself go. Tonight, she didn't want anyone to die, and for the first time in her life she enjoyed the feeling. Tonight would not be about destroying, it would be about gathering. She just wanted to know what she didn't know.

She killed the engine in front of a two-story house that had seen better days but was not on the verge of falling down. The car would not be out of place; there were plenty of muscle cars along the curb. As she put on the soft nylon jacket, she grinned and looked around. No one was on the street. She pulled her kit bag onto the passenger seat and unzipped it. She extracted a dented tin can of face paint and smiled as she recalled the first time she'd used it.

They were a group of hastily thrown together MPs on a makeshift aggressor detail in the middle of the German forest. Their mission was to attack a superior and experienced Air Force contingent. In the middle of the nowhere, they'd gathered around and dipped into the paint tin. As they streaked their faces, someone muttered in a low tone, "There's no way Air Force pukes are going to beat US Army cops. I'll die of shame first." A young and easily influenced O'Malley turned to the young man on her left when he finished his statement.

"Sean Barnes." He introduced himself. "You wanna kick some ass?" he asked with a flashy grin.

They drew the attack in the dirt at their feet, and it looked a lot like the plays etched in the sand of the playground during neighborhood football games. As simple as the plan was, it worked. The Air Force was routed and the Army won bragging rights, if only for the day.

Her warm fingers, laced with heavy face paint, touched the skin of her face and she felt herself turn from person into shadow. The grin she spied in the rearview mirror was nothing close to human.

There had been few times in her life that she felt perfect. The first time was when she was a nineteen-year-old soldier trained to fight Russians and East Germans, carefully stalking her prey in the same German forest. Each step was an epiphany, every breath measured and calculated. The second time was beyond the Iraqi border. There had come a point, with Sean tossed over her shoulder and each step a torture for her torn body, that she knew they would all come out of it fine. Her hearing was attuned to the action behind her. She turned, trusting her instinct, and fired the last few rounds left in her weapon. The brief scream of pain reinforced the gut feeling that the bad guys were close.

O'Malley let her eyes focus again, and the past was gone. She checked her reflection to make sure that she hadn't missed any skin. Her face was a mottled pattern of black and dark green. *If only my mother could see me now. She would pee in her pants.* The low chuckle that slipped past her lips surprised her. O'Malley stuffed the needed gear into her pockets, then slipped the earpiece snugly in her ear where she wanted it. She pulled open the car's fuse box and, counting to her left, tugged the correct fuse out of its spot. The dome light did not come on as she opened the door and eased out.

The walk in the shadows to her spot in the park went without incident. There were very few people out and about. She moved easily from tree to tree, bush to bush. She was in her element; Trey could not have picked better ground for her. Her eyes rested on the red-hot glare of dying coals. She headed in that direction and settled into a comfortable position for spying. She slipped the night vision goggles on and let her eyes adjust to the surreal green glare. Moving carefully, she plugged her headset into the small but powerful listening device. *I'll have to give Cage something really good for this one.* With all the gear in place she was able to make out the players she recognized. Trey and Thumper were there, and a couple of other minor club associates. The other four voices she did not recognize.

"Spyder wants that bitch to host a get-together. We'll be there." Trey's voice resounded in her ear. "Wait for my signal, and then we jump her ass."

"What's the signal?" a slurred voice asked.

"Whatever the fuck I decide," Trey snapped. "She's good, but I don't think even the great fucking O'Malley can take on five guys. After we kick her ass and have some fun with her bitch, Spyder will have his hands too full to pay much attention to us. Just don't get caught or I'll leave you hanging. That's the deal."

"So we have to kick her ass, fuck with her bitch, and not have the dime dropped on us? You're fucking rich, ain't ya? What's the payoff?" Thumper's voice was completely sober.

"Ten keys of pure China White, free and clear. Hank's so jumping at shadows, he's not going to notice that his safe is empty. We use his cash, Spyder's connection, and then we can cut loose of these posing fuckers," Trey announced with cocky surety. "Spyder is gonna call that bitch by the end of the week; we have to be ready. I can count on you boys, right?" There was an implied threat in his tone.

A round of agreeing voices reached O'Malley through her earpiece, and she would have moved if the hair on her neck hadn't stood up on end. Even though her body told her to scuttle off, she waited. The booted feet an arm's length away froze her in her place. She didn't look up; she almost didn't breathe. *The difference between life and death,* she recalled someone once said, *was the blink of an eye.* She knew it was all over if he looked closely to his left. After what felt like forever, he moved off. Still she waited, just in case.

In the waning light of the embers, Trey and his boys were drinking and boasting loudly as O'Malley's hands moved slowly in the dirt. She managed to gather her gear and ease it into the roomy pockets of her jacket. Without disturbing the area, she moved out. For a while it was toes and elbows, until she was out of the danger zone. There would be hell to pay for it later, but the information she had gathered was worth it.

Once she was safely inside the Camaro, she breathed a sigh of relief. She could take her time now. It took four wet wipes to clean most of the war paint off her face. She knew that if the cops stopped her, they wouldn't accept a "trick or treat" explanation. She eased the fuse for the lights back into its spot, then turned the key.

* ~ * ~ * ~ *

The sensation of someone slipping into bed beside her woke Terri from her light doze. She had spent the previous two hours waiting for O'Malley to return. Letting out a small sigh of relief, she rolled over. O'Malley looked fine and appeared to have all her parts intact—for the time being.

"You have a lot of explaining to do," she said bluntly.

"In the morning, Terri," O'Malley answered with a yawn and a stretch.

Terri shifted her eyes to the clock and read the numbers. "It *is* morning."

O'Malley blew out a frustrated breath. "All right, what do you want to know?"

"How about what the fuck is going on?" she hissed.

O'Malley ran her hand through her damp hair. "I went spying on Trey. I needed someone to take my place with you, just in case he's got a tail on us. Of all the people I know and use, Cage looks the most like me."

"That's an understatement. Why are you spying on Trey?"

"Because my gut tells me he had something to do with my ass getting tossed in jail. Knowledge is power, and I'm gonna beat that little fuck at his own game," she answered as she fluffed her pillow.

"Next time, O'Malley, just tell me what's going on. I was worried," Terri said softly.

"Sometimes, the less you know, the better."

"Didn't you just say knowledge is power?"

"Who said this was a democracy?" O'Malley snapped, immediately appearing to regret it. "I'm sorry. You know what I do for a living, Terri. It's dangerous. And at any point, if I look weak or like I can't do the job, they're gonna be all over me like sharks in a feeding frenzy. If you know what I know, you're a target too."

"Damn it, O'Malley, I'm already a target. You really think Spyder would believe me if I said I have no idea what you're doing?"

"No, he won't, but he'd kill you quicker. He would just get rid of you instead of having you tortured to death," O'Malley said quietly.

Terri let out a slow, shocked breath. "That makes me feel much better, thanks."

"Any time. Now can I please get some sleep?"

"Sure. I'll just lie here and panic." Terri's attempt at humor failed miserably.

O'Malley shifted in bed, wrapped an arm around Terri, and pulled her close. "If I think it's coming, I'll get you out of town first. I still have some favors owed to me."

Terri nodded, trailing her fingers absently over O'Malley's skin. She focused on O'Malley's breathing to try and take her mind off the words still lingering in her ears, but her mind churned the rest of the night and sleep was a long time in coming.

Chapter 14

O'Malley speared a sizzling steak off the grill and let it fall onto Cage's plate. "I hear you hooked up with Maria today."

Cage flashed a grin. "She told, huh?" While O'Malley and Terri had slept during the day, she'd gotten tired of waiting for them to wake up. Always the enterprising sort, she simply got into the Camaro and drove out to see the bar owner. They had a good time at the diner playing catch-up. Cage was amazed at the difference in Maria. She no longer looked to be on the verge of burnout, and her easy smiles were contagious. "Yeah, it was nice to see her again. She's totally stoked about the bar and worried like crazy about you."

"I keep telling her not to worry. Why doesn't anyone ever listen to me?" O'Malley asked, not expecting an answer.

"'Cause it wouldn't make any difference. I love her to death, but she is a total mother hen. I guess it makes her still feel like the chief nursing officer, you know," Cage mused. "And let's face it, bud, you were a mess for a long time. She's always gonna worry about you; it's her gift to the nurse."

O'Malley became very still as she thought about Cage's statement. "I know that I was fucked up and that I'm lucky not only to be here, but to still have friends. But, Cage, I am real sick of paying that particular bill." There was no malice in her voice, just fatigue.

Cage took a long look at O'Malley. Part of her was angry at her words, but part of her would forever be grateful to O'Malley for her part in saving her little brother's life. She sighed and shrugged. She wasn't about to give up trying.

"Well, hell, O'Malley, we all have bills to pay." She turned away and took her steak into the house to eat. She set her plate on the counter, then went over to the fridge and drew out a couple of beers. She had just twisted the cap off the second when O'Malley came in and set her plate beside Cage's.

"Let me know now if this is gonna be a Cage Quinn special," O'Malley said evenly.

Cage looked at her friend and noted that her eye color had not changed. She might be safe. "I don't want to make this a CQ special, all right. I owe you more than you'll ever know, and this is my way of giving back."

O'Malley sighed as she grabbed the beer off the counter. "Maybe I just want to finish this and get on with my life." She took a long drink and stared at Cage. "I am as well adjusted as I'm gonna get for now. I need to get these fuckers, and then I can move on."

"What about Terri?" Cage asked as she sat down on the stool and stared at her dinner.

"What about her?"

"When all this is over, what are you going to tell her?"

O'Malley sank down on her own stool and stared out the window. "I don't know."

Cage grinned around a bite of steak. "How about the truth? I know it's a stretch and all, but hell, it might be worth a shot."

"Man, don't talk with your mouth full. It's disgusting." O'Malley cringed and laughed at the same time. "If she's lucky, she'll come to her senses and run as far from me as she can possibly get."

"Not gonna happen," Cage predicted, ignoring O'Malley's request to wait until she'd swallowed. "She's gone on you."

O'Malley sighed. "Can't we talk about something else?"

"How about land mines?" Cage picked up her beer and flashed an evil grin.

"You are one sick bitch, you know that?" O'Malley laughed again when her friend just nodded like a bobblehead. "Why do I put up with you?"

"Because, whether you like it or not, you like me. Not that you're my type or anything."

"Next subject, please."

O'Malley finally cut into her steak and they settled into the routine of eating their meal. It was an easy silence and they didn't feel the need to break it. The steaks were finished in short order, and Cage quirked an eyebrow when O'Malley walked the plates to the sink.

"That's pretty domestic," she said as she fished out two more beers and opened them.

"You can sleep under the car, you know," O'Malley threatened, not turning around from her chore.

"Maria would take me in," Cage taunted in return.

O'Malley shook her head and went silent.

Cage saw the tightening of O'Malley's jaw and the trembling of her hand and was beside her in an instant. As her knees buckled, Cage caught her and eased her to the kitchen floor. The inhuman sound that tore up out of O'Malley's chest broke her heart. Cage rocked O'Malley gently, as she had done for her brother when they were kids and he'd had one of his nightmares. She wondered how long it had been since her friend had let out her grief and anger and frustration. From the sight of the typically strong, stoic woman on the floor crying hot tears and sobbing deeply, it had never happened.

Cage would forever owe her brother's life to the woman in her arms, and at first it was gratitude that had brought her to O'Malley. Thomas Quinn was not an easy man to impress, but his letters home from Fort Hood certainly piqued his sister's curiosity. He described his new squad leader in glowing terms, and Cage had wondered if the woman could actually walk on water. On a whim, she had decided to take her leave time early and go visit her little brother. Meeting O'Malley had been a letdown at first; she didn't seem like the super soldier he'd described. Then she spent some time with her brother and his friends and got to see Callan O'Malley as a person rather than the object of hero worship.

Just before the unit had shipped out to the Persian Gulf, Cage's last words to O'Malley were to keep her brother safe. After their encounter with the Iraqis, in which all of the squad members were injured, a bandaged and weak O'Malley lay in a hospital bed, just waiting for Cage to rip into her. The fear in her eyes had been palpable. Cage didn't miss it, nor did the Air Force nurse who hovered nearby ready to jump her if her behavior was out of line. It was the fear she had seen in those blue eyes that had stayed with Cage. She knew then that O'Malley was one of those people who feared failing to keep their promises more than they feared death.

Sitting on the kitchen floor, she was suddenly struck by the realization that O'Malley had always brought them back. The people she felt responsible for had always come home alive—maybe not unhurt, but breathing. O'Malley had never let anyone important in her life die. She had promised Ellen that she would come home alive, and then Ellen was the one who had died. Cage closed her eyes and silently damned the Fates for their cruelty to her friend.

* ~ * ~ * ~ *

Terri closed the truck door and pushed the button on the garage-door remote. She was tired and definitely wanted a shower. The smell of cigarette smoke clung to her clothes and hair. It was the only real downside to working at Traders. Most of the regulars knew she was O'Malley's and the nonregulars found out quickly enough, so she didn't have to worry about anyone trying to talk her into going home with them. She smiled at the thought of belonging to O'Malley. She knew she should have been incensed with the idea that someone owned her, but in the lifestyle she was professing, it felt more protective than demeaning.

She had seen enough to know that while not every biker was a club member, criminal, or general lowlife, the majority of them were, for whatever reason. All Terri could really do was try to understand it. She sighed as she pushed open the door leading into the kitchen. She set the keys down on the counter and looked around for O'Malley and Cage. There were two mostly empty beer bottles on the counter, and the bike was in the garage. Guessing that the two old friends had probably drunk themselves to sleep while rehashing the good old days, Terri pulled off her shoes and headed for the shower in the hall bathroom. There was no way she would go into their bedroom smelling the way she did.

She stripped off the foul-smelling clothes as she waited for the water to get hot. She caught sight of herself in the mirror and shook her head. She wondered what it was that O'Malley saw in her. O'Malley could have any woman that she wanted, and apparently had frequently done just that. Terri knew, however, that if circumstances were different, if she weren't undercover, she would still have been drawn to her. There was something about O'Malley, and Terri was damned if she could figure out what it was.

Turning away from the mirror, she tested the water and stepped in, groaning in relief when the hot water cascaded through her hair. She lingered in the shower. Lately it felt like the only place where she could be alone with her thoughts without having someone ask what was going on in her head. She was aware that her head was a muddled place. She felt torn between her personal feelings and her duty. She had not expected to make friends during her undercover assignment, and yet she had. She hadn't expected to make enemies, either, especially not the man who was supposed to be her partner.

She snorted in some water at the thought of Trey, and coughed in surprise. She was getting damn tired of his shadow.

In a strange way, she was also grateful that Trey had screwed up as badly as he had. She was learning more about Spyder's operation working behind Maria's bar than she had acting as Trey's girlfriend. Even when she was with Trey, the other members of the inner circle seldom spoke of their plans. At the bar, away from Spyder's eyes and full of alcohol, some of his confidants let things slip while boasting, and she tucked them away in her mental file to pass on to George.

Terri let her head press against the shower wall and felt the full force of the shower beat on her back. It felt good. *I wonder if I could just hide here forever.* A little-girl giggle bubbled from her. She knew that while it was a pretty good idea, it was not going to happen. She picked up the soap and lathered it in her hands.

It took her a while to feel clean enough to get out from under the water and dry off. She quickly ran a brush through her tangled hair; she wanted only to crawl into bed and snuggle up to the warmth that O'Malley's body offered. In O'Malley's bed, she felt safe. She'd had lovers in the past and she was sure there would be lovers in the future, but it was hard to imagine anyone else who could keep her monsters at bay during the night.

She had become so accustomed to lingering fright and sleep deprivation that the first few mornings of waking up refreshed had completely thrown her off her usual mental balance. She was seeing things more clearly than before, and it was becoming a problem. Terri didn't know how she could do her job and not completely ruin people she cared about. Maria might not be involved with Spyder's bunch, but she would be found guilty by association, and some of the fringe members whose only apparent crime was bad timing would be condemned for the same reason. She refused to think about what would happen to O'Malley.

Terri wrapped a large towel around herself and brushed her teeth, trying not to think. *I'll have time to drive myself crazy later.* She stepped out of the bathroom and barely contained her scream of surprise as she almost ran into Cage. She was going to have to hang bells on O'Malley and her friends. They all seemed to have the same cat-footed ability to sneak up on a person.

"Sorry," Cage said softly.

As her heart rate returned to normal, Terri noticed something different about Cage. She was subdued and her face was etched with something close to worry. Glancing around, Terri still did not see O'Malley, and she began to panic.

Cage recognized the look. "She's okay, sort of. Why don't you put something on and we can talk."

Terri had a sinking feeling in her stomach, but nodded. Trying to prepare herself for whatever Cage might have to tell her, she walked to the bedroom door and slowly opened it. A sliver of light illuminated the room and she could see that their bed was empty. Her heart began to race again. She slipped into O'Malley's thick cotton robe and was belting it as she stepped back into Cage's sight.

"How much do you know about Callan?" Cage asked quietly as she sat down and motioned Terri over.

"Not much," Terri admitted as she crossed the room and sat in O'Malley's chair. "I know what she does for a living." Cage's eyes widened in surprise. "I asked, and she told me. I know that she used to be in the Army and that she was kicked out. I've met Sean and Joan. I know that there was a lover once, and she died."

"Ellen," Cage interrupted. "Yeah, she was something." Her voice held a wistful quality.

Terri didn't know how to interpret the remark. "What's going on, Cage? Where's Callan?" She didn't realize that she'd used O'Malley's first name.

"I put her in the guest room. She's had a rough day. I'll tell you what happened in just a bit, but first I need to explain something to you so that maybe you might understand." Cage rubbed her eyes with a shaky hand. "O'Malley got hurt in the Gulf War."

"I know; I've seen the scars. She told me that her vehicle ran over a mine." Terri wrapped her arms around her midsection.

"When they got her to the hospital in Germany, she was a mess, even with the emergency care she'd gotten in Turkey. Ellen was her nurse. She took care of O'Malley's pain and protected her—from others and from herself. She helped O'Malley more than anyone else could have. Ellen was everything that she needed at the time, even if the dumb-ass was too banged up to know it. Maybe because of the intensity of their contact, or because they became friends first, their relationship is something I still can't describe.

"All I know is that for Callan, Ellen was everything. When Ellen died, something in O'Malley snapped, and for a long time she just closed off. She wasn't the person we knew and loved. Half the time we hated her, and the other half...we were worried that she was going to get herself killed."

"Cage, these are things that O'Malley should be telling me," Terri said as gently as she could. The caring and concern were evident on Cage's face, and Terri didn't want to hurt her feelings.

"I know, and I wouldn't be telling you all of this if I thought she would." Cage sighed and leaned back against the couch. "O'Malley doesn't usually talk about Ellen. Has she ever even said the name out loud to you?" Terri's silence was her answer. "I didn't think so. She can be such a stubborn shit, stubborn enough to not let the grief out. I think that maybe she's cried a little in what she would call a weak moment, but not all-out grieving.

"It's been a long time since Ellen died, and Callan finally snapped today. I don't know what made her cry, but I for one am damn grateful that it happened. It wasn't just crying, Terri, it was full release. If I know her, she's going to be fucked up for a few days; she might even take it out on you. She won't mean to, and she'll be damn sorry afterward.

"I know that O'Malley feels something for you and I don't think it's just the situation Trey put you both in. You've gotten under her skin. I know the look, and she hasn't had that in her eyes for a long time. You deserve to know what's going on with her so that you're not wondering what the hell is happening." Cage looked at Terri. "I think that's the most I've spoken at one time in years."

Terri stood and padded into the kitchen, for a moment considering the bottle of whiskey. She decided on beer instead. She pulled out two beers and opened them, mostly to have something to do. Cage's bombshell had left her unsettled. She had no idea how she could compete with a ghost. Her hand shook as she handed one bottle to Cage. She did not sit as she took a large first drink.

"What am I supposed to do now?" she asked, at a loss and frightened.

"I don't know. She's never done this before." Cage rolled the beer bottle in her hands.

"I don't know if I'm strong enough to handle this. What if she doesn't want my help?"

"Then you let her work it out until she's ready to," Cage advised as she set her bottle on the coffee table.

"I've seen her work things out, and, Cage, I won't just stand by and watch her punish herself. I'm not going to let her go through this alone."

Cage smiled tenderly and her eyes softened. "You just might be the only one she'll let close enough to help."

"I'm going to bed. I think it's my turn to keep the monsters away. Would you put my beer in the fridge?"

"Hell, I'm gonna drink it," Cage purred. "I'll lock up before I go to bed," she promised.

"You're a good friend to her, Cage. Thank you," Terri said.

"I owe her; I'll spend the rest of my days paying her back. Even if I don't enjoy the moments, I'll never regret them at all."

Terri frowned in confusion and tucked the words away in her mental file for later. Some day she would ask Cage what she meant, but for the moment, nothing was more important than being with O'Malley.

She slipped into the guest room and softly closed the door. Standing by the bed for a few moments, she listened to O'Malley's breathing. She couldn't tell if her lover was asleep or not. Slowly, as her eyes adjusted to the darkness of the room, the form under the blankets came into view and her heart ached.

Terri slid under the blankets and scooted close to O'Malley. She could feel the heat emanating from her body and knew that somewhere in her mind O'Malley was fighting her demons. Not knowing what else she could do, Terri wrapped her arms around her lover and gently pulled her close. Even in her tortured sleep, O'Malley turned until she was nestled against Terri. Unconsciously, she clung to the offered safety that had nothing to do with the past.

When dawn's light finally broke through the curtains, Terri's eyes drooped and closed. For a while, there were no dreams and no memories, no doubts and no fear. The only sound was their mingled breathing, and nothing else existed.

Chapter 15

Cage followed O'Malley into Spyder's clubhouse. Even at that hour of the morning there were quite a few bikes in the parking lot. Her eyes stole to O'Malley and she smiled inwardly. Some things would never change. When her friend was on, she was cocky and confident, and it showed in the way she moved. She didn't walk as much as she strutted. *No one would be able to tell that she was a sulking, brooding mess for the last two days.* Cage felt partly responsible, but she wouldn't feel guilty. Whether or not she would admit it, O'Malley had needed the breakdown.

She did feel bad that Terri was taking the brunt of O'Malley's confusion. She had watched O'Malley drift between sullen silence and smart-assed comments. Many times Cage had opened her mouth to take her friend to task, but each time Terri would just shake her head. It was easy to see how difficult it was, but Terri acted as though nothing was out of the ordinary and forced O'Malley to maintain a routine. Not once did Terri snap back.

Cage almost stumbled on a crack in the sidewalk and forced herself to focus on the matter at hand: she was finally going to meet the infamous Spyder. Even with O'Malley's description, she had no idea what he was really like. She was dying to get into his head and figure out what made him tick. It was like a game to her, and she loved games.

O'Malley pushed open the door and stepped into the dim light of the front foyer, flashing a hard grin at Boomer. He nodded, then opened his eyes a little wider as a second woman followed. He didn't miss how closely the two resembled one another.

"You didn't tell me you had a sister, O'Malley."

"I don't. Boomer, this is Cage. Cage, the mountain in front of you is Boomer."

Cage tilted her sunglasses down and let her brown eyes trail up

and down his body. Boomer was Cage's type. He was a large structure with an air of danger. Cage had always been attracted to the
flame. She lived her life on the edge, and she would never change.
It was refreshing, in a sick sort of way.

"Hi there." Cage's purr was in full force and it worked on
Boomer. She watched him flush and wondered what visual had just
passed through his mind.

"O'Malley, you are finally traveling in company I can relate to."
Cage knew that Boomer was enjoying the way she filled out the
leather pants that clung to her like a second skin.

O'Malley ended their mutual inspection. "Get your mind out of
your pants before you break something. He's expecting us."

Instantly, Boomer was back to his duty, though his eyes lingered
on Cage. "Either one of you packing?"

"Depends on what you mean," Cage teased as she unzipped her
jacket and let Boomer have an eyeful. "I'm not carrying a weapon."

Boomer grinned like a high school boy looking at his first skin
magazine. "Yeah, I can see that."

O'Malley found it as amusing as hell. "I'll let her come back
and play with you later. Right now, we have business," she reminded
them both.

"Killjoy," Cage muttered without malice. She knew she would
be seeing Boomer again. O'Malley was always good about sharing
information, and her briefing on Trey's conversation now took on a
greater personal significance. According to O'Malley, where Spyder
went, Boomer was sure to follow, and Spyder was going to be at the
party he was going to demand O'Malley host. "I'll see you later,"
she promised with a wink, causing Boomer to almost drool.

O'Malley shook her head and tugged on Cage's jacket. "Come
on. He hates to be kept waiting." She released the leather and
walked into the main room, where Spyder sat at his usual table.
Strangely, he was not surrounded by his usual entourage, and his latest girlfriend was not by his side. O'Malley kept her smile to herself.
Sometimes inside information was a lot of fun. She pulled out a
chair and turned it, then sat heavily, a grin on her face and her sunglasses in place. Cage stood behind her.

Spyder's expression showed his lack of amusement. Then his
eyes flicked over to Cage and for just a second, his surprise showed.

"Spyder, Cage. Cage, this is Spyder. He's the one we talked
about."

Cage eased into a chair and tucked her sunglasses in her pocket. "Hi."

"What's going on, O'Malley?" His voice was tinged with suspicion.

O'Malley grinned. "You want something heavier; Cage specializes in heavy." She folded her arms over the back of the chair.

"Can I trust her?"

"Probably not," Cage supplied with a low laugh. "But O'Malley can. You want something she can't get without me. It's your choice."

He switched tactics. "Maybe I changed my mind."

Cage was not at all thrown off by his statement. She was used to mistrust, expected it. "Then I'm outta here. And I don't know you and I don't expect you to know me."

O'Malley cut through the games. "You changing your mind, Spyder?" Her voice was dangerously low.

"No. Just testing the waters." His attention shifted to Cage. "You can get what I want?"

"I talked to a mutual friend. He's got four he can part with and not get caught. Any more than that and it goes to shit. If you need more, give me six months and we'll see what I can work out."

"Cost?" he asked, then slammed back the shot sitting in front of him. He didn't even react to the liquor sliding down his throat. With a wave, he caught the attention of the girl behind the bar. He held up three fingers and she went to work.

Cage deferred to her friend. "That's O'Malley's game. It's her deal."

"Twenty each. I gotta cover shipping and middle costs. Cage ain't cheap," O'Malley said easily, as she turned her head and watched the action behind the bar. "She's new."

"Yeah." Spyder grunted and waited until the woman walked over to the table and set the glasses down. "You want a taste?" His tone and eyes issued a challenge. He obviously didn't expect the wolfish smile that crossed O'Malley's face.

Without a word, O'Malley reached out and pushed up the waitress's shirt. Her hand shot out and held the woman in place as she tried to move away. O'Malley pulled the new employee close enough for her mouth to attach itself to an exposed nipple. She sucked for a moment, hard enough that it would leave a mark around the areola. She released the nipple and slid the shirt down.

"Very nice," she commented without acknowledging the woman, who was waved away by Spyder.

A flush spread up his neck. "What's the matter, O'Malley? Terri not enough for you anymore?"

O'Malley's grin was predatory. "Oh, she's more than enough. Since you seemed to be in the mood for sharing, I just hated to piss off the host."

For a long second, Spyder appeared to be at a loss. He picked up the shot glass and stared at the dark liquid.

"We have a deal on one condition." He looked hard at O'Malley, who still wore her dark wraparound sunglasses. "I want to have a party at your place. Tonight."

O'Malley had known it was coming, yet she let her head hang low for a second, as if she were considering his demand. "No fucking way."

"I'm not sure you get it, O'Malley. You don't get a choice in this one. I'm starting to get the idea that you think you ain't tied to me. You do this and maybe I won't be on edge about you." The threat in his voice was undisguised.

"Maybe I don't give a shit about what you think, Spyder," O'Malley drawled slowly.

"I say the word and your little business here dries up," Spyder countered. "I have enough connections to put you out of business." His eyes told enough of the truth.

O'Malley's face gave no hint of her surprise. In three years, he'd never admitted that his reach extended further than California and Washington. She pursed her lips as though she was in deep thought, giving him the time to think that he had forced her to accede.

"Dammit, I don't do parties, Spyder, not even for people I like, and I don't like most of your people."

He laughed. "Hell, O'Malley, even I don't like them. It's not a full blowout, just some of my best boys and their old ladies. I'll even tell 'em not to kill the furniture."

"Eight tonight. It'll take me that long to get ready. Hey, Spyder, they fuck up my house and I'll take it out on the bikes." She knew that threat might be enough to keep them in line, if only temporarily.

He grinned easily. "I take it that we have a deal then, both ways."

Cage could see how he had moved up the food chain and taken

over. He was charming, and handsome enough. He probably had not looked like a threat, and she knew from experience that it was just that sort of person that ended up in the lead dog spot. She guessed that he had watched and learned, and when the previous leader had a weak moment, he had moved in.

"You meet the cash and it's done on my end," O'Malley said. "I do the most fucked-up things for money," she said as she took up her shot glass. "We have a deal. On both ends."

Spyder smiled. "Cheers."

O'Malley grunted. "*Sláinte.*"

"*Na zdorov'ye,*" Cage tossed in with a lick of her lips. She just loved how the Russian toast sounded. It was the only thing she remembered from language school, but it had been worth the nine months. Together, the three kicked back their shots, but only Cage and O'Malley shivered when the Southern Comfort hit the back of their throats. Cage let out a low breath; O'Malley simply inhaled.

Spyder set his shot glass on the table and looked hard at the gunrunner. "Where's my nines?" he asked without humor.

"You think I'm gonna cheat you, Spyder?"

O'Malley's voice was flintier than he could ever remember. "I'm wondering where my product is. I already paid half. Business is business."

"I've never fucked over a client, Spyder, and I don't plan on starting now. You'll get your product." She stood suddenly and stepped away. "You might be able to dry me out with your kind of people, but there's more people looking to buy my goods than just bikers. Just keep that in mind and we won't have a problem." O'Malley waited a moment to let her words sink in, then turned to Cage. "You coming with me or do you wanna hang here?"

Cage slipped her sunglasses out of her pocket and let them settle over her eyes. "I'm with you. We still have some business to talk about." She turned back to Spyder. "She's a handful when she hasn't had her coffee. Bring Boomer with you tonight and maybe we can talk freelance contracting." She flashed a grin that usually brought men and most women to their knees before she turned and followed O'Malley to the front door.

She halted in front of Boomer and took in the appearance of well-worn jeans and a large but lean body, and she grinned. Boomer obviously took care of himself; she liked that. She leaned in close over the counter and let her eyes fall to the magazine.

"You really should go for the real thing. It seems there's a party tonight. I expect to see you there." Her words were both teasing and promising. She didn't wait for his reply before she pushed away from the counter and walked out the door.

O'Malley had already started the engine of her motorcycle when Cage came out of the clubhouse. Cage eased onto her own bike.

"Where to?" she shouted over the sweet noise of twin Harleys. She made a mental note to do something cool for Gato. She loved his bike, and someday she was going to convince him to sell it to her. For now, it was enough to borrow the dream machine.

"Gotta go suck up to Terri; she's gonna kick my ass over this party thing. And I gotta check in with Sean, see where he's at."

Cage nodded and laughed. For the first time in two days, she got the idea that everything might be okay. She snugged her chin strap, waited until O'Malley turned into the street, and then followed.

~~*~*

Terri, wearing tight leather pants and a half vest, turned and looked her reflection in the mirror, trying to keep the worried frown off her face. O'Malley's announcement had come as a total surprise, and it took every ounce of her willpower not to rage like a fool. The two village idiots, as she was calling O'Malley and Cage for the time being, had spent most of the day shopping and cleaning for the impromptu party. If it was going to happen, Terri was not going to run herself ragged. They'd gotten themselves into this, and she wasn't going to give much in the way of sympathy—or help. She was too busy worrying about Trey. If Spyder was going to show, then Trey would be around at some point, and Terri was trying to figure out what she was going to do and say.

O'Malley walked into the room and stopped cold in her tracks at the vision standing in front of the mirror.

"Quit drooling and get over here," Terri demanded with a smug smile. She allowed O'Malley into her arms and pulled her close. "You so owe me for this one, you know that, don't you?"

"Yeah. In more ways than one."

Terri leaned up to whisper into O'Malley's ear. She didn't see the leer that resulted from her request.

O'Malley smiled. "Count on that one. You should have asked

earlier." Her mouth latched on to Terri's lower neck and she sucked for all she was worth.

After a long moment of the sweet torture, Terri pulled away. "Mmm, good. I was thinking you might not want to have that kind of fun."

"You should know by now that surprises are a part of my life." She moaned softly. "I want *that* with you and I want you like that so very badly." O'Malley grinned.

For that instant, O'Malley was nothing more than the woman Terri wanted. "That makes two of us." She let her hands trail off O'Malley's shoulder and moved away, feeling like the consummate tease. If all went well later, it would not feel that way. They would both get what they wanted. She walked out of the bedroom with a wiggle to her hips and brushed past Cage, not bothering to say anything as she faded into the kitchen.

* ~ * ~ * ~ *

The party started slowly, as everyone expected. At first it was just Spyder, with Angela absent from his arm. Terri and O'Malley both suspected she had outlived her usefulness to the leader of the gang. Slowly, the others trickled in. Each one, in varying degrees of sobriety, walked into the house and handed over a bottle of something. It was a tradition.

O'Malley finally just left the door open and wandered around in the crowd, quickly losing patience with the whole thing. She filled her glass many times. It wasn't long before she lost sight of Terri and lost track of time. On one of her many rounds around the house, she spied Boomer and Cage standing extremely close and lost in each other. The smirk on her face would have been priceless if anyone else had seen it. She looked around for Terri, and not finding her was a disappointment.

* ~ * ~ * ~ *

It seemed like forever ago that the party had started, and Terri needed to get away from the claustrophobia she was feeling in the crowded house. She, Rhea, Candace and, to her surprise, Donna stretched out on the grass of the backyard. They passed a bottle of red wine around their small circle. Terri was looking up at the stars, only half listening to her friends chatter.

"Hank's been such an asshole lately," Donna said, which made Terri listened closer.

Candace took a sip of wine before asking, "What's up his ass this time?"

Rhea turned her head to look at Candace. "Are you kidding? He gets like this around this time every year." Candace still looked clueless. "Like, three years ago, one of his girls tried to take off and he had a hell of a night trying to get her back."

"I hadn't heard that," Terri said as she struggled to sit up.

Rhea helped her. "Well, you haven't been around that long, so you wouldn't know."

"I know what night you're talking about," Donna offered quietly. "God, he was a son of a bitch for a while after that." She waved off the offer of the wine bottle. Her green eyes locked on Terri. "It was like he was looking over his shoulder for something that was scaring the hell out of him. I can't remember her name, but she came to the club like the others. She was some runaway who ended up in our version of hell. Hank took an instant liking to her, and it wasn't long before he got her strung out and had her doing more than dancing, if you know what I mean."

The others nodded, knowing she was talking about the prostitution ring Hank was running out of the club. His favorite pastime was the women who could make him more money than the club ever would.

"She finally woke up and took off. From what I hear, a woman on the highway picked her up. When he found out that she'd taken off, Hank put out the word, and one of Spyder's boys sort of discovered the car by accident. They followed her half the night and finally ran the car off the road. You know where Moody's Gap is?"

"Yeah, nasty road. It's all snake turns and some serious drop-off cliffs," Rhea said.

"Well, that's where they ran the car off. I heard the woman driving was still alive when they got down there. Hank's girl was already dead."

"What happened?" Terri asked. She wanted to know, and at the same time she didn't want to know. She couldn't shake the morbid curiosity.

Donna looked around to make sure they were still alone. "The story from a couple of the boys who were there is that Hank called

Spyder to see what he should do. Spyder told him to wait there and make sure the woman was dead. So, that's what he did. Boomer said that if they had gotten her to a hospital, she might have lived. But what Spyder says gets done. She bled to death, and they covered their tracks and got the hell out of there."

"So why is Hank all jumpy?" Candace asked, grabbing the almost-forgotten bottle of wine.

"Because the woman driving had a family, and from what the papers said, a lover who threatened to find out what happened. He's all weirded out that this guy is gonna find out about it and come get him," Rhea explained in a frustrated tone. "Can you imagine what you would do if someone killed your lover?"

Lost in the visuals that popped into their heads, no one said a word. Terri had to admit that she didn't know what she would do. Until just recently, her job had been her lover.

"I remember it all now," Rhea said. "The driver's name was Ellen something. I thought they said it was a tragic accident."

"Like Spyder and his boys don't own almost everyone in this town," Donna commented.

Terri felt her world shrink. It couldn't be a coincidence. She thought back to the bits and pieces she had picked up from listening to O'Malley's friends. This story was too close to not be the truth of it. She tilted her head back to try and clear her mind.

Candace changed the subject. "So, spill it, Terri," she cajoled as she settled next to Terri.

Terri was sure she had missed something. "Spill what?" She felt a finger tickling her neck as her hair was moved away.

Candace giggled as she traced the outline of the hickey. "Nice markings."

"So, has she made you scream yet?" Rhea asked as she passed the bottle to Donna.

"You have no idea. Actually, yes, you do," Terri answered with a wicked grin. "Sometimes all she has to do is look at me and I'm there."

"God, you are so lucky. She looks at you like you are so on the menu."

Terri wasn't sure who said it, but that was how she felt. She grinned smugly. "I am appetizer, entrée, and dessert. Life is hell."

Rhea barked out a laugh. "You are so full of shit. You're enjoying it, and I say it's about time. One of us should be getting something satisfying for a change."

"Amen to that one," Donna agreed.

"I'll agree, too," O'Malley said as she walked up. She almost laughed when all four women jumped.

"Jesus, I hate when you do that," Terri snapped at O'Malley. She could hear the dancers catch their breath.

"Guess I'll have to make it up to you then." O'Malley stalked over to her lover's side, dropped to her knees, and planted a serious kiss on Terri's lips.

Terri wrapped her arms around O'Malley's neck and pulled herself closer, only pulling out of the kiss when Rhea cleared her throat loudly.

"Get a room," Candace teased.

"Girls, go away," Terri ordered in a playful voice. "And kill the porch light when you go in, please."

The dancers took the bottle of wine and walked the distance to the back door, tossing out some lewd comments. Terri watched them go and smiled when the porch light went out and the door closed, cutting them off from the party.

"Needed some fresh air, did you?" O'Malley asked, not moving from her position.

"Yeah. The party was getting to me. Too much of everything, you know?"

"Yeah, I definitely know." O'Malley swooped in for another kiss, her lips painting themselves to Terri's. Terri's tongue slid into her mouth and her body pressed closer. "This is much better," she managed between kisses, and wrapped her arms tightly around Terri.

Terri let out a small squeak as O'Malley rolled them over and put Terri on top. Looking down into O'Malley's eyes, she watched as the blue turned darker, and she shivered happily. The darker the biker's eyes, the more aroused she was. Terri had the feeling that it was going to be a very long night, and she was more than happy to be along for the ride. She leaned in, then bypassed O'Malley's lips, settling instead for the soft skin under her chin. She drew a wet line along her jawline, teasing with her lips and teeth. When noisy engines signaled the arrival of several more bikes, they both looked up toward the front of the house in time to see the headlights of a truck.

"Guess we have more company," Terri said as she calculated the number of people already in the house. With a few exceptions, she was certain that everyone had already arrived.

"In more ways than one."

Trey's familiar voice assaulted Terri's ears as she was yanked away from O'Malley. She felt herself tossed into the rough arms of someone else, colliding with his chest as she heard the unmistakable sound of a boot making contact with flesh and bone. She frantically turned her head and saw O'Malley rolling on the ground away from Thumper.

O'Malley managed to make it to her feet, then stood still for a moment to try and clear the spinning in her head. She lost a lungful of air when someone tackled her from behind. Her chin hit the dirt and she barely kept from biting her tongue in half. Blood flowed from jarred teeth.

Two pairs of hands pulled her up, and she let them. She stared at Thumper. The gloating grin on his face was enough to really piss her off.

He quickly closed the distance between them. The grin was still on his face when he planted his fist in her stomach.

Terri tried to rip herself out of the firm grip that held her, but she couldn't break away. Tears of frustration and anger rolled down her face as O'Malley doubled over in pain, only to be pulled back up. Even in the dim moonlight she could see O'Malley turning red from a lack of air. Terri struggled harder and felt a hand yank hard on her hair, the pain cutting off her shout for help.

$* \sim * \sim * \sim *$

"Not so tough now, are you, war hero?" Trey's voice held an edge of triumph as he finally emerged from his spot in the shadows. He grabbed a handful of O'Malley's hair and pressed his face close. "First that little bitch is gonna watch us kick your ass, and then you're gonna watch us take turns with her. Just a little reminder of what she's missing." He nodded at Thumper and then stood back to watch.

When Thumper punched her a second time, O'Malley doubled over again. This time she managed to suck in some air when they pulled her up. She tightened her grip on the forearms of the bikers who were keeping her from moving.

Thumper moved in again, only to meet the bottom of O'Malley's boot. His head snapped back and he stumbled. She brought her foot down hard on the instep of the biker to her right and felt his hold weaken. Shooting her right arm up and across her body, she jabbed four rigid fingers into the throat of the biker on her left. She was suddenly free as he brought his hands to his throat in an effort to stop its gurgling noises.

She spun and felt the sting on the back of her hand as she made contact with someone's face. She calmly scanned for more opponents. Thumper moved back into range, and she ducked his fist and let her body drop low. O'Malley kicked the vulnerable inside of his left knee and knew from his cry of pain that she had most likely crippled the joint. She stood quickly, only to have a sucker punch snap her head violently to the left.

O'Malley fell to her knees, and Trey shook his right hand to relieve the pain. He grabbed a handful of hair and punched her again, ignoring the rush of blood that flowed from her nose over his hand. He let her fall to the ground again and kicked her in the ribs, then grinned as she rolled to the side and settled in the dirt.

"Nice try, but you're the one in the dirt," he sneered. He lifted his foot, intending to cave in her chest, but she brought her hands up at the last instant, caught his boot, and twisted him off balance. He landed hard on his side, his legs tangled around each other. Trey and O'Malley managed to stand at roughly the same time, but he was a fraction quicker and rushed her. He lowered his shoulder and caught her square in the chest.

Their momentum slammed O'Malley into the wood fence. She saw one bright star explode in front of her eyes and in desperation brought her knee up hard into his chest as her elbow crashed into his back.

Terri stomped her foot down hard on her captor's and, feeling his grip loosen, raked her fingernails across his upper lip. He grabbed her and gave her a powerful shove, then rushed in to help Trey.

O'Malley saw him coming and moved out of the way at the last second. Trey's would-be helper crashed into the fence and bounced back a couple of steps.

Terri picked herself up off the ground and ran for the back door. She looked back over her shoulder and watched in horror as Trey swept O'Malley's feet out, sending her crashing again. Her hand closed on the doorknob.

O'Malley felt the arms wrap around her shoulders and neck, and as she was lifted off the ground, she knew she was in trouble.

Trey gulped in air as he stood in front of O'Malley. He planted his fist in her stomach and watched her eyes close and her face twist up in pain.

As she was yanked upright, O'Malley sucked in some desperately needed air. "That...all you...got?" she panted as she opened her eyes. Their typical light blue had turned almost black. Trey's fist caught her with an uppercut and she let her head snap back and up. The arms holding her from behind immediately released her when the back of her head made contact with a chin. The man who had been holding her dropped like a sack of potatoes. O'Malley barely kept her feet, slowly recovering her strength. As she stared at Trey, she let the rage seep out slowly. "You are...a dead man," she promised in a low, ragged whisper.

Trey managed to take one step before something cold and hard pressed against the back of his skull. Turning his head, he found himself staring at the black steel of a 9mm.

"You really have a death wish?" Cage asked, pressing the pistol hard into his cheek. "I can make it happen."

Terri and Joan rushed to O'Malley's side as Sean and several others moved into the backyard to check on Trey's boys. O'Malley winced as two sets of arms wrapped around her body. She pushed down the urge to vomit and willed her legs to stay steady. Together, the three of them slowly made their way to Cage's side. O'Malley was in agony, but she turned her gaze to Terri to make sure she was unhurt. When she was certain, she untangled herself from the two women supporting her. She reached out and took the pistol from Cage without letting it move from Trey's face.

O'Malley was running on pure adrenaline. "Do you know what my favorite saying was in the Army, Trey?" Her voice was deceptively calm as she pressed the end of the pistol harder against his face. When he shook his head slowly, she could almost smell his fear. "The United States Army...affords the enemy every opportunity to die for...his country. Guess who the enemy is right now." The answer was obvious. Her finger tightened on the trigger.

Spyder's voice stopped her. "I can't let you do that, O'Malley."

She didn't take her eyes off Trey's face. "It's not up to you, Spyder." Despite her overwhelming rage, her tone was even. She didn't have to look around to know that his bikers were taking up positions behind and to the side of him. She also knew they were most likely armed.

"He might have been more of an asshole than usual tonight, but he's still one of my boys. I can't let you kill him." His words held no anger, just determined resignation. "You're letting this get personal."

"You know, Spyder, if he had just come after me, it would have just been business. But when he tells me that he and his boyfriends are gonna take turns with my property, it gets damned personal." O'Malley's tone was not pleasant.

"If you want to keep doing business with me, you will lower your weapon," he said.

When O'Malley failed to lower her weapon or answer, he nodded his head once, but his bikers never had the chance to move as Sean and the group he'd brought with him cocked their weapons and quickly brought them to bear. Spyder looked around and noted that the opposition had superior firepower. He didn't miss the looks of grim determination on their faces. As dedicated as his inner circle was, they had never looked like that.

"Spyder, I want you to meet some of the best soldiers I've ever seen or trained." O'Malley felt a fresh rush of warm blood fall past her lips as she grinned. "We've seen hell together, and we don't mind dying right here. Do you?" She let the question linger in the silence before she looked at Spyder. "I'll make you a deal. You keep this asshole away from me and mine, and he gets to live."

"Done."

The bloody and beaten O'Malley had won the round, and she knew that Trey was going to pay for his fuck-up in the most painful and humiliating ways Spyder could think up.

"You can let him go now."

O'Malley lowered the pistol from Trey's face and started to turn away. She waited until he exhaled the breath he had been holding, then spun faster than she thought she had the energy for. The barrel of the 9mm caught his face with a satisfying crunch. He was unconscious before he hit the ground. Without a word, she handed the pistol back to Cage.

"This party is over," she said flatly. Her knees buckled, and she accepted the support Terri offered her.

Spyder barked out orders for everyone to clear out, and all parties relaxed a little. O'Malley's friends lowered their weapons only when they could see that the night was going to end without further bloodshed. They did not, however, move from their posts.

It didn't take long for the bikers to gather up their things and leave. Spyder was one of the first to go. The next group dragged Trey and his boys out. Those who couldn't walk were carried.

Boomer was the last to leave after talking to Cage and offering his apologies to O'Malley. She stood at the kitchen counter, her battered hands braced on the surface. Cage offered to walk him out and closed the front door behind them.

* ~ * ~ * ~ *

Sean opened the freezer and pulled out the bowl of ice. From the look of her rapidly swelling left eye, O'Malley was going to need it. He filled a ziplock Baggie and was closing it when O'Malley's legs finally gave out. Ice clattered into the sink as Sean dropped the bag and grabbed his friend in one fluid motion.

Joan had been expecting the collapse, and she leapt into action. She pushed Terri into the bedroom with orders to pull down the blankets and get a trash can.

Thomas Quinn picked up O'Malley's legs, and together he and Sean carried O'Malley into the bedroom. She was out cold.

Joan ordered the men out, ignoring the worry etched on their faces. When they hesitated for a moment, she said, "Sean, I'm not going to deal with this and you two underfoot. I know you want to help, but just let me work in peace. I'm going to need my med bag." She didn't raise her voice, but her words had the desired effect. Exchanging sheepish expressions, the men left reluctantly.

Terri softly closed the door. "How bad is it?" she asked, her voice trembling.

Joan shook her head. "I don't know yet. Help me get her clothes off and we'll see."

Thomas walked into the kitchen to rescue the ice as Sean stepped out the side door to get Joan's bag. He cringed when he noticed his hands shaking. It had been forever since that had happened. His days of combat were long past; there wasn't much opportunity for that kind of action sitting in a computer lab.

Sean reentered without letting the side door slam. Their eyes locked and he caught the ice bag that Thomas tossed to him. He knocked softly on the bedroom door and waited a moment before he opened it and stepped in. His eyes narrowed at the sight of bruises forming on O'Malley's ribs and chest. He handed over both bags, then ducked his head when Joan stopped checking the damaged ribs and glared at him. He stepped out of the room and sank down on a stool.

Cage walked through the front door a few minutes later. The four men who followed her in fanned out around the living room and dropped down to rest. The ride to O'Malley's had been on relatively short notice and they had pushed hard to get there in time. They were beginning to realize how close they had cut it. "The perimeter is secure," Cage announced, then stopped short as she noticed the looks on two very worried faces. "She crashed, didn't she?"

"Yeah. Hard," Thomas Quinn answered. "Joan's working on her."

"Good." Cage sank into the couch. The adrenaline was wearing off and she suddenly felt extremely tired. She turned her head and smiled when Thomas sat next to her. "Nice to see you, little brother."

"You, too. Next time we all have a reunion, how 'bout we just do dinner or something a little less exciting." He grinned as he looked at his sister. It took a moment, but the chuckles turned into laughter. It was a tension release and they all knew it. The laughter faded away slowly, then Sean started the ball rolling down memory lane. It didn't take long for more stories to be told. Most of them had something to do with O'Malley.

Terri heard the laughter as Joan was wiping dried blood from O'Malley's face. For a moment, she felt a surge of anger before it dawned on her that these were O'Malley's friends. When Joan's hand touched her arm, Terri sat back out of the way.

Joan leaned over and opened one of O'Malley's eyes, then flicked a penlight beam back and forth. "I have got to teach this one to stop leading with her face." Joan smiled and worked to open the eyelid on O'Malley's swelling eye, where she repeated the action.

"Shouldn't we take her to the emergency room or something?" Terri wondered as she went into the master bathroom to rinse out the bloody towel.

"That would be my first choice, but there are too many questions she won't want to answer. Also, they would probably bring the police in." Joan looked up at Terri. "From what Maria's told me, O'Malley's just a little too popular with the cops lately."

Terri nodded slowly and eased back onto the bed. "Yeah. So what do we do now?"

"Well, I'm going to have to get some stitches into her. I'm glad she's not awake."

"Why?"

"She hates needles." Joan chuckled. "The first time I had to give her those wonderful yearly inoculations, she almost took my head off. Of course, as soon as she saw the needle, she about passed out."

A wry smile crossed Terri's lips. "But she's got how many tattoos?"

"She got those while she was good and plastered." Joan reached into her bag and started removing the things that she would need. She checked the date on the medication bottle and tore open the suture kit. "It's not as sterile as I'd like, but this is the best we can do. You ready for this?" she asked as she uncapped the syringe.

Terri was fine until the curved needle bit into O'Malley's flesh. She turned away before her stomach could revolt. Each time Joan switched to a new section of torn flesh, Terri helped move O'Malley. The most difficult section was just over the bridge of O'Malley's nose.

Finally Joan let out a low breath and tossed the needle into the trash, then checked the the ice bag. Judging the condition of her battered friend, she knew they were going to need a lot more ice and Baggies.

"Her ribs are bruised to hell and back, but they're not broken. It's the concussion that worries me. We have to keep waking her to make sure nothing more serious is going on, and we're going to have to keep her iced until most of the swelling goes down. I'm going to give her a shot of antibiotic, and then we can ice her." Joan reached into her bag again. "Do me a favor. Let Sean know that I'm going to need him to go to the store and get me a couple of big bags of ice. And some beer."

Terri had never heard of using beer for reducing swelling. "Why beer?"

"Because I'm thirsty, and all you have out there is the hard stuff." Joan laughed as she rolled O'Malley over gently.

Terri looked away just as the needle penetrated the skin on her lover's hip. She couldn't watch. It hurt deep inside to see O'Malley so helpless against something she knew would be painful.

"She's going to be fine, Terri. She'll be grumpy as hell for a few days, but she'll get through this. We aren't leaving until she's pretty well recovered. We're not leaving her or you alone," Joan promised.

Chapter 16

George did not have time to answer the sharp rapping on his door before it was pushed open and Terri barged into the probation office. He was on the phone and scarcely looked up from his conversation as she stalked around the desk.

She pulled the receiver out of his hand and put it to her ear, then managed to sound almost pleasant as she dismissed the caller. "He'll call you back." She slammed the phone down on its cradle and glared at her boss. "You find that son of a bitch before I castrate him."

"What in the hell do you think you're doing? Do you know who you just hung up on?" he asked indignantly as he pushed out of his seat.

"You take one good look at me and then tell me if you think I give a fuck," Terri spat in return.

Repressing the urge to strangle his officer, George took a deep breath and did as she demanded. In the short-sleeved shirt Terri was wearing, the bruises on her arms were hard to miss. They were obviously black-and-blue impressions of a pair of hands. His eyes drifted up to meet hers. "What happened?"

"Trey happened. I think you can safely say that he's crossed the line. Last night, he and four of his boys jumped us at Spyder's little command get-together. His plan was to beat O'Malley to within an inch of her life, and then let her watch them take turns with me." Her voice caught as she finished, then she sank into the closest chair.

"Are you okay?" George asked, realizing that it was a stupid question even as it passed his lips.

Terri looked up with a wry, sad smile. "No, I'm not. Thanks to O'Malley and her friends, they didn't get their chance, but I'm not okay. You have to pull him in. Talk to the office, trump something up, and get him off the streets. If only for his sake. Spyder has him now, and as much of an asshole as he's been, I don't want to see him killed."

"Terri, you're talking in shorthand again and I'm not getting it. Do me a favor and try explaining from the beginning."

Terri nodded and took a deep breath. "You're not going to like any of this, George. I already told you about the stolen weapons, but from what I'm starting to hear at the bar, Spyder is into a lot more—drugs we don't know about, prostitution, and protection rackets. Word around the bar is that he's got guys not just here, but in Vegas, Washington, and New Mexico. Trey never mentioned any of that to me and I'm guessing he didn't tell you either."

George's silence was as much an answer as if he had spoken.

"My gut is telling me that O'Malley's business with Spyder is more personal. I'm not sure what that's all about," she said. Finally, she looked up at her boss and took a shaky breath. "You need to know that I'm sleeping with her." She managed to blush only a little while admitting that her relationship with O'Malley had turned physical.

He let out a low whistle. Cases had been lost on less. "I think it's time we called in the feds on this one."

Terri immediately objected. "I can break this, I know I can. I really just need a little time."

"This one's getting too hot. You're a damn good cop, Terri, but you're one apparently crooked cop away from becoming a nicely folded flag on your mother's mantle." Dishing out brutal honesty was sometimes his job.

Terri's fervor ebbed. "I know that," she said softly. "Spyder and Trey have both managed to piss me off more than you can imagine. I know what they're capable of and I'm not taking them lightly, but I'm not coming off this one."

He looked into her eyes and saw a new determination there. Even her body language was different. Six months earlier, the Terri he knew would never have barged into his office and acted as she had. He nodded slowly at her request, mentally crossing his fingers. There were reinforcements he could call in, even if they weren't feds. She might even forgive him for doing so some year in the future. All he had to do was figure out whom to bring in that Trey didn't know.

"Two weeks. That's all I'm going to give you. Then we do it my way." His tone left no room for debate.

"One more thing."

"Now what?" His growing frustration showed.

"Get me what you can on an Ellen Rivers. She died in a car accident three years ago at Moody's Gap. From what I hear, Hank Stillman and some of Spyder's boys were in on it. One of Hank's dancers was killed in the accident as well. If we can't get them one way, maybe we can get them another," she said.

George thought about the implications for a moment. "Sounds like a good idea. It's gonna take a little while for the office to get the files pulled, but I think I might know someone who can get it for me."

"Good. And George, I'm sorry about earlier. Who was on the phone?"

"Just the governor." He had to choke back a laugh at the horrified expression on her face.

"Please give him my apologies. I'll never do it again," she promised.

* ~ * ~ * ~ *

O'Malley leaned against the bathroom sink and stared at her reflection, then groaned out loud at the sight. Both eyes were black, and the one was still swollen shut. She could tell that the damage across her nose was going to scar. Joan had stitched it up as well as she could, but the skin in that area could stretch only so far. She shook her head at her appearance. *And I feel even worse than I look.* Every square inch of her hurt, and every injury was stone cold from the ice packs that had been used to keep the swelling down. She hadn't been that cold since winter survival training in Alaska.

Exhausted, O'Malley didn't even have the energy to pursue her anger at Trey or herself. She had known going in that Trey was going to jump her, she just hadn't figured he would do it so early in the evening. She pushed away all thoughts of the previous night. There were things she needed to do, and as bad as she felt, she had to get them done as soon as possible. Moving as slowly as she could, she pulled open the bathroom door and walked out into the living room, where several sets of stunned eyes turned to her.

"What?" she demanded peevishly as she eased into her favorite chair.

They looked at one another, and then Joan spoke up. "Just

thought you were still resting. You shouldn't be up."

"Yeah, but my vacation in the Bahamas doesn't start for another year. I've got things to do, Joan." She wished she could grin, just for the effect. "You got anything for pain that won't knock me out or make me fuzzy?"

"Hey, O'Malley, maybe just once you should listen to someone when they suggest downtime." Thomas's concern showed as he leaned forward.

"Quinn, you know me better than that." She looked around at her friends and sighed. For once she was glad that Terri was absent. "You all know why I'm doing this, and I thank you all for being here. I mean that more than you can know. Yes, I feel like I hit more than one land mine today. Yes, I would love nothing more than to lie in bed and just medicate like a horse. I don't have that option. Let's consider today a planning session. Tomorrow night we are all going to Stillman's club. We are going to act like we are having the best time of our short little lives, and Sean is bringing Spyder's product in his truck.

"In a little while, I'm going to call Spyder and tell him to meet us there. That will most likely piss him off. My presence alone is gonna freak a lot of people, and that's good. I want them rattled. We are going to drink hard and play hard. Cage, when I tell you, I want you in his office and his safe. I need a count of how much cash he's got in there. No, you don't get to keep any of it."

"Killjoy," Cage muttered with a grin. "How long will I have?"

"I really can't say. But if you get caught in there, we'll get something else going to give you cover time. I have the layout of his office, which I'll give to you in a little while. Cage, Sean, Joan, and I will be wired for sound. Cover teams will not. I'd hate to have to try and explain to any cop why you guys were wired. I'm not saying we'll get busted, but just in case."

"Anyone bring bail money?" Thomas asked with a boyish grin.

"I'll call Mom." Cage laughed when he stuck his tongue out at her.

"Children, do not make me laugh," O'Malley ordered, and they instantly returned to the issue at hand. "Jack, I'm going to give you a name and an address. I want you to ghost this guy. I want to know when and where he meets his mules. If you can find out where he makes his big sales, I want that too. If you have any trouble—" She stopped when she saw him frown.

"O'Malley, you wanna be in my lap while I do this? I am one of the best in the business, you know."

O'Malley was just smart enough to know when she'd gone too far. "Sorry. Habit. You can yell at me later when I don't have a headache. I trust you, I really do." She watched Jack nod and wondered when he was going to get rid of the platinum dye job.

"I'll pick the cover teams, if you don't mind," Cage said without fear of pissing anyone off. She looked around, and seeing no disagreement, she continued. "Once I get the layout, I'll spread it out. I will pick one leader for each cover team. I want three ways out from each team leader. Vehicles will not be valet parked. I want us to know where they are, and I want them ready for a fast exit, just in case." Everyone nodded in agreement.

"Cage, once you've picked your teams, recon the club today before they open for business, preferably while all the little worker bees are asleep," O'Malley ordered quietly. She was losing energy fast, and it showed.

Joan asked the question no one else was willing to ask. "What about Terri?"

O'Malley looked at her and blinked. "She's going with us. If she's not with us, it won't take long for Trey to hear about it. I really don't want to risk Maria or her bar," she answered grimly. After the previous evening's surprise attack, she wasn't sure she could predict Trey's behavior, and she certainly didn't trust Spyder to control him.

From his position behind his wife, Sean asked, "You going to tell her about this?"

"Nope. If she asks, I'm always like this when I have business to do."

"Oh, that's a stretch," Cage drawled, sarcasm dripping. Soft chuckles could be heard from all corners of the room.

"I think that's it for now. We'll regroup later tonight after the recon. Let's get it done, people." She started to move slowly out of her chair, then sank back down. "Someone get me some coffee, please?"

Cage grinned like a fool. "That was damn close to whining." She was on a roll since O'Malley was in no condition to go after her.

"Cage, just keep in mind that I'm going to heal, and I do know where you work." Cage swallowed her grin and went outside to hide. O'Malley laughed, even though she tried to keep it in. "Oh fuck, that hurts," she groaned.

* ~ * ~ * ~ *

Though she noticed there were fewer vehicles outside as she pulled into the driveway after her visit with George, Terri walked into the house expecting to see at least a few of O'Malley's friends. Not a one was in sight, and she wondered where everyone was. She let her purse fall onto the couch with a muted thud and then went to the bedroom door, opened it quietly, and peeked in at O'Malley. A smile tugged at Terri's lips. Her battered lover, hair poking in all directions, was deep in Sleepyland and snoring lightly. Joan had warned her that snoring would be a consequence of the broken nose. Terri closed the door and let out a low sigh.

"I heard that." Joan chuckled and almost laughed when Terri jumped.

"Damn it, I hate when you do that," Terri griped when she caught her breath. A moment later, she joined in the laughter. "It's sick, but I think I needed that. Thank you."

"Any time," Joan promised with a smile. She wrapped an arm around Terri's waist. "Come on, you look wiped out. I bet you didn't have any lunch."

Terri peeked at Joan with an arched eyebrow. "It's scary how you can do that."

"I'm Lakota. For me this is normal. I grew up on a reservation surrounded by elders who tried, and are still trying, to keep some of the old ways alive," she explained. "My grandmother was gifted with the vision, and it still gives me shivers to think of how many times she told me things that came to pass. My grandfather was one of the best trackers the people had. He earned his eagle feathers for Korea. You think I'm quiet? Compared to him, I'm a herd of buffalo."

"Well, for a buffalo, you sure are light on your feet," Terri quipped, and let herself be led to the kitchen. "How's O'Malley?" She tried to keep the worry out of her voice.

Joan opened the fridge and handed over a beer. "Drink that one slowly." She stood in front of the door and surveyed the shelves. "She's a little better. She was up a couple of times today." Joan turned her head to make eye contact. "It's good for her to move around. It'll reduce the stiffness, and she won't be nearly as much of a pain in the ass. How about a roast beef sandwich?"

Terri nodded and let herself rest. She hadn't gotten much of that the night before as she lay in bed watching her lover until at last she could no longer keep her eyes open, and even then she only dozed lightly, listening for O'Malley's breathing. She had stayed pretty much in one spot, not wanting to move and cause her lover more pain. In addition to her vigil, someone would come in every four hours to ask O'Malley questions until they got relatively coherent answers. Several times, O'Malley woke long enough to throw up in the trash can. Sometime around five, O'Malley's responses had finally started to make sense.

Terri's eyes moved to the clock on the kitchen wall. She really didn't want to go work the bar with O'Malley in such bad shape, but Maria needed her. A stray thought rolled around her brain, and suddenly work wasn't such a bad thing. Maria would be able to answer some of her questions about O'Malley's group of friends.

Joan set a sandwich in front of Terri and took a seat next to her. For a moment it looked like Terri was just going to push her food around, until Joan glared at her.

With a sheepish expression, Terri dutifully bit into the sandwich, then groaned with delight. "This is good," she managed with a full mouth.

Joan chuckled. "You sound like Sean at dinnertime. You eat, then I want you to go and get some rest. I know you didn't get any last night and you have to work tonight, right?"

"Yeah. I'd rather be here, but Maria really needs me."

"You go. We'll all be here," Joan promised.

"By the way, where is everyone?"

"They were driving O'Malley nuts with their concern, so she told 'em to get out and do something," Joan answered easily.

"Sounds like O'Malley. How lousy a patient is she?"

"When she gets sick, just book a vacation somewhere. Alone."

There was no teasing in Joan's eyes and Terri suppressed the urge to shudder. "And you want me to go in there and sleep?" Terri pouted. "Joan, I thought you liked me."

Joan laughed, but didn't answer. She wandered out to the backyard to spend some time with Sean.

Terri sat on the stool, idly enjoying her lunch and letting her mind wander. Each time a job-related question popped into her head, she pushed it away, too tired to try and contemplate an answer. She would tackle her professional life after she got some rest. By the time she finished her sandwich and beer, she was more than ready for her nap.

As she walked quietly into the bedroom, she gauged how much time she would need to shower and dress, then set the alarm to allow her every possible minute of sleep but not be late to work. She slid out of her clothes and got into bed, then tugged the blankets up as she rolled over and stared at O'Malley. Even as beat up and bruised as she was, she still looked good to Terri, who ran a gentle finger over her eyebrow and whispered a wish for good dreams.

~~*~*

Maria barely gave Terri time to drop her purse in the office before she started asking questions. It had not taken long for the rumor mill to start grinding full force. Maria would have been out at O'Malley's in an instant, but she couldn't leave the bar. The night before had been busy for everyone.

"So, is she dead, or does she just wish she was?" Maria grumbled.

Terri took a seat. "The latter. Joan took care of her. I'm sorry we didn't call you, it's just been a damn long night and day."

Maria waved off her apology. "I understand. We were packed here, anyway. Had to finally get Gato to kick some guy out on his head, and I mean that literally. I've heard the rumors, but I want to hear it from you. How bad is she?"

"Joan said she has some bruised ribs, an egg-sized lump on the back of her head, a broken nose, and you don't want to see her left eye. I think she put in close to thirty stitches in all. O'Malley's nose looks the worst. Nasty cut across the bridge," Terri explained. When Maria remained silent, only quirking an eyebrow, Terri went into detail about the fight, ending up with, "I was petrified that O'Malley really was going to pull the trigger on Trey."

Maria exhaled her surprise. "Damn. She hasn't done that in a long time. He must have really pissed her off."

"Well, Trey said they were going to make her watch them take turns with me. That's when she got really serious about fighting," Terri said quietly.

Maria shook her head. "That boy just isn't right in the head."

Terri chuckled. "It doesn't seem so, does it? Maria, Joan's a good nurse, right?"

"Yeah. She is. If she worked on Callan, then it's gonna be okay. Just don't get within arm's reach of that big baby if there's a needle around."

Terri was bewildered. "I don't get it. She's—well, let's face it, she's a badass, and she's afraid of needles?"

Maria gazed at Terri for a long moment. "We all have our weaknesses, Terri. Even O'Malley."

"Yeah, I guess we do," she allowed, after giving it a brief moment's thought. She stood and flashed a tired smile. "I'll get to work now, and I promise that we'll keep you updated."

Maria nodded and waved Terri to work. When the door to her office closed, she leaned back in her chair, closing her eyes in relief. She would call Joan later and get the full update, but at least she knew that the rumors weren't entirely accurate. If O'Malley held true to form, she would already be up and moving, despite everyone's protests.

She smiled at the memory of a certain Army sergeant who was a complete pain in the ass until she was allowed to actually move around the halls of the hospital ward at Ramstein. O'Malley had been a handful, and there had been times when Maria had pulled rank to get her to slow down. She could still see the wistful smile on Ellen's face when she gazed at the stubborn soldier. Maria knew her favorite nurse was in love before Ellen herself ever realized it.

Maria sent a mental prayer up to Ellen and whatever power was listening to keep O'Malley safe and then turned back to her paperwork. It was a long time before she was able to think clearly enough to make a dent in preparing her liquor order.

Chapter 17

O'Malley led the way into Stillman's strip club. Since it was still relatively early, there were plenty of seats available, which allowed the group to commandeer three tables and drag them together. Terri, sitting next to O'Malley, was wondering if maybe the biker needed to go to the hospital after all. She had been shocked when she announced that the entire group was going to the club. She wasn't sure if it was the look in O'Malley's eyes or the lack of protest from the others that had frightened her the most. She was sure that something was going on.

"What ya thinking, baby?" O'Malley asked as she leaned in close to Terri's ear.

"I'm thinking that you are out of your mind," she answered honestly. "Is this smart?"

"Probably not. You remember what I said about a feeding frenzy?" She waited until Terri nodded. "I'm trying to cut it off before it begins. Spyder's boys hang out here a lot, and he'll be here later. I'm going to finish some business with him, and then we are all going to have a good time."

"I still think you should be in bed resting rather than out here."

O'Malley leveled her eyes at Terri. "This is not open to debate, Terri. Business is business." There was a hard edge in her voice.

Terri nodded once. "One of these days I'm going to remember that," she answered flatly. "And everyone is here for backup?"

"That, and after being there to save my ass, it's also a thank you." She waved a waitress over.

The waitress took one look at the group and let out a soft sigh. It was going to be a long night. She walked over and took their orders in sequence. Most of the orders were for the hard stuff.

O'Malley didn't miss the sly, catlike grin on Cage's face. "What?"

"Boomer's here," came the unmistakably pleased answer.

"You can go play, but..." O'Malley didn't bother to finish the sentence.

"Just let me know when business is business," Cage tossed over her shoulder as she bolted from the group.

Terri shook her head and laughed with the others. From what she had been hearing from Thomas and the others, Cage was not one to waste too much time on the formalities. She wasn't sure that she believed all the stories, but with Cage, it seemed that anything could be possible. Terri looked around and took a good look at the crowd, mentally dividing them into different categories. She could figure who was going to be an ally and who was going to be an enemy.

She was listening with half an ear to the conversations going on around her when Hank Stillman walked out of his office. Barely noticing when the drinks were delivered, Terri kept a surreptitious eye on him, noting that her friends had been right: he looked like a ghost was chasing him. Terri suppressed a smile. A part of her hoped that he suffered every night for what he had done. In the time that she had worked in the strip club, he had always seemed so arrogant and cocky; now all he could do was look over his shoulder and sweat.

When she felt a hand gently squeeze her thigh, she turned her gaze back to O'Malley. She smiled as she tried to figure out what it was that she had missed.

"You okay? You were like a million miles away," O'Malley said, her mouth close to Terri's ear.

"Yeah. I just got a look at Hank. What did I miss?"

"Not much, just another bullshit story. You can't trust these guys. The stories get bigger every year."

There was a teasing quality to her voice, and Terri knew that the biker would have smiled if she could. "You really love these guys, don't you?" she asked.

"Can't stand any of 'em," O'Malley joked, and took a careful sip of her beer. "They're okay," she began, then was cut off when the music changed. It was grinding and raw. Most eyes turned to the stage and Donna stalked out as the lights flashed. Her tight bodysuit left little to the imagination, and Terri was sure she could hear the salivating begin.

The group watched, drank, and played until Spyder walked in with a couple of his bikers in tow. He passed O'Malley without a word, and Terri knew that he was not a happy man. He was used to giving orders and having them followed, not to being ordered around. From the look on his face, he was less than pleased with O'Malley. O'Malley cleared her throat softly. Sean and Joan looked up from their conversation and both took a sip of their drink. Cage wiggled her way out of Boomer's grasp and whispered something in his ear. She cleared her seat as Spyder made his way to the table.

Cage greeted Spyder, who grunted in response.

Terri wasn't sure what caused Sean and Joan to chuckle and she had no idea what to make of the twinkle in O'Malley's eyes. She decided to just chalk it up to an inside joke and let her eyes roam over Rhea's body as she performed her pole dance. She had seen Rhea onstage before, but she'd never really taken the time to actually watch. She was supposed to have been involved with Trey; there would have been too many questions to answer if she'd been caught staring. Now she could appreciate how good Rhea looked. There was no doubt the woman was hot, and Terri could understand O'Malley's one-time interest.

"See something you like?"

O'Malley's voice growled in her ear and Terri started. She turned her head and answered into O'Malley's ear, "I was just figuring out why you would want her." When she let her tongue trace a wet trail along the lobe, she was sure she felt the biker shiver.

"She was fun, but let's just say that I could tell she was more into men," O'Malley said. "You, on the other hand, are definitely into women. I enjoy that."

"Nice save, O'Malley." Terri teased with her voice and her tongue.

"God, I wish I wasn't tin-canned," O'Malley groaned. Both women missed the grins from their friends.

"Get a room," Cage grunted as she plopped down next to O'Malley. The hint of a blush stained O'Malley's face. Terri on the other hand was in full-blown crimson. Cage let out a roar of laughter.

"I can still kill you, Cage," O'Malley returned.

"And I am more than willing to help her," Terri tossed in with a fierce smile.

Their banter was cut short as Spyder stood up from his table. He made his way through the club and had a few words with Hank, then turned toward their table. As he came closer, he nodded but did not speak. Cage turned her head to keep an eye on Spyder's boys. Only Boomer left the table and slipped out the back exit.

"Sean, let's go." O'Malley was suddenly all business. Sean nodded and gave Joan a quick kiss. She handed over the keys to the truck and patted his leg.

"Be careful," Terri requested, receiving a gentle kiss in response.

"Roger that," O'Malley said.

"Well, she must like you," Jack piped in. At Terri's questioning look, he explained, "She only uses Army talk with people she likes."

* ~ * ~ * ~ *

O'Malley and Sean followed Spyder out the door and walked past him without a word. They continued walking until they reached the truck, confident that if he started anything they would be able to finish it, especially with the backup inside the club. O'Malley doubted that he was making the pickup alone, but regardless, he didn't have the advantage that she did. They halted in front of the truck and Sean used his key to open the passenger door.

"I was beginning to wonder if these were ever going to come in," Spyder said slowly.

"I don't fuck around when it comes to business, Spyder. It's bad for my reputation," O'Malley answered in a low tone.

He said nothing as he opened the two cases and inspected the 9mms. They looked to be in good condition and the serial numbers had been removed. He closed the cases and set them on the ground by his feet.

"You're beginning to worry me, O'Malley." He met her gaze with hard eyes. "It's not like you to deliver late, this thing with Trey got personal, and now it looks like you've got a posse with you. A man in my position might come to think that you wanted to take over."

O'Malley barked out a laugh despite the pain it caused. "You can have this shithole of a town. I'm not interested in your band of delinquents. I can make my money anywhere, Spyder. I've said it all along: you don't want to do business with me, fine. But get this straight, I freelance because I don't want any more jail time. What you do with those is none of my business, and to tell you the truth, I don't want to know. As for my posse, they're friends and business associates. Trey is a nonsubject. I don't expect to see him again, and if I do, there is nothing you can say that will save his ass again." Her eyes were unreadable, but her voice remained calm.

Spyder's voice was just as calm. "You're a loose end for me. I don't like that."

"You don't get it both ways. You say you want me tied to your club, but you don't enforce your rules where I'm concerned." They both knew what she was talking about. "Maybe I'm a loose end because I don't see where there's a benefit for me to be a full-fledged member. Hell, Spyder, I copped to your dope and did the time for it."

"And that's the only reason you ain't dead yet, O'Malley," Spyder grumbled.

Sean tensed and O'Malley waved him off. "It's cool, Sean. He's just telling the truth. If I was in his position, I'd be saying the same thing." She turned back to the biker. "Do you believe in honor among thieves, Spyder?" she asked.

"No."

"Neither do I."

* ~ * ~ * ~ *

Cage picked her drink up and walked toward the bar with her half-empty glass. She took a deep, calming breath as Thomas and Jack joined her. She had been waiting for O'Malley's signal but was almost surprised that it had come so soon. She whispered her short instructions in her brother's ear and peeled off toward the women's room.

The men took their drinks from the bartender and made their way over to the stage, where they stood off to the side and watched the action. Jack exchanged a glance with Thomas, then pushed his way closer, jostling a couple of men who stood in his way. From the expressions on their faces, they were not happy about being shoved around. When he did it again, they pushed back. It was all the excuse Jack needed.

If O'Malley and Cage wanted a distraction, he was more than willing to provide them with one. With one good shove he knocked one of the men into the side of the stage. The dancer quickly fled, tables emptied, and bouncers rushed in. In no time at all, a brawl had started.

Cage exited the women's room and saw that the diversion was more than she had hoped for. For the final act, Thomas threw his glass in the direction of a large drunk, aiming a little high. As planned, it hit the wall behind Cage, and as it exploded into a million shards, she appeared to be fleeing as she ducked into Hank Stillman's office.

Working quickly, she found the hidden safe and went to work. The small electronic device she carried looked like a beeper, but it was much more. Cage sent a silent thanks to her CIA training as she felt the safe open. As she shifted the stacks of cash, she did the math in her head. She managed to stifle the low whistle at the total. There was no way she would keep seventy grand in her safe; Hank Stillman was an idiot. Cage was about to close the safe door when two black cases caught her eye. She would have ignored the first one if not for the date on the label. It could not be a coincidence.

From the sounds outside, Cage knew she had to make a quick decision. She pulled the case out and took the videotape that was inside, careful not to disturb anything else. It took her only a couple of seconds to hide the tape in her leather jacket. She closed the case, set it back in its place, and quietly shut the safe. After turning the tumbler back to the number it had started on, she settled the carpet patch in place.

"Coming out and off wire," Cage whispered, then stripped off the wire assembly and tucked it into her jacket next to the tape. She took a breath and listened until she heard the action in the club grow louder. She counted to five and opened the office door. Jacket in hand, she stepped out, closed the door, and ran right into Boomer.

His eyes narrowed in suspicion. "What the fuck are you doing in there?" he shouted over the noise.

"Someone threw a glass and this door was the closest place to hide," she said. "Is it safe now?"

Boomer's eyes swept the ground, taking in the glass shards and splattered liquor. Seconds later, another glass crashed against the wall, and they both ducked. "I guess not. C'mon." He grabbed her hand and pulled her quickly down the hall, pushing his way through the worst of the crush.

"What were you really doing in there?" he demanded once they were clear of the fracas and out by the bar.

Cage leveled a dangerous gaze on him and set her jacket down on a chair. "I told you what I was doing. If you don't believe me, go ahead and frisk me," she said without breaking eye contact.

He grunted and searched her as she had invited. His hands did not linger as he traced the contours of her body; he was all business. He stopped at her hip. "What's this?" he asked harshly.

"It's my beeper." Cage's tone implied his idiocy.

He heard the insulting tone but ignored it and continued his search. Only when he was satisfied did his eyes change expression. "You're clean," he said needlessly, turned to the bar, and ordered two beers.

"Thanks so much."

Thomas slid to a stop next to his sister. "You okay?" he asked breathlessly.

"Yeah, are you? What the hell happened?" she asked innocently as Boomer handed her a cold beer.

"I think Jack got stupid. One second I'm watching the dancer, and then all hell broke loose. If he gets busted, I am not bailing his ass out again." Thomas Quinn's ire sounded genuine.

Boomer smiled and grunted his agreement. "I'll catch up with you later," he said to Cage.

"Whatever." Cage's voice was flat as she remained in character. She watched the large man shrug his shoulders and walk away into the crowd.

Thomas's voice showed real concern once the biker was out of earshot. "You really okay?"

"Yeah, that was a close one," she admitted, then took a sip of her beer. She caught sight of O'Malley and Sean as they walked into the club. Even though the two knew what was going on, they did a very good job of looking both surprised and concerned.

Sean and O'Malley moved quickly to their respective partners and made sure that they were not hurt in any way. It took a while to straighten everything out, and O'Malley had to hand over a large quantity of cash in order to keep Jack out of jail. He managed to look sheepish as she made verbal mincemeat of him. When he offered to leave, the offer was accepted, and those on his team volunteered to go with him to keep him out of trouble. Thomas retrieved his keys from Cage's purse.

"Keep this with you. No one else knows. Our eyes only," Cage whispered in her brother's ear as she subtly exchanged their matching jackets.

He nodded once. He owed O'Malley his life, but he owed his

sister his sanity.

* ~ * ~ * ~ *

The rest of the group stayed only long enough to make it look believable. To prying eyes, they looked like any other group of friends out on the town. They laughed and drank with easy camaraderie. Finally Terri noticed O'Malley's energy start to flag and called an end to the evening. There were only halfhearted protests as they settled up the tab and gathered their things.

Terri settled her head on O'Malley's shoulder during the drive to the house. "How are you?"

"I'm tired and my head hurts," O'Malley answered honestly. "I probably shouldn't be driving."

"You want me to take over?" Terri asked, quickly alert.

"Nah. We're not that far from home."

"Did you get finished with Spyder?" Terri yawned through the question and snuggled in closer.

"Yeah. It's done for now." O'Malley matched the yawn and rolled down the window for some fresh air.

"Good. What do you say we take some downtime soon?" There was hope in Terri's voice. "Just you and me."

"Just you and me? What would we do?" O'Malley teased.

Terri whispered her answer in O'Malley's ear and watched the biker flush.

"Can I keep you?"

"Well, if you don't, I don't know who will." Terri lightly stroked O'Malley's hand. She was finding it harder and harder not to show physical affection when she was with her.

O'Malley's fingers played back, and the women settled into a comfortable silence for the rest of the drive.

Chapter 18

As she walked into the room, Terri noticed right away that the naked woman under the blankets had confiscated her side of the bed and her pillow. Instead of being irritated, she leaned against the door frame and watched O'Malley sleep. The worry she'd felt since the night of the party was finally starting to ebb, but the nagging feeling that O'Malley and her friends were up to something had not waned.

Terri could see it in the way their eyes would not meet hers. She had been trained to look for half-truths, and she was not fooled when they tried to joke away touchy questions. It had been five days of stories that matched too closely, like they had been rehearsed, and they all seemed to leave out the same information. If it had been one story of O'Malley's Army exploits, or two, she wouldn't have noticed, but almost every single one was missing something. She wondered what it was that O'Malley and her circle of friends were hiding from her. She had not missed the quiet meetings when they thought she was otherwise occupied, nor did she miss the subtle coded signals that passed through the group. *They must have been something to contend with in the Army,* she thought with something akin to admiration.

The way they all deferred to O'Malley had confused Terri until Thomas explained the rank structure of the military. The only ones who did not defer were Cage and the man Terri knew as Jack. There, standing against the door frame, she suddenly realized that aside from Cage, Thomas, Sean, and Joan, she didn't know any last names. She let out a slow breath to stifle the sudden panic. It failed. There were too many reasons for the deliberate omissions.

"Why are you standing by the door and not here in bed?" O'Malley asked without opening her eyes.

Terri didn't flinch, even though she felt like someone should peel her off the ceiling. "I was just looking at you sleep."

"In that case, you have got to be incredibly bored, and I'm not asleep." O'Malley's voice was teasing.

"I can see that now." Terri pushed away from the door frame and crossed to the bed, shedding her nightshirt on the way. "How are you feeling?"

O'Malley rolled over and opened her good eye when she heard Terri move. "If I never hear that sentence again, I'll be happy."

"Well, if you never get your ass kicked that badly again, *I'll* be happy," Terri countered as she sat on the bed. She let her hand run through O'Malley's hair, then traced a gentle line down the battered nose. "Promise me you won't ever do this again."

Ice blue eyes locked on to Terri's. "I can't promise that." O'Malley held fast to Terri's hand when she tried to move it away. "It's not always up to me."

Terri cast her eyes down and nodded in understanding, then felt herself being pulled into O'Malley's arms. She nuzzled her head against a strong shoulder and sighed. They lay together in the silence, listening to each other breathe. Terri heard the steady beat under her ear and smiled, wishing she could lock out the rest of the world forever. Fingertips danced on her back in a gentle pattern. Somehow she knew it was Callan touching her, not O'Malley, and that quelled her fears for the moment. If Joan's description of the alter ego was accurate, Callan seemed to be surfacing more and more. Terri placed a soft kiss on the biker's shoulder and closed her eyes.

"I should move. Your ribs have got to be killing you," she whispered without looking up.

"I like where you're at, so don't move," O'Malley whispered back, tightening her hold.

"Your hand stopped," Terri murmured. "What's wrong?"

"Starting to doze."

"Did you know that your breathing changes when you start to fall asleep and when you lie?" Terri asked quietly as she lifted her head. "You're thinking about her, aren't you?"

O'Malley's expression remained neutral. "Who?"

"Your girlfriend. The one who died," Terri answered, searching O'Malley's face. When O'Malley said nothing, she brushed her fingers along the scarred chin. "It's normal to think about her; I would be worried if you didn't think about her. You had three years together, O'Malley, she deserves that."

O'Malley shifted slightly. "I do think about her."

"Then why lie about it?" Terri asked the obvious without judgment.

"It doesn't bother you that you're laying here in my arms and I'm thinking about another woman?" O'Malley's tone was indefinable.

"Yes and no." Terri placed a finger over O'Malley's lips to forestall her words. "Let me finish. You said you loved her like crazy, and I believe you. I know that if she were still alive, she would be here instead of me. I'm in your life because we got tossed together. I'm in your bed because that's where I choose to be. I know you don't love me, O'Malley, but you treat me with respect, and I think that somewhere inside, you like me. I'm okay with that. There, I'm finished now."

O'Malley was silent for a few moments. "How the hell did you get so smart?"

"A lifetime of losing, O'Malley. It'll grind you down, or it'll make you smarter. It's up to you to decide which one it's going to be." Terri rested her head on O'Malley's shoulder.

They settled back into silence as O'Malley turned the words over in her head, and Terri closed her eyes. The even heartbeat and steady breathing under her ear were making for a very good lullaby. She was almost asleep when the cell phone rang, jolting her awake.

"I'll get it," she offered, and reached across O'Malley to pick up the offending machine. "Hello." She listened for a moment and then handed over the phone. "It's the public defender's office for you."

O'Malley took the phone. "O'Malley." She listened in silence to the voice on the other end.

Terri watched her face, frustrated when she could get no hint as to what the conversation was about. The specter of trumped-up charges lingered for the last week, but with everything else that had been going on, they hadn't talked about it.

"Okay, thanks." O'Malley cut the connection. She moved to put the phone back and stopped suddenly. "Note to self, don't move in that direction."

Terri took the phone and set it back on the nightstand. "What was that about?"

O'Malley smiled as much as her damaged lip would allow.

"They dropped the charges. Seems Bates can't come up with the complaint."

Terri settled back in bed and propped her head up on her hand. "Nice to see justice finally working for a change."

"Yeah. I figured they would call, but damn, did they have to take so long?" O'Malley turned slowly in bed, mindful of her sore ribs.

"We should celebrate," Terri decided. "Or at least let Maria know. I think she was planning a protest on the courthouse steps."

O'Malley laughed, then groaned almost instantly. "God, Terri, don't make me laugh. Parts of me still hurt."

"What parts?" Terri asked with studied innocence.

"My ribs."

Terri ducked her head and placed a series of soft kisses on the named area, then with the tip of her tongue traced a wet line between O'Malley's breasts and up to her neck. She felt O'Malley suck in a deep breath. Sliding up the bed, she laid her lips softly on O'Malley's in a gentle kiss and heard the subtle moan. She reluctantly pulled away. "As much as I would love to continue this, I think we should both get some rest. You're broken, and I have to work tonight."

O'Malley chuckled. "You are in for a long night when I recover."

"I am so looking forward to that. Should I ask for the next day off?"

"When I'm done with you, you might have to ask for the next week off."

"Promises, promises."

* ~ * ~ * ~ *

Cage shut the hotel room door and listened to the ice fall into glasses. Turning her head, she watched as Thomas made their drinks, noticing that his hands shook slightly. She held in a frustrated sigh, mentally damning politicians and their choices. Her heart went out to her little brother for everything he had experienced and seen. Some things were just not fair, and the part of her that cared the most railed against the Fates.

She moved their bags to the space between the beds so she could unpack. For a woman who lied as a matter of job description, she was feeling an inordinate amount of guilt for lying to O'Malley. She owed her so very much and she knew that the biker might not forgive this betrayal. She unzipped the first suitcase and dug under the clothes to find her weapons. They were comforting in her hands as she let her skin become reacquainted with their cold metal.

"You really think you're going to need those?" Thomas asked.

"I hope to hell not, but after the other night, what do you think?" Her question really didn't require an answer.

"I think you might need bigger guns." He poured a generous amount of alcohol into both glasses, then poured in a soft drink to cut hers. He left his full strength. "She's gonna be pissed, you know."

"Boy, do I." She exhaled loudly. "Don't worry, little brother."

"Famous last words." He chuckled and passed the glass to his sister. "*Sláinte.*"

"*Na zdorov'ye.*" She took a sip of her drink. "That has got to be the second worst drink I've ever had," she sputtered after swallowing.

He smiled. "What was the first?"

"Something called a hardship. Basically you mix every dark liquor you have and kick it back really fast."

"You spooks have some really odd habits." He settled on his bed.

"Yeah, and you MPs are mine magnets," she riposted.

"Cold, big sister, very cold. And that's multipurpose," he corrected before turning his attention back to his drink.

Cage had to smile when he wasn't looking. She had learned the hard way that treating her brother with kid gloves only bothered him. His time in the Persian Gulf had affected him more than he would admit to others. Even their parents had no clue that on each anniversary of the war he would shut himself away until the memories, and the tremors, passed. Cage was the only one who knew the depth of his memories and his fears. It was her cabin to which he retreated, and one time he'd admitted that other than his team, she was the only other one who might be able to understand.

"You sure you're up for this?" she asked as she took the stolen videotape from her bag. It felt heavy in her hand.

Thomas looked up from his drink. "No, but put it in anyway. I'll be okay, Cage," he promised with a boyish smile.

Cage nodded. She took a deep breath and pushed the tape into the machine, turned on the TV, and hit the play button. The screen went from royal blue to a recorded night on a two-lane highway. She sank onto the bed next to her brother and drew up her legs, wrapping her arms around her knees as she watched.

The view was from the backseat of a car looking through the windshield, and the picture bounced around a little. Cage sucked in a hard breath when she recognized the vanity plate that read NURSE. She could make out two figures in the front seat of the car being followed. She knew that Ellen was the driver, and for a moment wondered if she could really watch the video.

"Run that bitch off the road."

Hank Stillman's voice, full of callous anger, cut through any doubts Cage might have had. The picture jumped when the vehicle slammed into the back of Ellen's car. The two women in the front seat bounced, and Cage could imagine their panic. Recorded laughter and boasting sounded out. The driver continued to rear-end Ellen's car until finally, at a curve in the road, Ellen lost control. Her car plowed through a guardrail and went over the side, leaving a trail of debris in its wake.

The camera caught Stillman and several others looking over the edge as he ordered someone to check the car's occupants. Boomer's large form started down the embankment, and the camera followed his progress to the wreckage. He stepped over and around the car parts that littered the area until finally he reached the passenger side, and he ducked his head in through the shattered window.

"Your girl's gone," he shouted, then moved to the driver's side. "This one is still alive."

The camera moved to Stillman as he pulled his cell phone out of his pocket and hit speed dial. "Spyder, it's me. We caught up to 'em and did like you said. Wait a second, this connection sucks." He moved up the roadway a few feet and then stopped. "Can you hear me? Okay, look, we ran 'em off at Moody's Gap. Tina's dead and the nosy bitch is alive." He listened. "You got it." He cut the connection and walked back to the edge.

Boomer's voice came up from below. "We gonna get an ambulance out here or what? She's bleeding bad."

"Spyder says we make sure no one gets out of that car," Stillman shouted back.

Boomer was apparently shocked at the order. "What? No way, man. I'm not getting tagged for murder."

Stillman turned to the camera. "Get some of the boys to back-track and pick up all the glass and shit. If we've got any empty beer cans, toss 'em around. It'll look like they were drinking and had an accident." He turned his attention back to Boomer. "You just tell me when she's dead and then get your ass back up here," he ordered.

"I'm not gonna watch some woman die," Boomer protested.

Stillman pulled his 9mm, pointed it down the embankment, and stopped Boomer in his tracks. "You fucking do what I tell you. Spyder doesn't want any loose ends, and I don't either."

After what seemed like an eternity, Boomer left the wreck and made his way back up the hill, a defeated slump to his shoulders. He stepped around what was left of the guardrail and looked at Stillman. His voice was low and rough as he said, "She's gone." He moved away.

"Don't you ever—" Stillman began.

Boomer turned on him. "What are you gonna do, kill me? Like you let her die? Fuck you, I'm outta this."

"No one gets out," Stillman answered. "You like the money and the chicks. You're not going anywhere, and if you try, Spyder will make you disappear." Stillman turned to face the camera. "Turn that fucking thing off."

The picture suddenly went blank.

For a long moment, neither Quinn said a word. Cage turned to face her brother. Tears flowed down his cheeks from behind closed eyes.

"Those motherfuckers," he croaked. "She was such a sweet woman. They just let her die out there."

"I know." Cage found it difficult to speak. They had all known that it wasn't an accident as the official police report stated, and now they had the truth. Cage felt a ball of fear form in her stomach. There was no way she could let O'Malley see the tape. It would destroy her or send her right over the edge.

"What do we do now?" Thomas asked after finishing his drink in one long swallow.

"*We* don't do anything. You go home; I'll take care of this."

"No way."

"Thomas Glenn Quinn, you are going home."

"I can't. I owe Callan my life, and I owe the Nurse. She—before you got there, she kept me sane. She would come in to check on me, and during that little while every day, it was like everything was normal again. She did that for all of us." He pushed off the bed and walked to the table to pour another drink. "Night was the worst. I could hear Sean breathing, and those damn machines kept going off. He was so doped up he just slept through the racket.

"Me, I would just lie there and remember. I closed my eyes and I was there again, running like hell. Hanson was in front of us. He kept turning his head, 'cause he couldn't hear from the mine going off. The sarge and me, we had Sean between us. He was busted up the worst. The sarge was always telling him to line the floor with sandbags, but he never listened. That's what saved her ass, you know. She had zero legroom and her knees were almost to her chin, but she was right." He sipped his drink.

"You don't have to do this, Tommy," Cage whispered.

"Yeah, I do." He sighed and sank onto the chair. "When two five started shelling those bastards, most of 'em got too busy to think about chasing us. The ones that did chase us were pissed, and they didn't give up until it was almost too late. O'Malley kept turning and capping off rounds. I don't think she hit many, but she hit enough of 'em to keep them back a little. When she got hit, it was like she tripped. I mean, one second she's up, and the next she's in the mud. All I could think of was that we were fucked if she was dead. Then she rolled over and capped off major rounds, screaming like a fucking pissed-off banshee. I don't know how she got up and helped me drag Sean out." He took another drink, trying to ignore the shaking of his hands. Then he looked at his sister with tortured eyes.

"I didn't know how bad she was hurt at the beginning. I thought the blood on her uniform was from getting us out of the Hummer. She was the only one who could have gotten us out of there. Sean was fucked, Hanson couldn't hear shit and he'd torn up his knee, and I was seeing five of everything and my shoulder was blown. All I could do was help her with Sean. I felt real low about it every night in the hospital."

"And Ellen helped you with that." It was not a question. The nurse had seen what the night in combat had done to the young soldier and had given Cage tips about how to help her little brother.

He nodded. "Yeah. Every night Ellen would come in and just talk to me—about everything and nothing. Sometimes it was just silly word games; sometimes we would talk about that night. I talked and she listened. It kept me from going nuts." He sighed. "I just have to be in on this."

Cage knew he was done talking about it and that he might never tell that story again. She slumped against the headboard, thinking. She would give anything to keep him from reliving the hurt, from feeling powerless, because he always would. But she also didn't want to put him in harm's way, and he was lobbying hard to be there. Cage closed her eyes, damning Hank Stillman and Spyder for ending the life of a woman who had given so much to the people around her. The decision was unavoidable.

"You're in. You earned it. Now make me another drink and together we'll figure out how to get these fuckers."

Chapter 19

O'Malley kept her eyes closed as Maria cut through the stitches across the bridge of her nose. They had already taken care of the rest; these fifteen were the last.

Maria was as gentle as she could be, but there was still pain involved. She saw her friend's complexion pale. "You okay?" she asked in the calm, soothing tone she had used as a nurse.

"Nope. If I feel the urge to pitch cookies I'll let you know," O'Malley promised.

"Just remember who has the scissors, Sergeant," Maria threatened playfully as she eased the last stitch free. "Okay, you're done."

O'Malley opened her eyes, blinking several times as she scrunched up her nose. She sighed. "Much better."

"Doing your exercises?" The bar owner chuckled as she swept everything into the trash can and pulled off her rubber gloves. "Joan did a good job on those. They're not going to scar badly at all."

O'Malley looked pointedly at her friend. "Since when has that bothered me?"

"Pardon me. I forgot who I was talking to." Maria sketched an exaggerated bow. "How are the ribs?"

"Not bad. I won't be doing crunches anytime soon, but they're better than I expected. I'm more pissed about my nose," she groused, pulling on her shirt. "All those years of breaking up bar fights and I never broke it. I was hoping to go my whole life without doing that."

"Quit leading with your face then," Maria advised with a sly grin, rising from her seat. "You up for tequila night?"

"Oh no. Not ever again. I must have puked up most of my stomach lining last time," she said. "Besides, I want to take Terri out someplace nice tonight. She still has tonight off, right?" There was a hopeful expression on O'Malley's face.

"Yeah, she's got tonight off. You really like her, don't you?" Maria asked softly.

O'Malley suddenly found her boots interesting. "Next question," she mumbled.

"I think it's cute."

"You would. *Cariña*, what good would it do for me to say it? We are worlds apart. When this is all said and done—"

Maria interrupted. "You will get back to your life, and you don't have to live it alone. Would it be so bad to share it with someone like Terri?"

"Quit," O'Malley snapped. "I don't have a life after this. I had the one I wanted, and it's gone now. I wouldn't know how to live." She leaned against Maria's desk. "It's all up in the air, you know. Anything could go wrong."

"And everything could go right. You have always been a pessimist." Maria finally lost patience. "I love you, *chica*, but you are such a pain in the ass sometimes. Ellen was a wonderful woman, but she had her faults, as you did, and still do. Don't go putting her up on some level where no one else can touch that place she held in your heart."

"The place she *holds*," O'Malley muttered, voice tight, arms crossing over her chest. "It's still there."

"I know it is. She will always have a piece of you, but she would not want you to be alone. It was one of her greatest fears," Maria said. "Don't look at me like that. We used to talk about you all the time. You were her favorite subject."

O'Malley stiffened. "So she could tell you what she couldn't tell me?"

"She wanted to tell you, but you went to Bosnia sooner than we all expected. She didn't get the chance. It's no one's fault, Callan; it was just fate." Maria suddenly wished that they'd had that conversation a long time earlier.

O'Malley nodded. Between her preparations, professional and personal, there had been little time to spend alone with Ellen. Both of their schedules had become impossible. Her shoulders slumped in defeat and she sighed.

"What if I can't let her go?" She sounded scared.

Maria smiled gently. "You don't have to let her go; just let someone else in."

"I'll think about it." She walked to her friend and wrapped her arms around her. "I promise."

"I'll accept that. For now." Maria smiled and returned the hug.
"Now get out of here and have a good time with your girl." She
handed over the black motorcycle helmet.

* ~ * ~ * ~ *

O'Malley didn't look back as she made her way out of the office
to the front door. Her mind was alive with questions that she had
avoided for a very long time. She knew that Maria was right, though
she hated admitting that even to herself. She tugged on her helmet,
then touched the starter button and felt the Sportster roar to life. It
didn't have the same vibrant sound. With the million thoughts rolling around in her brain, everything else was muted. She mechanically went through the motions of getting the bike off the stand and
into gear.

Driving through the city streets, she was aware of how alone she
felt. There was a time that riding had been a joy, but that was when
she'd had that special lady sitting behind her. The warm hands that
once held her tight were no longer there. She rode for a long time
while her brain kept up a litany of questions and nonanswers.

*What are you going to do, Callan? Live alone without anyone to really
love until you die and rejoin her in heaven? What if you do that and then you
find out there is no heaven? What if there is and she's mad at you for hiding
away?*

She pulled to a stop at a traffic light, a headache forming deep
behind her eyes. She rubbed them with her fingers, and an unexpected realization came to mind. As much as she had been in love
with Ellen Rivers, she hadn't told her so during her stay in the hospital. She'd had months to speak her mind and heart and had said
nothing. After her return to the States, she had kept her at arm's
length in letters. Ellen had told her almost everything in those
pages. They had been filled with hopes and dreams, fears and joys.

When the car behind her honked impatiently, O'Malley opened
her eyes. She pulled forward and changed lanes, knowing she had to
get off the road for a little while. She managed to keep her composure until she got to the house.

* ~ * ~ * ~ *

Terri closed the file and let out a harsh breath. Looking up at her boss, she read in his face that he'd seen the contents. Without a word, he took the file and locked it back in the cabinet. Her stomach roiled. She had seen many things in her time as a beat cop and then as an undercover cop, but there wasn't much she'd witnessed that could compare to what had been done to the two women on that road.

"I don't believe they are still getting away with this." Her voice was as bewildered as she felt.

"No one will talk. Hell, Terri, he's got upper brass in his pocket. The politicians and cops he doesn't own have their heads so far up their asses, they couldn't organize a cluster fuck." His frustration was evident. "Now you know why we only met with Simpson. He's the one we know for certain Spyder doesn't have."

"Did you know this when we pulled the assignment?"

George shook his head without breaking eye contact. "No. There were a few rumors, but nothing solid. While you've been playing biker babe, I've been doing some quiet digging. I have enough on a couple of city councilmen to get the state attorney general salivating. If we're lucky, they'll turn on each other for consideration." His disgust at the idea showed up in his voice.

"And in the meantime, Spyder and Stillman get to play their little games and hurt how many more?"

"I don't know. We have to do this right or they'll walk. And then they will be even more cautious. When the club started here, it was nothing more than a bunch of delinquents playing games and riding bikes. Milton came in from the Angels and organized them, but he was more into using dope and women than anything really criminal. He was a wannabe. It changed when Spyder took over after Milton got busted on statutory rape. If you ask me, Spyder set that one up." When her expression turned curious, he explained, "No real evidence, just a gut feeling."

"I'm guessing right now he feels pretty bulletproof."

"Yeah, and right now it seems like he's out to prove it. His girlfriend's been seen with another biker, so I guess he's done with her. He's stepping out more and more to places he gave to other associates for safekeeping. He spent a long time building up, then sort of sat back to reap the rewards. Now he's back to being actively in charge. Whatever is going on with him might work in our favor." George fell into silence for a long moment. "You have any thoughts on the accident?"

"You mean other than that it wasn't an accident?" She couldn't stop the sarcasm but immediately regretted the tone she had taken with her boss.

"I mean, you brought it up. Is there something you know about it that I don't?" He watched her closely.

Terri closed her eyes. "I heard two dancers talking about it at the party. One of them seemed to know enough details for me to believe that it went down like she said. The file confirms it for me. The autopsy of the passenger found major track marks between her toes. I heard Stillman got her hooked on drugs and then sold her nightly."

"Will your dancer talk?" There was both curiosity and hope in George's voice.

"Maybe, if we can bust Spyder and his circle. If she feels like she can be protected, we might get testimony."

"That's all you have?" It was a cop's question.

"Rumor has it there were club associates on hand that stood by and watched the driver die." She bluntly laid down the card that she hoped would be enough. She didn't want to have to use O'Malley. She did not want to have to admit to her boss that the ghost trailing Hank Stillman was the woman she was sleeping with, the woman who was bringing out feelings that she'd thought she'd forgotten about, the woman she was trying to protect.

"Get me a name and I can work from there," George ordered. "You're down to four days, Terri. I'm not budging on the two weeks."

Terri opened her eyes and saw by his expression that he was serious. She nodded and picked up the truck keys. Holding them loosely in her hand, she wondered for an instant if she was doing the right thing. She could back up right now and tell him everything she knew or thought about Callan O'Malley.

Her hand tightened around the key ring and she walked out the side door of his home, not completely confident in her choice. It might blow up in her face, and if it did, she would take the consequences. Terri drove mechanically, barely aware of her surroundings as she made her way back to O'Malley's.

Pulling into the drive, she saw O'Malley crouched next to the Sportster. There was something comforting in the knowledge that the biker was home. The smile that greeted Terri was enough to let her know that on some level she had made the only choice she could. It would have to be enough. She rolled down the truck window as O'Malley stood.

"Hi there. What's wrong with the bike?" Terri hoped that she sounded normal.

"Just tweaking her a little. She sounded kinda rough today." O'Malley rubbed most of the grease from her hands with an old rag. "How's your day?"

Terri killed the engine. "It was okay." She exited the truck and closed the door. "You look hot, want a beer?"

"I'm done. How about I push the bike in the garage and join you for that beer in the house?"

Terri nodded with a smile and walked through the garage, side-stepping tools. She heard O'Malley groan a little as she moved the bike. The normality of the actions hit Terri as she was twisting the caps off the beer bottles. For a moment, she could pretend that this was her life. She would come home from a day of errands and find her lover waiting for her. Sighing, she let the caps fall into the trash can and her dream along with them, having learned long ago that there was nothing to be gained by pretending.

O'Malley snatched a bottle, stealing a kiss in the process. "You okay? You look a little down." There was real concern in her voice.

"Yeah. I just wish..." Her voice trailed off. "I don't know what I wish." Terri looked O'Malley up and down and figured out why she looked different. "You got the stitches out."

O'Malley smiled with less pain than usual. "Give the girl five points for observation."

"Wow, five whole points." Terri smiled and took a sip of her beer. "Mmm. That tastes good."

"Points are important. You get enough points and you can trade them in." O'Malley winked as she walked into the living room to pick up the mail on the floor. She shuffled through it, stopping short at a letter for Terri. The yellow mail-forwarding sticker came as a little bit of a surprise. "You know anyone in Michigan?"

Terri's almost bowled O'Malley over in her enthusiasm to take the letter. She looked at the return address and grinned. "My mom. I don't believe it." She ripped the envelope open and pored over the words. When she was finished reading, the smile was still there as she blinked back tears. "She wants to see me." Terri's whisper was disbelieving. "I've looked for her a long time. I was ready to give up."

"Are you glad you didn't?"

"You better believe it." Terri practically bounced around the room, letter still in hand. "She wants to see me. You have no idea what this means to me. I haven't seen her in so long." She suddenly stopped and looked at O'Malley with a new insight. "Actually, you might be the only person I know who would. She wrote that she's got some vacation time coming. I really want to go see her."

"Why wait?" O'Malley watched as Terri's happiness turned to hesitation. She offered, "I could get you a plane ticket to Michigan."

Terri could only stare. "You would do that for me?"

"It makes you smile, of course I would." O'Malley awkwardly rolled her beer bottle in her hands. "I was going to ask you if you wanted to go someplace nice for dinner, but we can make it a celebration dinner. Just tell me when you want to go."

The rushed words and shy admission burned themselves into Terri's heart. "O'Malley, I would be more than happy to go to dinner with you, even without the celebration." Almost instantly the self-doubt rose. "You should know that I'm nothing special, and I know that some day you'll get tired of me being around—"

O'Malley cut in. "Is that you talking, or him?"

Terri lifted her head and found herself caught in the gaze of ice blue eyes. "Him?"

"Yeah. Is that your thinking or your father's, or each and every guy who ever told you that?" O'Malley closed the space between them and wrapped her arms around Terri's waist. "When I look at you, Terri, I see someone special. Maybe I can't be what you might want me to be, but it's not because of you. I told you that I didn't want anyone in my life because my life is fucked right now."

"I remember." Terri was horrified to find more tears coming, and she buried her head against a strong shoulder.

"If my life wasn't fucked up, if I *could* love someone, you would be her. It would be because of who you are and not because I get off on doing the knight in shining armor thing. Maria's busted her ass getting me to understand that you don't need me to save you. When Trey and his boys were kicking my ass, I was fighting almost as hard as I know how and I still couldn't save you. You did that yourself." O'Malley's voice was tight.

"Do you ever cry, O'Malley?" Terri asked, knowing that if she had been the one speaking those words, they would have been accompanied by a well of tears.

"Sometimes, when no one is watching, and even then it's only on the inside."

"Who taught you that?"

O'Malley's body sagged just a little. "No one had to. It's just the way I've always been."

"You can cry with me. I won't tell anyone," was Terri's whispered promise.

* ~ * ~ * ~ *

Cage tailed him from a distance, knowing that in the nondescript sedan she wouldn't attract much attention. She still had the touch; he had not noticed her all day. Smiling, she admitted to herself that it felt good to be back in the field. She missed that part of life. The chase was thrilling. O'Malley and her friends might have their night rides, but she thrived on walking the shadows. She was the consummate actress, never quite seeming to be what was expected. She could become anyone—anything—and she got off on it.

She'd left a hundred stunned expressions in her wake. She doubted whether any of them knew that she was the one who had brought about their downfall. Her favorite had been the small group of would-be spies in New York. It had taken her months to get the mannerisms and accent just right. It took her only weeks to break through their carefully constructed maze to get to the truth. They had played a dangerous game, not understanding the consequences until well after the gavel fell.

Cage pulled into a convenience store and jotted down the location of her quarry's latest stop. The soft drink she bought felt good going down. Not as good as hundred-year-old vodka, but it would do in a pinch. She tracked his progress in the rearview mirror as she sat in her car and tried to predict his next move. Whether they knew it or not, her prey always had a routine. She had learned long ago that everyone fell into complacency when going about everyday life.

She gave him a minute's head start before resuming her tail. When he pulled out onto the street, Cage knew where he was going just by the direction he turned. When he eased into the parking lot of Hank Stillman's strip bar, she smiled and slowed with traffic. She watched him stiffen his shoulders before pulling the door open. It made her feel just a little better about what she was going to have to do to him.

She found an out-of-the way place to park her car, near enough to watch the comings and goings. Settling down for what she knew might be a long wait, Cage focused her thoughts. There were things she needed in order to make her plan work, but the list wasn't very long. As she tugged her cell phone free, she reflected that forgiveness was going to be a long time in coming, but she had a job to do. She dialed the number without guilt and waited for the answer at the other end.

"Demler." The tone was brusque without being rude.

"Cage. I'm in. I need four SAWs ready for me by the end of the week." She let her seat recline just a bit.

"How 'bout you just ask for a tank?" Demler choked out.

She couldn't help herself. "Well, if it'll end this sooner, sure." Sometimes it was just too easy to push Demler's buttons.

"Do you have any idea how hard that might be?"

"Unless you want me to toss all this hard work out the window, they'll be ready. You want to be the one to tell the boss why an entire network of gunrunners got away?" The question was rhetorical. She listened to the silence on the other end. Sometimes the silk in her voice was not an entirely pleasant thing.

Demler sighed. "Fuck. End of the week. You picking them up?"

She could just imagine him sweating behind his desk. "Yeah. I'm flying in, picking them up, and delivering back here. I need 'em used but clean, if you get my drift."

"Yeah, I get it." He grunted in surrender. "They'll be ready," he said, just before he hung up.

Cage pocketed her phone and watched the sun set in a brilliance of colors.

$$* \sim * \sim * \sim *$$

Terri settled between O'Malley's thighs and leaned back against her chest. Warm arms circled her body and held her close. Despite the turmoil she instinctively knew lurked in the coming daylight, she felt content. In the dark there with O'Malley, she was safe from the real world. The entire evening had only proven something Terri knew intuitively: O'Malley was a better person than she let on.

"Thank you for tonight. Dinner was wonderful. I don't remember the last time that someone made me feel special. I especially liked that whole chivalry thing." She chuckled at the memory of O'Malley opening her doors and pulling out her chair.

O'Malley laughed. *"Hey, my mother raised a gentleman—even if she didn't know it at the time. Imagine her surprise when she found out the gentleman was her daughter rather than her son."*

"So, where does the whole knight in shining armor thing come in?" Terri asked with a smile.

"Too much television."

"Did you ever think about being the evil knight?" she teased playfully.

"Nah, he never got the girl."

"So, the truth comes out. You're just in it for the reward."

"Wouldn't you be?" O'Malley asked, ducking her head to whisper the words into Terri's ear, knowing full well that she loved that.

"Depends on the reward and the knight," Terri managed, even as her breath caught. *"What was the usual reward?"* Her tone implied she already knew the answer.

O'Malley traced Terri's ear with her tongue, leaving a wet trail. *"I could show you,"* she offered, her voice husky. *"Of course, there are degrees of reward. What would this knight have saved you, the fair damsel, from?"*

Terri almost forgot the question as O'Malley's hands stroked from fingertips to shoulders. *"That feels good,"* she whispered, trying to remember to breathe. *"Ogres?"*

"Ogres are very low on the scale. You want to try again?" O'Malley asked with a smile, clearly enjoying the little game they'd fallen into.

Terri tried again. *"How about an evil guardian and a disgruntled wizard?"*

"At the same time?"

She chuckled. *"If it's higher on the reward scale, oh yeah."*

"Well, in that case, the knight's reward would be..." O'Malley's voice drifted off as she shifted slightly to reach the back of Terri's neck, where she planted tiny kisses. Her hands slid down and off Terri's arms, moving across her belly until they met in the middle. She switched direction, her palms dusting over ribs and breasts. Terri's nipples hardened as O'Malley circled them playfully.

Terri arched her back as O'Malley's hands closed over her breasts, cupping and gently squeezing at the same time. The multiple sensations were exactly what she wanted. Desire rushed through her body in abundance as O'Malley's touch alternated between gentle and almost rough.

Terri woke suddenly, not sure what had roused her from her dream. The weak light edging through the curtain told her that the sun was not yet up, and she listened to the sounds of the house. Everything sounded normal, even the soft snore that came from the warm body next to her. Settling her head back on the pillow, she stared at O'Malley with a satisfied smile.

The previous night had been more fun than she'd had in forever. The times with O'Malley and her circle of friends were good, but they were all socially oriented. Last night, it had been just the two of them. There was something about sharing parts of their lives with no one else around to laugh or tease or take pity. Terri shared her memories about life with her mother before her parents split. She had even recalled a thing or two she thought she had forgotten.

With an air of insecurity, O'Malley talked about being the second of three children in a family where only the best effort was accepted. In her eyes, she had never been able to live up to those expectations, too much of a free spirit to be caged with rules. Over dinner and dessert, the women laughed at their most embarrassing moments.

Terri emitted a happy little sigh. It had been a good night, one she would treasure. Their activities after dinner would be fodder for those lonely nights when self-exploration was her only outlet. If she closed her eyes, she could hear the sounds of two women taking pleasure from, and with, each other. She had never thought of herself as being vocal during sex, but O'Malley was starting to bring that out in her.

The woman sleeping next to her was in no way shy about voicing her pleasure and was explicit in her desires. Terri was almost embarrassed at the silent admission that she found it incredibly sexy to hear the husky whispers of want and need. She snuggled closer and wrapped her arm around O'Malley's waist, wanting to feel her skin and just be close to her. She closed her eyes again, praying to whoever was listening for a way to avoid hurting the knight of her reemerging dreams.

Chapter 20

Boomer parked his bike next to Cage's car in the hotel parking lot. The playful glance she shot in his direction sent all the blood in his brain south, and he grinned in anticipation as he followed her through the halls and to her room. Her call had come as a very pleasant surprise.

Cage flashed a seductive grin over her shoulder as she keyed the lock, then pushed the door open and motioned him inside. She felt a twinge of disappointment as she closed the door and secured the dead bolt. Her original plans for him had not included what she was about to do. It was a shame, really. He was definitely her type of guy and it would have been fun. She pushed the thought away and let her professional self fall into place.

Boomer took a couple of steps into the room, then stopped when he saw a bottle of whiskey and two glasses, one of which was half full. He shrugged it off. Turning to face Cage, he found himself staring into the business end of a silencer, and froze. There was nothing playful in her glance now.

Cage enjoyed the fear and instant realization in his eyes that he was totally screwed. "Not exactly the night you planned, I'm sure," she said casually. "You can come out now, Tommy."

Thomas stepped out of the dark bathroom. He silently circled around his sister and tied Boomer's wrists together with flexible plastic cuffs, ignoring the man's grunt of pain as he tugged it just a notch tighter than necessary. Thomas winked at his sister before moving away to take his seat next to the glass of whiskey. This was Cage's game to play. He was only there as backup and to be a witness.

Cage finally broke the silence. "Boomer, I'll explain to you how this is going to work." She watched his eyes flick in her direction, still laced with confusion and fear. "I am going to ask questions and you are going to answer. Honestly, I should add."

"Who the hell are you?" he asked.

She settled the end of the silencer against the side of his right cheek. "See, now that's not part of the game. You don't get to ask anything. If and only if I feel like it will you get any explanation. Do you understand this game now? You can nod if you do." She watched him wrestle with the idea that he was not in control. He nodded carefully.

Not bothering to remove the weapon from his face, she pushed him backward until he was roughly two and a half feet from the wall, then grabbed a handful of his shirt and stopped him. She braced her foot behind his left heel to keep him in place and pushed his shoulders and neck against the wall, knowing full well what the position would do to his body and his mind. His face flushed with the immediate pressure.

"You want a drink, sis?" Thomas's casual tone matched Cage's.

"Maybe later." She moved back into the biker's view. "I think I can take this away for now." She waved the pistol slightly to make sure she had his attention. She heard the whiskey pour into the glass but didn't take her eyes off Boomer. Wanting him to be painfully uncomfortable and close to the edge of breaking, a position he had probably never been put in before, she waited before beginning the interrogation. The first time the technique had been used on her, she had lasted about half an hour.

"Spyder owns you?" she asked suddenly after the prolonged silence.

Boomer answered without hesitation. "Yeah."

"I think he's getting the idea of this little game, Tommy."

Thomas's reply was noncommittal. "We'll see."

Cage nodded her agreement. "Maybe that one was too easy. Okay, Boomer, let's try something harder, shall we? You were there the night Hank ordered that car off the road at Moody's Gap?"

Boomer struggled against the wall for a second; it only increased the pain and pressure. "Yeah. I was there." His answer came out as a low grunt and he lowered his eyes.

"Look at me, Boomer." She waited until he complied. "I can play this game longer than you could believe possible."

"You're crazy."

Cage chuckled. "Of course I am, but that's really not the issue here. I have the tape." She didn't raise her voice or change her casual tone, and she could tell it scared the hell out of him. Men were so easy sometimes. Take away their sense of control and they would tell you anything, especially if confronted with their own perception of the truth. "Why did Spyder order that car off the road?"

Boomer struggled against the burning sensation in his lower back and tried to breathe. "She was running. ... They thought she knew too...much."

"What did she know?"

"Names. She knew the names of guys Spyder has...in his pocket. I don't know how she got them. Damn it, I can't breathe." He gasped for air.

"You have something in common with the two women who died that night, then," Thomas pointed out before taking a steadying sip of his drink.

"Tommy always has been the observant type," Cage purred as Boomer's face turned another subtle shade of red. She wasn't worried about him. All she would have to do was pull him forward slightly to ease his pain, and then she would start again. "What was so important about that?"

Boomer closed his eyes as he answered. "Cops...politicians..." He blew out a shallow breath. "They protect Spyder...for a cut."

Cage moved to the most difficult question. It wouldn't be the last, but she really wanted the answer. "Why did you let her die?"

"Didn't want to. You saw what happened," he rasped.

"I saw gutless, I saw spineless, I saw zero balls," Cage replied coldly.

"Couldn't..." he wheezed. "Too much time..."

Cage stepped on his toes, stretching him further. As his body moved to accommodate the new strain, his eyes popped open. She knew it would clear his head, if only for a moment or two. He drew in a measure more of air and his color evened out.

She leaned in closer, letting him see her eyes. "Too much time what?"

"Too much time...invested," he whispered, then swallowed hard.

She released her foot and he slumped back against the wall. Even that small impact stole his precious air again. He managed a groan before the pain settled back in and the sweat trickled down his neck.

"Kinda hurts, don't it?" There was an almost clinical quality to her voice. "Makes you wonder how much it hurt to bleed to death.

The autopsy report said she had five broken ribs and a punctured lung. That's not what killed her, though, was it? It was the blood rushing out of that gash in her throat."

"Who the hell...are you?" he asked.

Cage's smile didn't touch her eyes. "I'm the only chance you have."

"Wallet," he managed as his world faded to black.

Cage saw it coming and quickly helped him down to the floor. She wanted answers more than she wanted to hurt him physically. If need be, that could be arranged later.

Tommy was by her side almost immediately. "Hey, Cage, let me know if I ever piss you off." He sounded serious.

"Don't worry, Tommy. Mom would kill me if I did this to you." With a small smile, she said, "Check his wallet." She rolled the biker onto his stomach, and the leather wallet containing his papers and money fell to the ground. Looking at his hands, she knew that Thomas had exacted a small amount of revenge with the tightening of the cuffs. Boomer's wrists would be screaming if she ever let him go. She heard Thomas turning the wallet inside out and riffling through the contents; then suddenly he stopped. A plastic card appeared over her shoulder.

"You know, we might have to cut him free," Thomas said flatly.

Cage took the card and flipped it over. The face on the card was definitely Boomer, even if he looked scruffier in person. Richard Mathis seemed like such a normal name for the figure on the ground, and the initials DEA stared up at her.

"Well, this certainly makes life interesting, doesn't it?" she asked her brother.

* ~ * ~ * ~ *

Candace pounded on O'Malley's front door, mindful of the pain that flared in her hand. She knocked again, not sure if Terri and O'Malley were even home. All the lights were off, including the front porch light, and the truck wasn't parked in the drive.

Donna whimpered softly as a car pulled up to the stop sign down the street, then turned in the opposite direction. She was grateful for the dark as she pressed deeper into the shadows. While standing on O'Malley's porch wasn't her first choice, she understood that it might be her only choice. She just wished that someone would answer the door before Hank found her and made good on his promise. She also wished that the whole thing would all go away, but she knew that wasn't going to happen. She watched Candace pound on the door again.

"Awful late for a visit, ladies," O'Malley said quietly as she stepped into view.

"Jesus, that's not nice," Candace scolded after she caught her breath.

"It's after two in the morning, Candace." O'Malley tucked her Sig into her waistband.

"I know. I'm sorry, but we—"

"Come on around this way," O'Malley interrupted as she glanced around. "We can talk inside."

Donna hesitated, suddenly aware that O'Malley could just hand her over to Spyder, who would in turn give her to Hank.

"You have a choice, ladies. You can stand out in the open and let whatever's chasing you catch up, or you can come in." O'Malley's tone was even.

Finally, Candace made the decision for Donna. "Come on," she muttered, as she grabbed Donna's arm and pulled her down the porch steps. "O'Malley doesn't like Hank, so I don't think she'll give you up to him."

Donna sighed, relinquishing control of her fate. "I hope you're right."

The two women made their way across her yard and through the side door of the house. O'Malley waited before following them, checking to make sure that they had not brought any unexpected company with them. After a moment of mental venting, she walked into the house and closed and locked the door behind her.

As Terri settled the two women on the couch, O'Malley lit a candle and placed it on the counter so that at the very least, they wouldn't kill themselves on the furniture. It took a long moment for everyone's vision to adjust to the dim light, and that gave them all time to shift mental gears. Without a word, O'Malley started a pot of coffee.

Donna leaned back into the couch and tried to arrange events in some sort of order, then suddenly realized as she looked at Terri and O'Malley that her sudden appearance had interrupted something. Even in the dim light of the candle, she could see that O'Malley's T-shirt was inside out, Terri wore a short robe that covered a minimum of skin, and the house smelled of sex. She closed her eyes, wondering when her friends would tear into her for disturbing them. The hand that gently patted her on the knee came as a surprise.

"It's okay," Terri said softly. "I'm going to get some clothes on and then we'll talk."

Donna nodded mutely. Terri's reaction was not what she had expected, nor was O'Malley's silence. For a while, the only sounds were the coffeemaker and Terri rummaging around in the bedroom. A muted thud and a colorful curse broke the stillness. Terri emerged in sweats and one of O'Malley's shirts. Her limp gave them all an idea of what had precipitated the curse.

Terri smiled in the candlelight as O'Malley handed her a mug of coffee. "Thanks," she whispered.

"Any time. You okay?"

"Yeah, but your disgruntled nightstand attacked me." She chuckled as her lover reached for another coffee mug.

"I have it programmed to protect my shirts," O'Malley answered as she poured coffee. Handing it to Terri, she gestured toward the two dancers. "You take those two; I'll get the other two."

Terri nodded as she took the second mug. Watching where she walked, she managed to get the mug to Donna without spilling or taking out any more furniture. She sat next to the shaken dancer, not missing the tremble in her hands when she accepted the coffee. O'Malley handed a mug to Candace and then took up residence in her favorite chair. She waited until Donna, obviously scared, was ready to talk.

Finally, Donna was composed enough to speak. "I'm sorry for coming here like this, but Rhea and Candy said you could help me. I'm desperate enough to believe them." She took a deep breath, wishing there were something stronger than coffee in her mug. "Hank's been after me to turn tricks for some of his high-dollar clients. I kept telling him no. I might take my clothes off to earn my money, but I'm not whoring for it. Tonight he said that if I didn't turn tricks, he would tell Spyder that I've been running my mouth about things I shouldn't." Fear shook her voice.

"Rhea and I think that someone heard us the night of the party. They told Hank, and now he's trying to use it," Candace explained.

"What's so different about tonight?" O'Malley asked.

"Huh?"

"How long has he been wanting you to trick, Donna?" O'Malley asked bluntly. She took a careful sip of her coffee as Donna considered her answer.

"Close to a year now. He had a couple of the other girls doing it already, but now he's after me," she said quietly.

"So, why now?" Terri repeated.

Candace looked at Terri and O'Malley like they were idiots. "He needs the money," she supplied.

"He's got a shitload of money." Terri snorted. "He keeps it in his safe. Everyone knows that."

Donna and Candace exchanged a look before Candace spoke again. "Where the hell have you two been tonight?"

"I worked 'til nine and then we came back here. You'll just have to use your imagination to figure out what we were doing after that." Terri leered and blushed at the same time. O'Malley managed to hold back a laugh.

"All night?" Candace asked as she looked hard at O'Malley.

O'Malley kept a straight face. "Don't look at me. I was ready to go to sleep two hours ago."

"We'll talk about that lie later," Terri threatened. "What happened tonight?"

Donna drew a ragged breath. "Half the club burned down. Everyone got out okay, but the place is totally trashed. When the fire department finally put it out, Hank went right for his office—well, what used to be his office. I guess the safe was open when it all started because he came out white as a sheet and started yelling at Trey."

"Trey was there?" O'Malley couldn't keep the surprise from her voice.

"Yeah. Thumper got out of the hospital today, so they were drinking and shooting off their mouths and having a good old time. Well, Thumper wasn't, but the rest of them were." Donna set her coffee cup on the table. "Hank talked to Trey, and a few minutes later he's in my face telling me that I'm going to turn tricks for him." Her eyes searched O'Malley's face. "I know there's nothing I could ever do to pay you back, but I really need your help. If he goes to Spyder, I'm dead."

O'Malley didn't take long to make her decision. As soon she'd heard Stillman's name, she had known that she would help Donna. She shook her head sharply to cut off the familiar jolt of anger that always surged through her whenever Stillman was mentioned. Hearing a quick inhalation from one of the women in the room, O'Malley refocused her attention. Donna was close to tears.

"Sorry, that wasn't a no. I had to think for a second."

"Jeesh, O'Malley, give the woman a heart attack, why don't you?" Candace scolded.

"It's almost three in the morning, Candace, cut me some slack, huh?" O'Malley shot back. Her brain churned. "Who knows you're here?"

"Rhea. She drove us over," Candace said with a small smile.

Terri was confused. "But she lost her license."

"My car's in the shop. Someone had to drive," Candace reasoned.

"If she gets pulled over anywhere close to here, we might be fucked," Terri said. "Spyder owns cops all over this town. It won't take a rocket scientist to figure out where Rhea was coming from."

O'Malley took in the information and digested it slowly. "Let's hope she doesn't get pulled over," she muttered, pushing slowly out of her chair. She walked into the bedroom to get her cell phone. Cage would probably kill her for calling at such a late hour, although she didn't really expect her to be asleep. She found her cell phone as she bumped into the corner of the nightstand. From the short laugh that sounded in the living room, she knew Terri had heard. She sighed as she dialed the number.

The phone was ringing as she walked back to her coffee mug and sipped on it. She hung up when the voice-mail message answered. She had to think for a minute before she remembered the second number. As she dialed, Terri rose from her spot and took the mug from her hands. She poured a refill and returned the mug.

"This had better be a fucking emergency," Cage slurred into the phone.

O'Malley cringed. She would have rather been guilty of interrupting Cage during sex than of waking her up. "It's me, and it is an emergency."

"Damn, O'Malley, do you know what time it is?"

"Yeah, I do. I need a major favor. You need to call me back when you're more awake?" O'Malley crossed her mental fingers. She could hear Cage sitting up.

"No, I'm good. What do you need?"

"I have three little refugees I need to hide away. Can they stay at your cabin, and can I have some cover for them?" O'Malley knew that she would be using up major favor points if Cage said yes.

"You can have the cabin. It might take me a little while to get some cover set up," Cage mumbled sleepily. "Get your refugees started on the way. I'll start working on the cover. You owe me steak and vodka for a year, just for waking me up."

O'Malley chuckled. "You're all heart, Cage."

"I could make it more, you know. Give me two hours to get some things worked out. I'll call you back. You're lucky I don't have to work tomorrow," Cage said just before she cut the connection.

"We're on," O'Malley informed her guests as she pocketed her phone. She looked at Candace. "Can you get hold of Rhea?"

"Yeah. I know where she was going."

"Good. I'm going to pick her up and then we're all taking a road trip." She ignored the stunned expressions on three faces. "Terri, this time, pack light."

* ~ * ~ * ~ *

O'Malley groaned as she stepped out of the truck, hoping to hell that her body would forgive her sometime in the near future. Five hours of driving with little sleep and a lot of stress was taking its toll. She tagged a mental note to talk to Cage about the seriously rutted road they had spent the last twenty-five miles bouncing around on. Warily approaching the front of the cabin, she let her eyes survey the surrounding land.

The area around the cabin, out to twenty yards, was clear of any vegetation, which gave her an unobstructed view. She knew from experience that the back side of the cabin would look the same. Cage liked a clear field of fire, and O'Malley approved. Walking a slow circle, she listened to the sounds of nature. It was quiet but not overly so. That was as it should be. The approach of the truck would have scared the animal population into silence. Inhaling deeply, she detected nothing human in the scents that surrounded her.

While Cage liked her solitude when she could get away, she was still paranoid as hell sometimes. O'Malley didn't blame her one bit. Her friend's profession was a dangerous one, and having a cabin so far away from civilization served more than one purpose. Here, Cage could unwind and work on her human side. She could also hide those who needed to disappear for a while.

Terri roused the three dancers and then joined O'Malley. Laying a gentle hand on O'Malley's arm, she got her attention. "How are you doing?"

"I'm okay, but could I talk you into lending me your hands later?" O'Malley's attempt at a smile failed. "My back is killing me."

Terri nodded. "Sure. I think those three are just going to crash for a while. Let's get settled and then I'll help you out with that."

O'Malley looped her arm around Terri's shoulder and together they walked to the front door, where O'Malley stopped for the hidden key.

Five very tired and stressed women entered the sanctuary of Cage's cabin. O'Malley watched with something akin to amusement as the others wandered around the space. Their surprised expressions were priceless and almost worth the trip. The cabin sported three bedrooms, two full bathrooms, and plenty of space in which to move around. The crowning glory was the almost medieval fireplace that dominated the living room.

"Welcome to Cage's place." O'Malley smiled tiredly. "You three can fight over the other two bedrooms, but Terri and I get the master."

Having expected much rougher accommodations, the three dancers agreed willingly. They chose rooms and drifted off to settle their few belongings. Each woman had left home with little more than the clothes on her back, and they all thanked the powers that be for twenty-four-hour Wal-Marts.

O'Malley sank gratefully onto the couch and closed her eyes for just a moment. She felt an overwhelming wave of tiredness wash through her. All she really wanted to do was curl up around Terri and sleep.

Reentering the common room after depositing their overnight bag in the master bedroom, Terri walked over to the couch and gently shook her lover.

O'Malley's eyes opened slowly, a sure sign that she was wiped out.

"Baby, you wanted to call Cage when we got here." Terri handed over the cell phone. "I'll check on the girls."

O'Malley rubbed her face as Terri walked away. If she weren't so damned tired, she would have enjoyed the view of the retreating ass. She dialed the number and waited. "We're here," she announced when Cage answered the phone.

"You made good time. You beat the cover team by about an hour. You remember Jimmy Herredia?" Cage asked with evident fondness.

O'Malley smiled. "Yeah. He's a good kid."

"Well, he's all yours until further notice. He's bringing three guys with him. If I know him, your refugees will be safe and sound for the duration." Cage's manner was all business. "Go ahead and fire up the surveillance system. I've modified it a little since the last time you were there, and I changed code words."

O'Malley memorized the code word immediately and took note of the changes as Cage rattled them off. As tired as she was, her brain still quickly registered the information.

"You carrying?"

O'Malley snorted a short laugh. "I've got the Sig with me." She tried to keep the sarcasm out of her voice and only marginally succeeded. "You know me, Cage, I'm always armed."

"If you get any company, there's firepower down in the cellar. Door code is 'gambit.'" Cage's voice edged into concern. "You gonna be okay?"

"Yeah. I'll wait up 'til Jimmy gets here and then I'm gonna crash. Terri and I have to stay a couple of days to keep to the story. After that, it's back to the grind. Cage, thank you." Her gratitude was evident in her voice.

"Stop it, Callan. I'll see you in a few days. I should have the SAWs soon. I'll call you as soon as I know."

O'Malley was surprised. Cage had excellent contacts, but this was even quicker than usual. "That fast?"

"Yeah. I had to sweeten the deal, but I figure the quicker we get it done, the quicker this will all be over." She sounded far away for a second and then returned to the line again. "Hey, O'Malley?"

"Yes?"

"You'd better change the sheets on my bed before you leave." Cage's teasing signaled a sudden shift back to her nonprofessional self. "And no, you can't use my toys." The line went dead as soon as that last sentence was out of her mouth.

Mildly shocked, O'Malley just stood there in the middle of the living room with the phone in her hand. After a moment, she chuckled and shut off the cell. *I'll make sure we change the sheets, but I'm not making any promises concerning those toys Cage keeps hidden away in the nightstand.* She sighed, knowing that it was an empty threat. *The next couple of days are business, not pleasure.* Her eyes stole to the clock. *Fifty-five more minutes or so and I can get some sleep.*

A hand on her shoulder made her start. "You don't get points for that," she grumbled at Terri's satisfied smile.

"Yeah, I do. I felt you move," Terri insisted through a yawn as she guided them to the couch. "The girls are out. Donna didn't even make it under the covers."

"I wish we could do the same, but Cage has some contacts coming over. They should be here in an hour or so. I know you're tired; you don't have to stay up with me," she said.

Terri shook her head. "I owe you a massage. If I go to sleep now, you won't get it. Is Cage very angry?" she asked, leaning against O'Malley.

"Not about us using the cabin, maybe about waking her up," O'Malley joked. "She said we have to make sure to change her sheets, and we're not allowed to play with her toys." Her pout was nowhere near genuine.

"We'll see about that," Terri teased with another yawn. "Can I ask you a question?"

"You can ask; I don't guarantee I'll answer," O'Malley said as she leaned her head back on the couch.

"Where does Cage get all these contacts?"

O'Malley considered the question, wondering why she felt almost confident enough to let Terri in on the secret. In her tired state, her brain wasn't working on all cylinders and she found herself answering honestly.

"Cage has had a very interesting professional life, not all of it good. Let's just say that once upon a time, she was a spook for the military, and she's kept some of those contacts," O'Malley answered quietly.

"Are you sure she's done with it?"

"I don't know," O'Malley admitted quietly. "They took so much from her back then, I thought it was over. But now, honestly, I can't say yes or no. Sometimes I think she's done, and sometimes I think she's still in. Some people live their whole lives and nothing interesting happens to them. They go to work, they go home, they go to sleep, and then it starts all over again. Cage lives for the edge, baby, and she loves it. If she's working for them again, I wouldn't blame her." There was something wistful in O'Malley's words.

"You miss it, don't you? Being on the edge." It was a question and a statement at the same time.

O'Malley sighed out loud. "Yeah, I do. It was a rush, you know? I can't explain it to you, but I was good."

"Tell me," Terri said.

"I was good," O'Malley repeated, sighing out her words. "Just take my word for it. I learned well, and I'm grateful for the things I learned. I was lucky in a way. ... I had good teachers."

"I'm glad you did," Terri said slowly, her eyelids were sliding downward.

"You go on in and go to sleep. I'll be in as soon as the guys get here," O'Malley urged without moving.

"No. I can wait with you."

Chapter 21

Terri lifted her eyes from the pages of the paperback to check the clock. Her earlier thread of worry was beginning to grow stronger. O'Malley was not yet back from the errands she'd said she needed to run, and now it was well after dark. Terri wouldn't have blamed her if her only purpose was to get away from the tense atmosphere in the cabin for a while. O'Malley had asked if she wanted to come along, and she had declined. Something in the biker's demeanor had screamed a need for alone time, and Terri needed some as well.

Five women in close quarters during good circumstances was bound to be difficult enough, but three high-strung, high-maintenance dancers in serious danger for what might well be the first time in their lives spelled disaster. Even the cover team had decided that it was probably safer to spend as much time as possible outside. Rhea, Donna, and Candace had spent the previous thirty-six hours, minus sleeping time, bickering with everyone. Terri knew it was stress related, but that didn't make it any easier to deal with.

She and O'Malley had taken the chicken's way out by spending as much time as possible out of the cabin. They had taken long walks in the woods during which they talked to each other about everything and nothing. In those hours, she had more often found herself thinking of her companion as Callan, feeling special that she was trusted with the bits and pieces that made her.

Sighing, she tossed the paperback onto the nightstand, leaned back, and closed her eyes. There was something going on in O'Malley's head, that much Terri could tell, but she couldn't begin to guess what it might be. There had been moments when it seemed that O'Malley wanted to tell her something, only to back off. The woman was driving her crazy, though not in a bad way, and she had no solution for the problem.

Terri suddenly felt that she was being watched.

"Open your eyes."

At the sound of her lover's voice, Terri relaxed. "You've been gone a while," she whispered.

"Please open your eyes."

Terri did as asked and saw O'Malley leaning against the door frame. There was something different in the way she held her body, but Terri couldn't put her finger on it. O'Malley's gaze was uncertain, almost shy, as if she was expecting some sort of rejection.

Terri couldn't keep the concern out of her voice as she leaned forward in bed. "O'Malley? Are you all right?"

"That's a very good question," O'Malley said as she straightened and softly closed the bedroom door behind her. She felt Terri's eyes watching her as she crossed to the bed and lay down with a sigh. "Too many thoughts going around in my brain. I think all of this is finally getting to me."

Terri shifted in bed to wrap her arms around the biker. "I'm not surprised. You don't have to do it alone, you know? I'm here." She curled around the chilled body beside her. "Baby, you're cold."

"Yeah, it's a little nippy outside," O'Malley answered quietly. "When I got back, I got one of the guys to bring in the groceries and I walked for a while. I just wanted to think. I was gone longer than I intended. Sorry."

"None of that, now. Why don't you get out of those clothes? I'll keep you warm," Terri promised as she released O'Malley. She noted the slight narrowing of blue eyes. "What's wrong?"

"Nothing, really. I just haven't heard that in a while." O'Malley closed her eyes and a small smile surfaced on her lips. "I think I'll take your advice." She leaned up and immodestly pulled off her T-shirt and sports bra at the same time. She let them fall to the floor, then made short work of her boots and jeans. Settling under the covers, she let out a low sigh of contentment when Terri killed the light and snuggled in close.

Wrapping her arm around the smaller woman, O'Malley let her eyes close and basked in the feeling of skin on skin. Inhaling, she took in the spicy sweet smell of the woman in her arms as a warm palm danced slow circles on her stomach. The touch was soothing, and she let her brain shut down bit by bit. They lay there silently in the dark of Cage's bedroom for a long time.

~~*~*

Ignoring the irritated expression on Thomas's face, Cage answered her cell phone on the second ring. "Cage."

Jack spoke with an almost detached tone. "We're a go. Boomer's info was good, and that fuckhead Trey is definitely the money man on this one."

"How'd you manage to get that?" She couldn't help asking. Jack could work miracles sometimes, but this information was almost too good to be true.

"He drinks, he talks. Easy, if you ask me. Cjerzoki was a little harder, but I have my ways."

"Jack, you sure you don't want to work for me?" she offered for maybe the millionth time.

He laughed into the phone. "Hell no. You people are way too scary, even for me. I like being almost sane. Besides, your retirement package sucks."

"I would have to agree." She was back to business instantly. "When?"

"Saturday night, 9 p.m., out at some place called the Dunes. I did some checking with my people and it seems that Cjerzoki brings plenty of firepower with him. This one might be a little iffy."

Cage shook her head. "I think I can deal with it now that I know when and where. I want your ass out of there now. If this goes down bad, I don't want you caught in the cross fire."

"I knew you loved me." There was laughter in his voice.

"Right. More like I'm afraid of your wife. Go home, Jack, and give her a hug from me." She cut the connection, then relayed the information to the men sitting at the table.

"So the fire was Trey's way to get the cash. Nice." Thomas's voice carried a hint of admiration. "What kind of power vacuum will it cause if Trey gets the drugs?"

Boomer shook his head. "I can't be sure, but it would cause a major shake-up inside Spyder's circle. I know him. He'd take out anyone with ties to Trey just to prove a point."

"So why not let the fuckhead get the drugs and let them have an internal gang war? It might make it easier to get Spyder."

Cage worked it out in her head as she said aloud, "The problem with that would still be Spyder taking out Trey's associates. Unfortunately, that would include Terri, which would put O'Malley in even more danger." Another idea sparked and her eyes darted to Boomer. "What's this Dune place?"

"Sand dunes just outside the city. We get freaky wind currents up here sometimes, and the Dunes are kinda the hot spot. There are only a couple of flat places. If O'Malley is right and Trey is going after ten keys, it's gonna take a car to get it out. Unless he's got a monster SUV, he can only take one of two roads."

Cage nodded. "Would you like Cjerzoki *and* Trey?" There was something childishly mischievous in her smile. "I just bet one of the two would roll over. My money would be on fuckhead."

Boomer grinned. "It would be nice to get out of this. It's been a long fucking time. I can get a team together for Saturday."

"I can set up the SAWs for delivery on the same night," Cage purred with a sly expression. "If we can, I would love to get them both on the same night. It would be even better if Spyder walked in on Trey's little buy. Cjerzoki knows Spyder, right?" Cage waited for Boomer's nod. "So the likelihood of gunfire is reduced. I like that even better."

"You sure about this, Cage? O'Malley's gonna be pissed," Thomas warned.

"I know. Believe me, I know, but I'll deal with it myself. And this time, little brother, you are going home." The edge in her voice told both men that she would not backing down from that edict.

"I'm already packed. I knew that's what you would say, so I rented a car while you two were out earlier. I'll leave in the morning." His grin was sad, but then it widened as he added, "And I got another room, just for me."

Cage looked at Boomer. "Such a good boy. Mom raised him from a puppy, you know." She felt at ease for the first time in days. "I want you to take the tape and mail it to the state police along the way. I really don't want it traced back to you."

"You got it." Thomas looked at the DEA agent sitting across from him. "What's that going to do to you?"

"I reported the incident and my involvement as soon as I could. The brass chose not to move on it. They said that this case was my only priority." Boomer's voice was shaky. "When it goes public, I'm sure I'm gonna take a lot of heat. I'll take it, though. I really didn't think they would just let her die out there. I would give anything to change that."

Thomas nodded, then kissed his sister good night. He walked

out of the door and to his new room, deep in thought. A lump formed in his throat at the thought that O'Malley was going to be extremely angry with Cage. Angry was too soft a word for it, he knew, but he had no other words for how O'Malley was going to feel.

~~*~*

Navigating by memory, Terri walked the path in bare feet, enjoying the coolness on her skin. She and O'Malley had walked to the hammock many times in the last day and a half. It was their temporary refuge. She made a mental note to have one set up in her yard if she ever got back to her own place. In the dark, she felt almost comfortable. There she could hide from the truth of who she thought she was. A low sigh escaped her lips.

Earlier, when her eyes had opened and her hand searched behind her for O'Malley's warmth, the spot next to her had been empty. Instantly awake, she had felt a momentary flash of panic, almost afraid that her lover would not return. After a short wait, she decided that if O'Malley would not come to her, she would go to O'Malley. She could do nothing else; there was no other choice. She wasn't used to chasing the women in her life, but then, she had never met anyone like Callan O'Malley.

As she walked, Terri let her mind drift over the enigma that was the woman who shared her bed. She was rogue and gentleman, hard and soft, tender and harsh, all at the same time. Terri would have closed her eyes to picture Callan, but the last thing she wanted was to trip and break an ankle. She was, however, sure that if that happened, a certain knight in scarred leather would come to her rescue. She turned the bend in the path and saw that the hammock was swaying gently in the night.

"Terri?" O'Malley murmured quietly in greeting.

Terri chuckled when her heart started beating again. "You know that is totally unnerving."

"Why do you think I do it?" O'Malley teased, and lifted her head. "Come on in," she invited with an outstretched hand.

Terri closed the distance quickly and carefully sank next to O'Malley. "You were gone."

"Sorry. I couldn't sleep. I didn't want to keep you awake."

"I wasn't, until I figured out you were gone. Aren't you cold?"

she asked as she shivered a little.

"Nah, been colder. But that's a story for another night." O'Malley smiled and relaxed a bit more.

"And why is that?" There was a teasing in Terri's voice.

"Oh, just one of those O'Malley-was-stupid kind of stories that you have to get me drunk to tell," O'Malley said without the usual wry, embarrassed smile. After a moment, she wrapped her free arm around Terri and eased her closer.

They snuggled together, watching the available stars in comfortable silence. O'Malley sighed, content to just lie back and do nothing but feel. She tightened her embrace in reassurance when Terri's fingers stilled their pattern on her arm. After a moment, the touch resumed, and O'Malley smiled as the goose bumps rippled in its wake.

Terri said nothing as she shifted in the hammock so that she was resting atop O'Malley's body. She wanted a kiss and more. She couldn't pinpoint why she felt like she needed to touch the woman lying beneath her, but her fingers found their way under the heavy cotton of O'Malley's shirt and she let her fingernails trace up and back down the tight stomach. She could feel the quivering her touch caused, and a surge of desire rushed though her. She tilted her head forward and her lips captured O'Malley's with a gentle possessiveness. She was surprised when the biker let her kiss and taste and nibble to her heart's content.

When Terri deepened the kiss, O'Malley's hands tightened in her hair, not taking control, only participating and giving consent. Emboldened, Terri kissed with everything she had in her. Even though they'd had sex many times, this time somehow felt different. There was something softer to each action, each touch and kiss. Opening her eyes, staring into a dark blue, she saw a reflection of what she was feeling. She pulled away and slowly lifted her shirt, almost shy in her offering.

Torn between wanting to take and wanting to give, O'Malley decided to give. Wrapping her arms around Terri's waist, she pulled closer and let her lips close reverently over the closest raised nipple. Where in the past she had teased quickly, this time she went slowly. Tongue and lips brushed lightly, savoring the treat that was offered to her. She alternated between the two nipples, taking her time and making sure that not an inch of breast was ignored. Terri's whimpers of pleasure told her when to speed up and when to slow down.

She wanted to take her time, wanted to give Terri every moment of pleasure that she deserved.

Moving against her lover, Terri looked down and caught the tender expression on O'Malley's face. Her heart soared as she suddenly understood what she was seeing: this was not O'Malley touching her, it was Callan. She slid her hand back under the T-shirt, but O'Malley stopped her.

"This is for you," she whispered into the night. "Please tell me what you want."

Terri groaned as O'Malley's palms brushed over her sensitive nipples. "You."

"You have me." There was a promise in her voice that Terri had not heard before.

O'Malley pressed her body up against Terri as her hands roamed over exposed skin. She touched her as though she had never touched a woman before. Her hands guided Terri's legs until her lover was straddling her. Slowly, so that they did not upset the balance of the hammock, she reversed their positions until Terri lay on her back. The gentle smile stayed on her face as she kissed as much of Terri's skin as she could reach.

Her hands played inches lower than her lips, a precursor of what she was going to do. She felt Terri shiver in anticipation as she teased the waistband of Terri's pajama bottoms lower, an inch at a time. Her lips and tongue followed, tasting and painting at the same time. She didn't have to look to know that her lover was wet and ready for her touch. She could feel the heat and the wanting. Terri's legs finally slid free of the restrictive material.

O'Malley slid between Terri's opened legs, drawing her body against the slick treasure that waited. She couldn't hold back the chuckle when a heated groan reached her ears. She slid her body back down the same path, not at all minding the wet trail left on her skin. She accepted the gift of Terri's arousal and planned on replenishing that gift tenfold. She curled up into a ball and leaned closer to what she wanted. Instead of diving in, she simply exhaled, letting her hot breath touch the most intimate spot of Terri's body. Fingers tightened in her hair as Terri lurched slightly in surprise. O'Malley breathed again over wet lips and swollen clit as her fingers gently massaged Terri's breasts.

"Oh, God, don't tease me." Terri's voice cracked with need. Whatever she was going to say next was cut off quickly.

O'Malley swooped in with a broad stroke of her tongue where she thought Terri needed it most. From the sudden sharp gasp, she knew she had guessed correctly. Sometimes she loved it when she was right. She kept up the fast, darting strokes for a few moments before slowing to a fleshy crawl. She took her time discovering all the places that made Terri shiver and beg for more. Wrapping her arms securely around Terri's waist, she drew her closer, and her tongue slowly entered the source of the tangy, sweet taste. A moan of delight escaped her as familiar, tight warmth folded around her tongue. She ignored Terri's "please," urging her to go faster, instead content to make it last as long as she could.

Terri felt as though she were flying. Her nerve endings were singing out and she was powerless over them. Regardless of her pleas and words, she was being given exactly what her body wanted. Deep inside, she knew this was not sex: Callan was making love to her. The knowledge made the sensations that much more intense. She felt everything and everywhere that O'Malley touched her, and she couldn't control her body's responses. When O'Malley pressed her nose against her clit, her whole body shivered. She was close, and there was nothing she could do to stop it. She gave herself over completely to the woman inside of her. She felt the tip of the talented tongue touch the spot she loved most, alternating between soft and hard, and her back arched violently.

Terri lost her breath as she came, and still she was able to feel O'Malley stroking her, teasing more out of her. The second wave started almost before the first subsided. She found her breath again, only to cry out loudly. It was the sound of pure ecstasy, and still O'Malley did not stop. Terri finally had to release her hold on her lover's hair to push her away, if only for her own survival.

Without words, she pulled O'Malley up and close. If there had been a way to slip into the biker's skin, she would have done it if she could have found the energy. Instead she kissed the mouth that had brought her to certain salvation. She had tasted herself on the lips of more than one woman, but it had never seemed so important as it did right then. She licked herself from O'Malley's mouth, chin, and cheeks. The flavor was something she knew she wanted more of for a very long time. She wrapped her arms around O'Malley's body and pulled her closer, tears forcing their way past her eyelids.

O'Malley moved easily, her fingers wiping away the tears without saying anything. She was lost and she knew it. The walls she had built were just bricks at her feet, torn down by the woman in her arms. There was nothing more and nothing less that she could do but accept that realization, for better or worse. For a moment she was unsettled by the thought, a flicker of guilt at letting someone else into her heart. Slowly then, Maria's words washed through her mind and the guilt eased, if only for a while. She held Terri as tenderly as she knew how. It was the only way her lover deserved to be treated.

Chapter 22

A smile plastered on her face, Terri pulled O'Malley toward Traders and barely avoided bumping into a couple of bikers who were on their way out. They were regulars at her section of the counter, always ready with an order and tips. With a silly expression, she mumbled an apology that was accepted in good nature. Artfully the four danced around each other.

O'Malley chuckled. "You're a goof lately." As they walked into the bar, the sound of heavy metal assaulted her ears.

"Yeah, and you're stuck with me," Terri teased, punctuating it with a quick lick of her lips.

O'Malley grinned widely. "Uh-huh, and I'll make you pay for it later."

"Promises, promises." Terri turned around to face O'Malley. She did not miss the almost evil gleam in the biker's eyes, and she almost tripped over her own feet.

"How graceful." O'Malley's words were playfully sardonic, even as she reached out to steady Terri. "You sure you can handle a drink or two?"

"O'Malley, you want to get lucky tonight?" Terri sounded as serious as she could.

"The thought had crossed my mind," she answered with a long look up and down Terri's body.

"Then be nice to me."

O'Malley laughed. She had definite plans to be nice to this woman—more than nice, in fact. She slowly drew her fingertips along Terri's sides. "Okay, being nice now."

Terri pulled away from O'Malley. "Good boy."

"That's a loaded statement."

"You have no idea." Terri was back in teasing mode, or perhaps it was a promise. She wasn't sure.

O'Malley leaned in close to Terri's ear. "I think you like it better when I'm a *bad* boy." A wet tongue followed her words and tracked down Terri's jaw.

"You could be right," Terri managed when she caught her breath.

Turning carefully, she weaved around the tables and led O'Malley to the bar. Together they pulled out bar stools, and O'Malley ordered their drinks.

"What ya smiling at?" O'Malley asked as she settled onto her stool. Her eyes searched Terri's for an answer, then she decided that she didn't need one; it was enough to see her happy.

"Just remembering," Terri answered as she rested her head against a strong shoulder.

"Anything in particular or just in general?" O'Malley dropped the money for the drinks on the counter as the bartender brought their beers. "Keep the change."

Terri waited until the bartender took the cash and walked away with a grin. "You sucking my fingers clean; you singing badly with the radio. We have to talk about that someday."

O'Malley chuckled. "No, we don't. I'm tone-deaf. That ain't gonna change." She groaned when her cell phone rang, and she let it ring for a few seconds before she decided to answer it. "O'Malley," she said gruffly.

"You have such a charming way of answering your phone," Cage purred in her ear.

"And you fight like a girl," O'Malley shot back, holding back a laugh. She mouthed "Cage" at Terri's questioning look, and watched her lover nod.

"Well, at least I don't run over land mines," Cage taunted.

"Nice try, but Sean was driving."

"That's a technicality. Hey, I talked to my contact and I got way lucky."

O'Malley couldn't resist. "Cage, your twisted sex life scares me."

"Eww. He's a troll," Cage's voice conveyed a shudder, "and we're talking business here. Keep up with me, would ya?"

"I'm trying, but you confuse me all the time."

"Just wait, mine magnet, I'm gonna get you back. I can get four out there by the end of the week. Does that sound good to you?"

"Damn, Cage, that's fast." O'Malley couldn't help wondering

whether her friend was going to be pudding from driving so far in such a short amount of time. "You gonna be okay with that turn-around time?"

"It's gonna be a little tight, but I'm good with it. I can pick up on Wednesday and be out to you by early Friday. Depending on when we set it up, I can sleep before delivery. I'm just asking for about eight hours of good sleep. I was talking to Boomer about a good delivery spot and he gave me some places, so I'll want to check them out before we call your boy."

O'Malley leaned against the bar, thinking quickly and trying to gauge whether that would give her enough time. She figured she could make it work. "We're a go. I think I can give you the eight hours. If you want, I can recon for you in advance, give you an idea of what we're working with."

"That would make it easier. I'm leaning toward something called the Dunes; that would be my first choice. Boomer said your boy uses it a lot. It'd keep him easy, if you know what I mean."

"I could do easy for a change. I'll check it out," O'Malley promised.

"I'll see you on Friday then."

"Right. See you." Before she could hang up, Terri motioned for the phone and O'Malley hesitated at the evil gleam in her eyes. "Hang on a second, T wants to say hi." O'Malley handed over the phone.

"Hi, Cage. I just wanted to thank you for letting us use the cabin." Terri listened for a moment. "The toys were incredible and we did wash them before we put them back, but I'm gonna have to buy you new sheets," Terri said in a rush, then cut the connection. Ten seconds later, the cell phone rang again. Terri looked at O'Malley, an impressively innocent expression on her face. "You might not want to answer that."

O'Malley almost fell off her stool with uncontrolled laughter. "No shit. I like breathing. You do know that she will get you back," she warned as she turned off her phone.

Terri flashed a cocky grin. "She can try."

"Okay, you two are up to something, and Terri's got that evil look on her face."

When Maria's voice reached them, they both turned their heads at the same time, like children caught with their hands in the cookie jar.

"Evil can be fun sometimes," O'Malley drawled slowly, the accent revealing the time she had spent in Texas.

"Yeah, but it always bites you in the ass later," Maria shot back with an easy smile. "You two look good."

"Run, Terri. She gave us a compliment, she wants something." O'Malley took a sip of her beer.

"Maybe she just missed us." Terri leaned over the bar and gave Maria a hug. "Hi there."

Maria returned the embrace, then pulled away slowly. "Nah, I don't want anything except to let you two in on something. Keep smiling and don't react. Let's just play like we're catching up." Maria's smile never reached her eyes. "Hank's been on a rampage lately. He's tearing up the town for a certain threesome. He's convinced that a certain ex-soldier had something to do with getting them out of the city. Keep an eye on your six, O'Malley. You too, Terri."

"What's a six?" Terri asked.

O'Malley pulled her girlfriend closer. "It's your back, baby. Thanks, *cariña*. I got our six," she promised in a low tone. "And God help him if he decides to fuck with us."

Maria lifted her half-full glass. "If he does, take him down hard, *chica*." It was a statement and a request at the same time.

"I will, on O'Malley honor, I will. Now, tell us why you look so damn happy," O'Malley demanded good-naturedly.

Maria casually leaned against the bar, her face giving nothing away. "You wanna be an uncle, O'Malley?"

It took a long moment for the question to sink in. When it did, O'Malley's slow smile faded with shock and then reappeared.

"I think you might have killed her, Maria," Terri teased. "Do I get to be the little one's aunt?"

"Hell yes. I want my kid to be well rounded. Like the gaping fish sitting next to you said, 'Evil is good.'" Maria laughed for real this time. Her desire to have a child with Gato was no secret to those around her.

"This calls for a toast," O'Malley declared as she raised her bottle. "To *my* kid. May the road rise up to meet her and may all her sunsets be to her face."

"Well hell, she is Irish, isn't she?" Terri laughed and lifted her own drink. "To your family, Maria. I hope your child is as good as you are. If she is, then she will be wonderful."

Maria took a sip of her water. "Joan says we're having a boy."

O'Malley groaned. "We're screwed. He's gonna look like Gato."

Maria laughed and set up two shot glasses. "Just for that, you shithead, you get to take a shot on me." She pulled up the bottle of tequila and ignored O'Malley's groan as she poured.

* ~ * ~ * ~ *

George slid the file across the top of his desk. "Commit that to memory, and you stick close to her," he ordered.

The plainclothes officer just nodded as he picked up the file. He scanned the contents for a long time. He knew he would have to read it at least one more time before he had it all, but it would be time well spent. George rarely asked for favors; he was usually the one granting them to other cops and agencies in the state. For him to ask, it had to be important.

"No one will touch her." He was too good an officer not to ask, "What about the biker she's with?"

"She's an unknown in all of this and to be honest, I don't care about her. Just keep an eye on Terri."

"I'm going to guess that she doesn't know I'm her new shadow."

"Do you think I'm suicidal? I'd rather she not know unless she has to," George said with a grimace. "I've got your cover in place. Try to keep a low profile."

A dark eyebrow arched. "I'll stay low, and I'll update you on a regular basis," the officer promised without giving away his irritation. He was one of the best in the state at personal protection, and while he understood the older cop's concern, his professional pride was still ruffled. As he stood, he offered his hand to his temporary boss.

"I'll owe you one." George had no difficulty saying the words.

"No, sir. It's my pleasure. I'm sure she won't remember me, it was a long time ago, but if it weren't for her, I'd be six feet down with a box wrapper. This one's on the house," the officer said in a low voice.

* ~ * ~ * ~ *

O'Malley was definitely feeling loose as she pulled the Sportster up to the stop sign, but not so much so that she could miss the strange car that was parked at the curb in front of her house. She leaned back to Terri and turned her head. For once she was glad that she had forgotten her helmet; at least Terri would be able to hear her.

"When I park, don't say a word. Just go into the house and don't come out," she ordered.

"What's going on?" Terri asked as she shifted closer on the seat of the bike.

"I've got a feeling we've got company we don't want," O'Malley answered.

"You good to do this?"

The grin O'Malley flashed was anything but pleasant. "I'm so good I'm dangerous, baby. You just do what I say. I can take care of this and them. Trust me."

Terri answered with a reassuring caress. Her hands tightened around slim hips as O'Malley pulled forward into the unknown.

O'Malley rode the bike into the driveway without keying the garage door. She didn't want to give Hank and his two boys an extra way into the house if she didn't have to. When Terri peeled out of the seat without a word, it was a comfort to O'Malley. She wouldn't be divided on two fronts. All she would have to deal with was Hank—and his two goons. Flicking a quick glance around, she knew she could take his company without too much trouble. She'd seen them around. They were yes-men and flunkies. She might hurt a little in the morning, but it wouldn't kill her.

She pulled the key from the ignition and slid off the bike. She didn't have to wait very long as the three of them stalked across the lawn with Hank right in the middle. The burn in her chest rose instantly to a boil, and O'Malley shut down every feeling except hate. She forced her body to stay relaxed and ready.

"That looked damn cozy," Hank muttered as the three men halted just a couple of feet in front of O'Malley.

"Why is everyone always saying that?" O'Malley asked, not expecting an answer. "You want something, Stillman?" She watched them carefully, waiting for them to make their move.

"I want those three bitches and I think you know where they are. All five of you disappeared at the same time." Hank's voice sounded almost normal.

O'Malley had to try, if only to make it look good in front of his sidekicks. "You wanna tell me when whoever the hell you're talking about disappeared?"

Hank took a step forward. "You know who I'm talking about, you bitch. Get them back here or—"

"Or what, Stillman?" she demanded as she matched his step forward. O'Malley showed no fear because she felt none. She could take him and his men out of sheer rage alone. "T and I spent the weekend at a friend's place, alone. You can't keep track of your girls, maybe you should get out of the business. I hear you have a habit of that. Losing girls, I mean. Try working on your charm, it might keep 'em around." She watched his face turn several shades of enraged purple before adding, "Now get off my lawn."

Hank's hand shot out and made a grab at her throat. He came up empty as she easily sidestepped the clumsy maneuver. The biker to his left rushed in, and O'Malley dropped quickly and planted the heel of her boot on the inside of his knee. He crashed to the ground with a scream of pain. She was playing for keeps. Rolling to the side, she regained her feet and spun, tracking the remaining two targets as she righted herself.

The second biker held back a little, maintaining a wary stance. He was just smart enough to not wade in without some sort of plan.

O'Malley deliberately stepped toward him while listening for Hank. Predictably, he went for her while her back was turned. She waited until the last second to stop short and half turn while she extended her arm. The move caught Hank between shoulders and chin. It wasn't a classic clothesline move, but it worked for her. O'Malley took a small measure of joy in his pain as he thudded against the ground before she quickly turned her attention back to the second biker.

For a moment he looked like he was going to run, but then he charged at her. She backpedaled a few steps and picked the moment when he was slightly off balance. She ducked under a punch and, while turning, planted a hard right into his kidney. O'Malley heard the pained grunt and hit him again in the same spot. She grabbed the back of his jacket, then swept his feet out and pulled backward at the same time, and he joined his friends on the ground. Sometimes the results of momentum were a good thing.

Gulping in air, Hank slowly picked himself off the ground. Looking at his two men, he could see that he wasn't going to get any help from them.

"What's the matter, Stillman? Just sinking in that I'm not like the women you're used to having around?" She punctuated the question with a well-placed jab that caught him just under the left eye. His head snapped back and his feet did a stutter step. Instead of following up the punch, she gave him time to recover his balance. She wanted her fun to last.

The flesh under Hank's eye begin to swell. "Fuck you," he growled, then rushed her. For a moment his hands were on her jacket, then he was pulled down and forward. He lost his breath when O'Malley's knee crashed into his chest, twice. When she let him go, he sank to his knees, trying desperately to breathe.

A cold smile crossed O'Malley's face. The confusion and pain on Stillman's was something she was enjoying. She knew most of the story of what had happened the night that Ellen had died, the night her life had died. Trey and his boys weren't the only ones who had been listening to the dancers the night of the party. They had only confirmed most of what she had been able to find out on her own. Looking down at the man responsible for Ellen's death, she could conjure no pity for him. She'd felt pity for the Iraqi soldiers she'd helped kill and for the enemy in Bosnia, but for Stillman she felt nothing.

"Break's over," she grunted as she pulled him to his feet and then took one step back. "I'll give you one free shot. Better make it count." She watched him blink as though he couldn't believe what he'd heard. It took him a moment to throw the punch. She blocked it with one hand, twisted his arm, kept her hold, and smashed her fist down over his elbow. He screamed as the joint gave. She let him fall for the last time. Taking a deep breath, she sank into a crouch over him, her eyes locked onto his. "I lied about the freebie. Now get your ass off my lawn and take them with you," she ordered in a quiet, even voice.

* ~ * ~ * ~ *

As O'Malley stood up and walked away from a broken Hank Stillman, Terri watched from the window, O'Malley's Sig in her hand. It was O'Malley's fight, but she had wanted to be ready if she was needed. She knew that Hank Stillman would probably never see the inside of a jail cell for what he had done that long-ago night, and for that reason, Terri temporarily stopped being a cop. For that one moment, she was a part of a deserved retribution. For the first time, she was very glad that no one in that neighborhood would call the cops.

The door opened as soon as O'Malley's feet touched the porch. O'Malley didn't say anything as she stepped into the house and locked the door behind her, though her eyes widened at the sight of Terri holding her pistol.

Terri shrugged and closed the drapes. Setting down the weapon, she took O'Malley's hands and inspected them for damage. She winced at what she saw. *We'll be using plenty of ice tonight.*

"I need a drink," O'Malley declared as she stalked into the kitchen.

The abruptness of the action startled Terri. "I'll make it. You get ice. What do you want?"

"Whiskey and water on the rocks." O'Malley's voice was tight.

Terri was confused and suddenly worried. "O'Malley, you okay?"

"Adrenaline, Terri. You might not want to sleep next to me tonight," O'Malley cautioned.

"I'm sleeping next to you, O'Malley," Terri answered with determination in her voice. She turned back to making the drinks.

Chapter 23

O'Malley turned off the main road onto the secondary road, keeping her eyes on both traffic and the Dunes. If a set of sand dunes had to have a name, it made sense to keep it simple. She shook her head as a sick sort of laughter started to filter through her brain. She was tired, and it was starting to affect her thinking process. She drove the circular road, ending up almost where she'd begun. She pulled off onto the shoulder and killed the engine, not bothering to pull the helmet off her head.

She took in the undulating mounds of sand, years of shifting winds having formed them into random shapes. Her training kicked in almost instantly. She had a momentary flash of a faraway desert and an exploding land mine. She shook her head. It took a little while for her mind to be convinced that the danger wasn't buried in the sand. *Focus, you dumb-ass.* The little voice in her head pulled her back to the present.

O'Malley tried to imagine the place in the dark. It would be interesting navigating, but with Cage's help she could manage it. Three of the dunes she immediately eliminated as possible meeting sites. They were too hard to get in and out of. Four more were ambush hazards. She wasn't about to meet Spyder with the SAWs only to get herself killed in the process. She wouldn't put it past him to set her up. She wasn't his favorite person at the moment.

That left three more possibles. They looked easy to get in and out of, they had plenty of cover away from the main road, and better yet, there were a few smaller dunes around them. If she needed to duck and run, she could probably play hide-and-seek for quite a while. She smiled beneath her helmet. Cage just might like the choices. She let out a slow breath as it dawned on her that it was almost over. Very soon she would have Spyder dead to rights, and this time he wouldn't be able to squirm out of justice. Retribution would be better, but she had promised Joan that no one would die, at least not by her hand.

Looking to the sky, she opened her mouth to say hello to Ellen. The word stuck in her throat. She swallowed hard and finally removed her helmet. Ellen had always hated it when she wore a hat when talking to her. It had always made her feel like she was talking to her as a soldier and not as a lover. She settled the helmet on the gas tank. She looked up again and settled her sunglasses on her face.

"Hey, Nurse. It's been a while since I talked to you, and I know you're probably wanting to kick me in the ass right about now. I also know you can see everything I've been doing down here." She whispered, not wanting to disrupt the peaceful silence too much. "Doing this, I kinda got away from being me, and I'm sorry. I am trying to get back there, you know. The thing is, I think I've met someone who might make getting back to me a good thing. I think you'd like her. She doesn't let me get away with anything.

"I miss you, Nurse, I miss you like crazy, but if Maria's right, then you'll understand. I wanted a lifetime with you, but I'm lucky that I had you for as long as I did. I guess I should be thankful for Sean's lousy driving skills." She chuckled and wiped the tears from her cheeks. "I'm not going to say good-bye, 'cause I know we'll see each other again, and I'll always keep talking to you. I like talking to you, even though you're kinda quiet on the answer side." O'Malley took a deep breath. "It's been hard, baby, so damn hard. I had every intention of coming back home to you, I want you to know that." She sniffled and quickly wiped her face with her jacket sleeve. "I kept my promise to you; I was careful. I just wanted to say it out loud." O'Malley fell silent for a long time.

"I gotta go, Ellen, but you'll be hearing from me again. I love you still. And if you've got any pull with you-know-who, could we make sure Maria has a girl?" she finished, sure that Ellen would get the joke.

Quiet and lost in her thoughts, O'Malley took off her sunglasses and replaced her helmet. She slid down the sun visor and tucked the sunglasses back into her jacket pocket. Her fingers grazed the box nestled in the soft material. She smiled just a bit and started the bike. There were things that she had to get done before meeting Terri after work. With a little luck, she could still be on time. Blowing out a harsh breath, she gunned the engine and settled back into being O'Malley as she tucked Callan away someplace deep inside.

* ~ * ~ * ~ *

Terri watched the sun set from where she stood on the back step of Traders. She felt torn, and damn tired of having to hide everything all the time. She felt as if she were in the middle of a really bad movie, and she wished she had the remote control so she could just stop it. She shook her head to try and clear her mind. It didn't work. Her thoughts were stuck in one long, obnoxious loop, playing the same story over and over in her brain. Something in her gut told her that it was all coming to a head soon and there was nothing she could do about it. Every worst-case scenario was running amok in her thoughts, and she was also experiencing a serious dose of self-doubt. She was close to crossing the line. She blew out a breath. Hell, she was straddling the line she had lived behind her whole career. There were rules: bad guys were bad guys, and good guys put the bad guys in jail. Her world was off kilter because of one woman. It would have helped if she knew which side that woman was on. There were moments she couldn't believe O'Malley was a criminal, and then there were others that convinced her the biker was nothing but.

Terri was tempted to bang her head against the wall as she leaned her back against it. She knew from experience that it would hurt. Closing her eyes, she wondered how her day had gone from good to a roller coaster of doubt. It didn't take long for her thoughts to remind her.

Waking up next to O'Malley earlier in the day had been more than good. She was still in that satisfied zone after a very good night. Those were rare enough, but to have the source of her satisfaction still beside her in bed was an added bonus. Normally her bed partners ran—or she did, but with O'Malley, she didn't want to leave. She needed to have O'Malley there, even with the light snore from the healing broken nose.

Terri almost smiled at the thought of the sound. At first it had caused concern, then annoyance; now it was simply a part of the biker. In a way, it was a comfort to hear the sound and know that O'Malley was just an arm's length away. They had shared coffee and kisses infused with something neither was willing to admit, at least not to each other, but she was sure she had felt the emotions lurking under the surface.

Her undoing had been brunch at Gus's. She had just finished

ogling O'Malley's ass as the biker disappeared into the restroom. As she shifted in her seat, the well-earned soreness in certain parts of her body gave rise to the thought that she could do this for a long time. Not every single night, but on those nights when they both wanted something a little more. Her brain had asked the question that had rocked her perfect little world. *When did this become a future?*

Terri opened her eyes and suppressed a scream of frustration. How was it that she had finally found the woman she could give and take with, not be afraid to admit her frailties and fears to, and the woman was a criminal? She idly wondered what she had done wrong in a past life that fate had cursed her so, but couldn't come up with an answer. The door opening suddenly caused her to jump.

Gato poked his head out the door and his expression turned to relief. "You okay, *chica?*" he asked in his gruff way.

"Yeah, just a lot on my mind, and Digger's been trying to cop a feel since he came in. Not a good combo, you know?"

"You want me to bounce him on his head?" The question was laced with a protective tone.

Terri chuckled at the thought. It was a nice offer and it was tempting. "Nah. Let's just let Maria serve him for the rest of the night."

Gato laughed hard. "I think we can do that." Digger would chew glass before ever trying to cop a feel from Gato's feisty wife. He had tried it exactly once and almost pulled back a stump. The expression of fear on the two-hundred-fifty-pound mountain had been priceless.

"Do you mind if I take a few more minutes? I'm pulling it together, but..." She trailed off to let him fill in the blank however he wanted.

"Hey, T, take what you need. It won't get stupid for another hour. You sure you don't need anything?"

"I'll be good in a bit. Thanks, Gato." She just had to think things out for a minute or million.

He disappeared back into the bar without another word, and the door slammed shut. Terri watched the sun burn down to the horizon, her heart sinking with it. *Sometimes I feel so damned lost.*

* ~ * ~ * ~ *

With a satisfied, grim smile, Cage slammed the back door of the

SUV. Checking her watch, she knew she would have to push to make time. The shipment had been delayed while the paper pushers had kittens over her arrangements. They had not been at all pleased that she had brought in a DEA agent and forced them into a joint operation. She snorted at the thought. *Not much has changed.*

Everyone was playing politics while all she was trying to do was uphold the law. Not that she was stupid enough to have blind faith in anything—she'd been hung out to dry too many times—but she had to have faith in something. So she had faith in herself, and faith in a certain antiquated honor that dictated that she keep her word. Maybe it was the stories her grandfather had told her. "Quinns never go back on their word" had been her childhood mantra. And she had given her word to enforce the laws of her nation.

From the corner of her eye, she saw a uniformed young officer hesitate as he walked in her direction. She resisted the urge to roll her eyes. Why were they so afraid of her? *Possibly 'cause you're a badass spook who can kill without a thought?* It was an entirely rhetorical question and she knew it.

"You're all set to go, ma'am. The colonel asks that you not lose his equipment."

She looked at his rank insignia. "Head or tails, Lieutenant?" she asked quietly.

"Ma'am?" He looked as confused as he sounded.

"Did you pick heads or tails to get this one?"

"Actually it was rock, paper, scissors," he admitted with a wry smile.

"You want some advice? Next time, just make a gun with your hand. It works every time and you never lose." She smiled as she took the paperwork he offered. Digging the vehicle keys from her pocket, she walked away from the young man who didn't look old enough to shave. "I need a serious vacation," she muttered.

Once settled into her seat, she pulled out her cell phone and made two calls. They both conveyed essentially the same message: she was on her way with the shipment. Cage pulled down the driver's visor and stared hard at the photo of an Air Force nurse. She let her fingers brush over the face, frozen in time and forever young. Every time she looked at the photo, she knew why O'Malley had fallen in love with Ellen, and each time, she renewed her promise and her word.

"Put in a good one with upstairs for me, would ya? I might

need it," she said, and turned the key. *It's going to be a long trip.*

* ~ * ~ * ~ *

Terri slid the sweating bottle to its buyer and accepted the money for the beer, including her tip. She was tired and almost headachy from the smell of smoke. It had been a busy night at the bar. Maria and Gato had been busy with problems and patrons too drunk to understand the phrase "you're cut off." It had been an almost wild night. She was more than happy to be off work in a little while. Some quiet time with O'Malley sounded like a very good thing.

"You look at the clock one more time and I'm gonna think you don't love me anymore," Maria teased as she pulled the receipt roll from Terri's register.

"It's not you, I promise." Terri tried to smile but failed miserably. "It's been a long day."

"T, are you okay?" Maria's voice was laced with concern.

Terri stepped back from the bar and turned her face away. "I'm in love with her."

Maria blinked twice as the words sank in, then a smile crossed her lips. "Good for you."

"You really think so?" Terri asked in a low tone, wanting desperately to believe it might be a good thing.

"Yeah. I do." Maria took note of the absence of the giddiness that should have been stamped on Terri's face. "Why aren't *you* acting like this is great?"

"Because I don't know how she feels." Her shoulders slumped.

"O'Malley doesn't always talk about what she's feeling; she's more about action. She's a doer, not usually a talker." Maria looked closely into Terri's eyes. "There's something else, isn't there?"

"She doesn't know all about my past. What if she finds out stuff that she doesn't like?"

"Is there something in it that would make her walk away?" Maria asked with concern.

Not like you think. In her past relationships, there had been judgments and conditions, recriminations and emotional closures, but with O'Malley there was only the truth as she could tell it. The truth Terri had not yet told was the one thing that could end it all between them, and she knew it. "It could be. I just don't know how to talk to her about it."

"Try starting at the beginning. That usually works best with O'Malley, or at least that's what I've found."

Terri sighed. "And if she doesn't—doesn't feel the same?"

"Then you have some decisions to make," Maria answered bluntly. "Are you happy enough for now, even if she doesn't feel the same way?"

Terri considered the question for a moment. Sometimes she couldn't get enough of touching the biker. There was something sensual about the warm skin under her fingers and the sounds they both made. It wasn't a good or bad thing, it just was. She tried to deflect the question without lying.

"I can't answer that. We have too much going on right now to even think about being happy."

Maria nodded in agreement. "You're gonna have to think about it at some time, *chica*. When all this is over, why don't you two take some time alone? Get out of this place and let it be just the two of you." Maria flashed an evil grin. "And don't spend all your time in bed, huh?"

Terri had the decency to blush crimson. "We don't spend all our time in bed," she said defensively. "We do get out to have breakfast or brunch sometimes."

Maria grunted in good humor as she brushed a sympathetic hand along Terri's shoulder. "Maybe you two should try talking for a change of pace." Maria swatted Terri with the bar towel and laughed.

After a moment, Terri joined her. What Maria said made a certain amount of sense. Since the first time she and O'Malley had made love, the emphasis had rarely been on talking.

When she stopped laughing, she had to lean against the bar for support. She felt better. With just a few sentences, Maria had gotten her to accept certain things that she had already known but not acknowledged. Cocking her head, she wondered where Maria had gotten her insight into the enigma that was O'Malley. A light clicked on in her head as her mind flashed to one of the faces in the background of Sean and Joan's wedding pictures. Another piece of the puzzle locked itself into place, even though Terri still had no idea what the completed puzzle would reveal.

Her police-trained mind knew that for some reason all of O'Malley's friends had a connection with Spyder and his club. She figured that it had to have something to do with Ellen's death, but what exactly they were doing was still a mystery and she wasn't sure what she would do about it. She had not yet given George the information on the money that O'Malley had received from Boomer. Deep in thought, she almost missed seeing a vaguely familiar face in the crowd. By the time she looked again, he was gone, and an unsettled feeling inched its way up her spine.

She spent the next hour and a half serving her customers and watching the crowd for the face. Something told her she should remember it, but the more she tried to place him the more she came up blank, and it bothered her. It affected her normal performance behind the bar, and she had to endure good-natured teasing from her regulars. They all assumed that her distraction had something to do with a certain dark-haired biker. She didn't correct them.

~~*~*

At nine on the dot, O'Malley walked into the bar, a smile crossing her lips as soon as her eyes settled on Terri. She couldn't help herself; it felt good to just look at her. As she strolled through the bar, O'Malley didn't take notice of anything else. For the first time in a long time, she felt free enough to enjoy being with someone without experiencing overwhelming guilt. She had always been honest with the women she'd shared her bed with, but the guilt was always there. Now the guilt was gone, and it felt damn good.

The smile was still on her face as she pulled out a stool and quickly took a seat. Leaning her elbows on the bar, she waited until Terri took notice and came over to her, flipping the bar towel over her shoulder as she leaned forward.

"Hey there, good looking." O'Malley kissed Terri.

Terri enjoyed the contact for a moment before pulling back. "Hi, baby. I'm almost done here. How're the hands?" she asked as she moved to fish two bottles of beer out of the cooler.

"A little sore, but they're good." O'Malley watched the caps fly off. "How's the body?"

Terri quirked a little grin. "A little sore, but good."

O'Malley chuckled and took the beer that was pressed into her hand. "You look good," she said suddenly as she noticed that even after an evening of hard work, there was something about Terri that glowed.

"Well...thank you." Terri didn't seem to know what else to say to the unexpected compliment. "I just have to do my register and then I'm all yours. Save my beer for me. I'll be back in a few."

O'Malley nodded and watched Terri pull her register drawer and take it into Maria's office. She had to smile at the way all of her lover's customers sagged a bit when they understood that it was time for her to leave. She knew they were disappointed, but she didn't care. *Tonight is for the two of us. I have plans for that brunette spitfire, and they definitely do not include an audience.*

As she sipped on her beer, O'Malley had the feeling that someone was watching her, but every time she took a subtle look around there was no one she could catch looking. That in itself made her nervous. She had long ago learned to trust her instincts. Even if she couldn't identify the threat, that didn't mean it wasn't there. *I wouldn't put it past Trey or Spyder to come after me or Terri.* Forcing herself to remain calm, she readied for any attack that might come. This time she would protect what was hers.

The minutes passed slowly, and she was almost surprised when Terri appeared suddenly at her side and took up her own sweating bottle. An impish smile was plastered on warm supple lips that O'Malley truly did enjoy sampling. As they slowly drank their beers, neither one said anything. There was nothing to be said. At that moment, there was only them and the music that filtered around them from the jukebox. Finally Terri slid her mostly empty bottle across the surface of the bar and wrapped her fingers around O'Malley's hand. She tugged her from the stool and led her out of the bar.

* ~ * ~ * ~ *

O'Malley pulled the Sportster to a halt and turned the key, killing the engine. For a moment there was only silence, then nature resumed its usual symphony. She shoved the stand into place with a little difficulty and settled the bike on it. Leaning back, she let herself enjoy the sensation of Terri's arms around her waist. There was something good about the subtle strength hidden in Terri's slight frame. Looking up into the night sky, all O'Malley could see was miles of stars. It was one of the reasons she had driven out as far as she had. The city lights normally hid the multitude of stars. It was one of the things she missed about being in El Paso. The blanket of winking light had always left her in awe. Some of her best memories had been forged under the stars.

Warm hands sliding under her shirt and a chin lightly resting on her shoulder pulled her from her distant thoughts. Turning her head, she had to smile. Terri looked so incredibly delighted as she let her eyes wander up to the heavens. There was something so innocent in her eyes, something that belied the things she had lived through. O'Malley felt her heart swell. Instinctively she knew this was an important moment.

"God, that's beautiful." Terri whispered as she kept her eyes on the pinpoint lights in the sky.

"Yeah. Almost overwhelming sometimes, ya know? I like to come out here at night just to not think." O'Malley shifted in her seat. "You like it?"

"Definitely. Thank you for sharing this with me."

"You're most welcome." O'Malley squeezed Terri's right hand gently. "I just wanted for you to see it like I do."

"Anyone ever tell you you're sweet, O'Malley?" Terri's breath tickled the biker's ear.

"Not lately," O'Malley said. "I'm not, you know. I'm set in my ways, I'm a slob, and lately I snore."

Terri chuckled. "Yeah, you're all of those things, but..." Her voice trailed off as she struggled to come up with the words to describe O'Malley. "Why did *she* fall in love with you?" she asked suddenly.

O'Malley wasn't sure she had heard right. "What?"

"Your girlfriend. Why did she fall in love with you? I'm sure she told you." O'Malley settled back in the seat, and Terri listened to the crickets chirp for a long, silent while.

"She said she fell in love with me because I cried for my guys. One night, she wheeled me into Sean and Quinn's room. I couldn't help it. The tears just came. I was so damn grateful to see them alive, and at the same time I felt guilty 'cause I hadn't kept us from getting hit," O'Malley said quietly. "I think it's 'cause I made her laugh. At the time, she was with someone that forgot that she was alive. I guess I made her feel special."

"You see, Callan O'Malley, you are sweet." Terri kissed O'Malley's ear and let her lips linger for a long moment. "Even if you hate to admit it."

O'Malley could feel Terri's smile on her skin. "How about we agree to disagree?"

"How about you agree with me just once?" Terri offered, as her tongue traced a ridge of skin.

O'Malley closed her eyes at the pleasurable sensation. "I can do that," she breathed out as Terri continued to leave little wet spots on her skin. After several long moments of gentle torture, O'Malley felt Terri pull away.

"I like it when you agree with me. We should have that happen more often." With that, Terri dismounted from the bike and walked a short distance away.

O'Malley was almost grateful for the break. She knew better than to play with fire, but Terri was almost too irresistible. Instead of following right away, she sat and watched Terri walk. Almost everything inside her urged her to run away, but her heart told her that this time it might be okay to stay put. Without her thinking about it, her hand strayed to the interior pocket of her jacket. She nimbly extracted the jewelry out of the box and touched the cool metal.

Walking silently, almost stalking, she went up behind Terri, smiling like a fool. She felt Terri tense for just a moment when she made contact with Terri's back. She took an end of the chain in each hand and draped the jewelry around Terri's neck, then fastened the clasp without a word. She let the chain drop to its natural position and kissed the spot on Terri's neck where the clasp rested.

"I'm not much on words that matter. All I've ever really known has been about doing instead of talking. This belonged to my great grandmother. She brought it over with her from Ireland when she was just a girl. It's yours."

Terri finally lifted the necklace and looked at it. In the near dark, she was able to make out the delicate knotting. "O'Malley," she breathed, "I can't take this. It's too much."

"No, I think it's just enough," O'Malley said with conviction in her voice. Her arms wrapped around Terri's waist. "You make me want to be who I am and who I was. I know that doesn't make too much sense right now, but I hope it will soon."

"Are you sure?" Terri was asking more than the obvious question and they both knew it.

"Yeah. I'm sure."

Turning quickly, Terri launched herself at O'Malley, needing to touch and kiss and give voice to the words she'd wanted to say for some time. O'Malley's tongue engaged hers in a delightful dance. It was primal and exquisitely erotic. Letting her head fall back away from O'Malley, Terri nearly purred with pleasure.

The shrill beeping of her cell phone killed the words on her lips. Tugging her phone from her pocket, she glanced at the caller ID.

O'Malley immediately noticed the change in her lover. Even in the dark, she could see the color drain from Terri's face. There was only one thing that could elicit that sort of reaction, only one person who could reduce Terri from spitfire to frightened child. The phone continued to ring. The look of fear in Terri's eyes broke O'Malley's heart. She reached for the phone.

"Yeah," O'Malley answered curtly. For a second there was silence. "Listen up, asshole, she's with me, and no matter how many times you call she's where she belongs." O'Malley took pleasure in playing with a mind here and there.

"I'm looking for Terri," the voice on the other end finally answered.

"Yeah, well, she's busy right now. You get me instead." O'Malley let her old training fall into place. "Who are you and what do you want?"

"Get her on the phone; she'll know who I am." The male voice on the other end remained almost charming. It was a soothing sound, meant to reassure.

"I have a better idea. You leave me a message and I'll make sure it gets to her. Or you can give Trey a message from me: back off or he'll be eating breakfast through a straw. He lost, and she's mine. It doesn't matter what he thinks or wants. She likes coming *to* my bed and coming *in* my bed. If he has anything more to say to us, he can do it on his own." She ducked her head to get Terri's attention and pulled her closer.

"I think I may have the wrong number. I'm looking for Terri Barclay."

"Yeah, who do you think I'm talking about?" O'Malley demanded as though he were an idiot.

"Could you describe her for me?" the caller asked, sounding very much like a cop.

"Petite brunette...blinding smile...four little moles running down the middle of her back...great tits," she said, and heard him choke on the other end.

He shouted into the phone, "This is her father!"

O'Malley tugged the phone away instantly. He had good lungs.

"Oh, in that case, *Daddy*, why don't you come down here so I can kick your ass on general principle," she offered casually.

"Who in the fuck is this? I want your name. Do you hear me?" His voice was frantic.

"I hear you, and you can want all day long. Call her again or touch her again, and I will make you wish you were dead. I would really like to see you try and hit someone over the age of six." O'Malley's voice took on a dangerous, quiet tone. "And just for the record, the only person she calls Daddy anymore is me." O'Malley couldn't resist getting in that final dig just before she cut off the connection. She only wished she could have seen his face. It didn't matter that Terri didn't really call her Daddy, it was enough that her bastard of an old man might have a coronary at the thought. She chuckled despite herself.

"You okay?" O'Malley asked as she looked at the top of Terri's head.

Terri's face remained against O'Malley's chest. "You remember when I said you were sweet?" she asked quietly in a neutral voice.

"Yeah," O'Malley answered, managing to keep her fear hidden.

"I was so wrong. That was damn cold, and I loved every minute of it." Terri lifted her head and O'Malley saw the grateful expression on her face. "Thank you. And if you don't mind, I'd rather call you something that is more fitting for a knight in leather armor."

O'Malley couldn't suppress the smile playing over her lips. "How many damsel rescue points is that one worth?"

Chapter 24

Cage pulled her SUV into O'Malley's driveway and let out a long, slow breath. She was completely wiped out. The drive had been an exercise in nerves as she tried to maintain her schedule and not get caught speeding by the cops. A small smile quirked her lips as she thought about the conversation she would have had if the toys in the back of the vehicle had been discovered. The smile died instantly at the thought of having to explain that one to her boss.

She crawled out of the truck and set the alarm system. It wouldn't do to have the damn things stolen right from under her nose. The four beeps made her feel slightly better. Actually, it wasn't the beeps that gave her a sense of security, but the protection system she'd had installed in her vehicle. Anyone touching the SUV would get one very nasty surprise. The thought almost put the smile back on her face. She walked up the porch steps, her feet feeling like they were weighted with cement.

Before Cage had a chance to ring the bell, the door swung open and O'Malley stepped back to let her into the house. An ice-cold beer was pressed into her hand before she crossed the threshold, and she took the first sip before the door was closed. It felt better than it should have.

"You look like hell, Cage," O'Malley offered good-naturedly.

"Thanks so much," Cage shot back as she sank onto the couch with a low groan. "Remind me not to do this again anytime soon, okay?"

"After tomorrow, we won't ever have to do this again," O'Malley noted aloud, and then she gestured back toward the kitchen. "You hungry?"

Cage grunted as she pulled her shoes off and wiggled her toes. "There had better be a steak in that kitchen somewhere."

"Count on it. I grilled some up just after you called." She went in and pulled open the oven door. "I guess I'm gonna have to wait on you."

"Definitely. I don't think I have the energy to move," Cage said as she lifted her beer and took a sip.

"No energy to move, and yet she still drinks like a champ," O'Malley teased as she pulled three plates down from the cupboard and started dishing up dinner.

"You know, when I'm feeling better, I can kick your ass," Cage purred.

O'Malley gave a mock shiver. "Keep in mind that I'm holding your dinner here."

"Okay, I take it back." As Cage leaned back and allowed her body to start the decompression process, she decided to change the subject. "Where's Terri?"

O'Malley plopped mashed potatoes onto the plate. "She's still at work, but she should be here pretty soon." She picked up the plate and grabbed the silverware as she made her way out to Cage, where she set the plate down on the coffee table. "Enjoy." She turned back to the kitchen to grab her own dish and a fresh beer.

Cage dug in and groaned her delight. The steak was grilled to perfection, and she was suddenly aware that her last meal had been a greasy breakfast at a truck stop some three hundred miles ago. She was halfway through her meal when she finally noticed O'Malley staring at her.

"What?" She managed not to choke on the question.

"Did you even taste that?"

"Yes, it's very good. Now that I've stroked your ego, can I finish?" She was still hungry, and most of her friends were bright enough not to mess with her when that was the case.

"By all means." O'Malley laughed and turned back to her own dinner, eating at a more leisurely pace.

They ate in silence. When she was done, Cage actually felt almost human. She had revived enough to pick up the empty plates and carry them to the sink. Then she reached into the fridge and pulled out two more beers.

"Thanks, O'Malley. I feel much better." She set the beers on the coffee table and resumed her seat.

"No problem, Cage. You look like you could use some sleep. You wanna crash now or wait?"

"I can wait. I'd like to go over what you found at the Dunes before your girl gets home," Cage answered cautiously.

O'Malley pulled out the map that she'd drawn earlier in the day. "I narrowed it down to three choices. We can take a look at them after you wake up. We've got two roads that lead in and out. From those, we have eight walking paths that have been grooved out by traffic." She traced out the spots she spoke of. "These three dunes here are looking like the best choice. Easy to get in and out of, and there are some smaller dunes that we can hide-and-seek in if we need to."

Cage looked at the map through tired, burning eyes. Nodding, she had to admit that O'Malley still had the touch. "Looks good. I can give you the yes or no after we take a peek. I say we go with your plan unless I see something I don't like. When do you want to call your boy?"

"Right after you say yes or no. You pick the time. I'm sure he'll show up with the cash. He wants his guns and he wants his business with me finished," O'Malley answered easily. "You sure you want to do this without backup?"

Cage nodded and tucked away a twinge of guilt. "Yeah. I think he wants the guns more than he wants to take you out. Besides, I'll be loaded for bear and I'm sure you won't go in without something tucked under your arm." She smiled.

"Good girl. You have been listening to me." O'Malley smiled and leaned back to take a sip of her beer.

"Yeah, I do that sometimes. And you look different. You gonna tell me why or just make me guess?" Cage asked casually.

"Let's just say that sometimes, I listen to you, too." O'Malley tried to keep the smile off her face but failed miserably.

"I'll be damned. You let her inside, didn't you?" Cage bounced around the couch like a kid who'd eaten too much sugar. "Callan's got a girlfriend." She repeated the singsong sentence until even she was sure it was obnoxious. Finally she stopped and looked at O'Malley's pained expression. "Sorry. Got carried away. I can't wait to tell Joan."

"Oh, hell, she probably already knows. Might have seen it in a dream or something," O'Malley said. "I gotta tell you, Cage, it feels really good, you know?"

"I'm sure it does," Cage answered, with something close to envy in her voice. "I was always jealous of what you and Ellen had, and now I get to be jealous all over again." Her words were light, but the tightness around her eyes gave away the truth of the statement.

"One of these days, my friend, you're going to meet the one," O'Malley promised with conviction.

"I'll let you think so. Haven't met the one yet, so I reserve the right to be skeptical." Cage slammed back the rest of her beer. She didn't miss O'Malley's expression. "Don't even say it, Callan. I'm not the perfect catch, and for right now I'll settle for having as much fun as I can. If it happens, it happens, but I'm not going to be tripping over myself to find the perfect guy."

"Well, when you do, just let the rest of us in on the secret, okay?" As O'Malley picked up the empty beer bottles, she heard the sound of her truck pulling into the driveway. "Oh yes, the little woman is home."

"She was kidding on the phone about the toys, right?" Cage asked seriously.

"Why should I answer that?"

Cage didn't hesitate to use blackmail. "Because if you don't, I'll tell her you just called her the little woman." She watched the quick look of panic on her friend's face.

"She was kidding," O'Malley admitted. "You're not gonna tell her, are you?"

"Chicken," Cage shot back. Beyond that, she didn't answer. She would find it amusing to watch O'Malley squirm for a little bit.

From the moment Terri walked in, O'Malley seemed like the person that Cage used to know. She was the old Callan, courteous and sarcastic, attentive and teasing at the same time. It was almost like stepping back in time. When Cage caught sight of the necklace around Terri's throat, she knew without a doubt that her friend had fallen hard, and she was glad that O'Malley had a second chance at being happy.

Cage spent the next hour catching up with them and almost fell over when she received the news of Maria's pregnancy. It seemed like it was the night for good things to happen to her friends. Finally the drive caught up with her, and she had to admit that she was exhausted.

The bed in the guest room wasn't the most comfortable thing, but after two days of hard driving, it felt like heaven to Cage. Sleep was long in coming, though. Each time she closed her eyes, all she could see was the road rushing up at her. Beyond the closed door, she could hear the murmuring of two quiet voices. She couldn't make out the words, but she was sure it would be one of those conversations that she hated being a participant in. Rolling over, she pulled the blanket with her and tried to will her mind to shut up so that she could get some sleep. The next day was going to be incredibly long.

~~*~*

When O'Malley heard the guest room door close softly and looked at Terri, she knew their conversation was probably not going to be a good one. O'Malley leaned against the doorjamb and watched while Terri started picking up after the impromptu party without saying a word. She did not feel like running headlong into an argument, but after the third cup was slammed into the sink, she was forced to move. She stepped behind Terri and wrapped her arms around her.

"Stop. If you're mad at me, don't take it out on the dishes."

"I want to go with you tomorrow," Terri blurted.

O'Malley released a sigh. "I know, but that's not gonna happen. I can't do this and worry about taking care of you," she said in a low tone.

"I am not the damsel we play with in bed, O'Malley. You can't protect me," Terri said bluntly.

"Maybe I'm protecting myself," O'Malley whispered. "If Spyder were to get his hands on you and hurt you, it would cut my heart out. I don't want anything to happen to you," she said, resting her forehead on Terri's back. "I lost one woman I cared about, I don't want to lose another one."

"What would she say if you told her what you've told me?"

O'Malley chuckled. "About the same thing, but with more colorful language. I don't think you're weak by any means, baby. I just don't know if I could be that strong. Please understand."

"I want to, but it's hard." Terri looked down at the floor.

O'Malley hated what the situation was doing to her lover. "I just found you, baby. I'm not gonna screw that up by doing something stupid," she promised as her arms wrapped more tightly around Terri's body.

"You better not, O'Malley. I've gotten used to you being around, and I like the feeling." Terri's voice cracked.

"We're going to deliver the guns and get the cash. That's all.

I'll be home before you know I'm gone."

"You're a terrible liar, O'Malley." Terri chuckled. "I'll know that you're gone."

"You know what I mean," O'Malley whispered, holding on for dear life. "I want to get this over with and then come home to hold you this close."

Terri turned in O'Malley's arms. "That makes two of us." She smiled shyly. "Just for the record, I'm not going to stop worrying, okay?"

"I can live with that." O'Malley placed a gentle kiss on Terri's forehead.

"I will remind you of that from time to time." Terri smiled and snuggled into the biker's arms. "Can't we just stay like this for the next...I don't know...decade?"

"I kinda like the sound of that. Might be a rough decade. I'm a little on the fucked-up side. I know what you mean to me, but I'm not sure I remember how to show you." O'Malley admitted her fear in a husky whisper.

"I have time, O'Malley," Terri said. "I'll do the dishes tomorrow. I'm gonna take a shower."

The sudden change of topic made O'Malley dizzy. She blinked and muttered her agreement. She reluctantly let Terri out of her arms and received a kiss on the cheek in return. Shaking her head, she watched her lover disappear into the bedroom. She shrugged and then fished a beer from the fridge as she heard the door close. O'Malley was sure that admitting that she was flawed had sparked some negative train of thought in Terri's mind. *Who are you kidding? You want her around and you don't even know if you can make it work?* Her doubts surfaced hard and smacked her in the back of the head, and she savagely twisted off the cap. She did the only thing she could: paced the floor and started on her beer.

* ~ * ~ * ~ *

Terri stepped out of the shower and quickly dried off. She knew she'd confused O'Malley, but at the time she couldn't devise a better way to make her sudden thought a reality. Her lips curved up in a mischievous smile as she slipped into a teddy, determined to make this night a most memorable one. She wanted to give O'Malley something to come home to, a reason to not take any stupid chances.

Almost anything could go wrong the next day, but for the rest of the night there would just be them. Just the thought of dressing like that for her lover was exciting. Terri wanted to be every one of O'Malley's best fantasies. She wanted it for the both of them. She couldn't recall the last time she had wanted someone so badly, or so often. There were moments when she worried about always needing to touch her lover or to have O'Malley touch her. There were other moments when she gloried in the feeling, while worrying that she might not be enough for the hard-living ex-soldier. But at that moment, the soft satiny texture of the teddy made her feel just sexy enough. In the past, she might have felt foolish or clumsy, but O'Malley had a way of reaching in and bringing things out in her that she didn't think she could do. Brushing her hand through her hair, she looked in the mirror and decided that she looked damned good. The smile that crossed her lips was genuine.

Surprised to not find O'Malley already in bed, Terri opened the bedroom door. She spied her lover sitting on the couch in dim lights, eyes closed and a beer bottle settled between her legs. From the crinkled eyebrows she knew O'Malley was thinking too much again. She softly padded to the edge of the couch. When her lover's eyelids twitched, she knew that her presence had been detected.

"What are you still doing out here?" Terri asked softly, her fingers brushing through O'Malley's dark hair.

O'Malley sighed aloud. "I wasn't sure you wanted me in the bedroom. You left kind of quick."

"I didn't mean to scare you, honey. I just had a sudden thought and I wanted to follow up on it. Open your eyes for me." The tone in her voice was pleading, as she was unsure O'Malley would comply. When the blue eyes finally opened, they went wide. "This was my sudden thought."

O'Malley had to swallow to speak. "I like the way you think," she said. "You look amazing." Her admiration was heartfelt. Terri in nothing but the teddy was skin and satin, angelic and sultry. As Terri inched closer to sit in her lap, straddling her legs, O'Malley's body responded more quickly than usual. Whether it was the teddy or the knowledge that the dangers of the next day were fast approaching, O'Malley didn't know, nor did she care.

Terri settled herself in O'Malley's lap, removed the beer bottle from its cocoon, and slid closer. She took a sip of beer, then set the bottle on the floor. Pressing her body close to O'Malley's, she took momentary control. Her hands slid up the biker's stomach to her ribs and then over breasts that became very interested in what was going on. She could feel O'Malley's eyes on her every move.

"Tonight I want to be your best fantasy; I want you to be my best fantasy. All this," she drew her hand away from O'Malley and slid it down her own body, "is yours. Tell me, baby, do you want it?" she whispered, as she wriggled her hips against her lover.

O'Malley groaned at the sweet pressure. Her hands finally moved and tangled themselves in Terri's hair. "Yes," she breathed. She pulled Terri closer, and her lips found their warm and willing target. She smiled around the kiss and couldn't resist the urge to lick Terri's lips. She was rewarded with a low moan, so she repeated the action. That sweet sound made her heart quicken and her body responded.

Her fingers teased Terri's body through the material that covered her skin. It was sensual and sexual at the same time. Both women loving the feeling, for just a little while they forgot everything but themselves.

* ~ * ~ * ~ *

Terri rolled over in bed and came into contact with a solid, warm body. She knew before her eyes opened that her lover was already awake. The fingers that trailed across her shoulder were a dead giveaway. Her internal smile never surfaced as her brain reminded her what day it was. She pulled herself closer, wanting nothing more than to just crawl inside O'Malley's skin and stay there. Finally she opened her eyes to find O'Malley staring at her.

"Hi, gorgeous," O'Malley whispered with a ghost of a smile, her fingers never stilling.

"You are deluded if you think I'm gorgeous when I wake up," Terri argued, even as her hands touched naked skin.

"I'm allowed to be crazy. I did drive over a land mine once." O'Malley settled a soft kiss on her lover's neck. "Mmm, you taste good."

Terri chuckled. "You said that last night." She tried to move to check the time, but O'Malley wouldn't release her hold. "What time is it?"

"A little after three," the biker said around butterfly kisses. "Cage and I have already been out. The meet is set."

Terri stiffened. "You didn't wake me up?"

"I tried, baby, but someone was zonked out hard. I think I wore you out last night," O'Malley explained with a grin.

"Sounding a little proud there, aren't you?" Terri asked as she rolled on top of her woman.

The smug look resurfaced. "Oh yeah."

Terri would have laughed if not for the rush of desire that coursed through her body. She should have been sated for the next month after their activities that had lasted into the wee hours of the morning. Instead she wanted more, and she definitely wanted more now. Without a word, she ducked her head and her lips suddenly latched on to O'Malley's right nipple.

Any protest or comment that O'Malley might have made was overridden by the short circuit that cut off her brainwaves. The sucking sensation went right to her clit, and she was quickly drenched. If she had any complaints, her body vetoed them. In no time she was a quivering mass of want. Her body arched into Terri, letting her know without words that she was giving herself up.

Terri groaned at O'Malley's surrender. It was so unlike the biker to give up control, she wasn't going to waste her opportunity. She kissed her way to O'Malley's left breast as her hands slid down tightly coiled muscles and between opened thighs. Her fingers found a wellspring, and she slowly teased her lover, ignoring O'Malley's pleas. As O'Malley's head fell back against the pillow, Terri finally eased two fingers inside. She knew the liquid heat pouring from her lover was all for her, because of her.

O'Malley's surprised gasp was not enough to keep Terri from going slow. This time, she wanted to make love. She fluttered her fingers time and time again, letting her lover slide close to the edge, only to ease her back. She wanted to make the feeling last as long as O'Malley could stand it. Her free hand mapped the contours of the body beneath her. Gasps and moans were her guides, and she used them to full advantage.

Terri slithered her way up her lover's body, her fingers never stopping. O'Malley's eyes opened and Terri was able to see what O'Malley had not yet said out loud. She kissed her gently and felt strong arms wrap themselves around her back and hold her as close as possible. They rocked slowly together, eyes locked, kissing, until finally Terri felt the familiar tremors start around her fingers. She waited until the last possible second to kiss O'Malley once more.

This time she did not pull her fingers away, and O'Malley gasped her pleasure around the kiss.

As slowly as she had entered, Terri slipped out and wrapped herself around her still-recovering girlfriend. She could feel the strongly beating heart as she kissed her way across O'Malley's chest, and she smiled against salty skin as she regained her own breath.

~~*~*

Cage quirked an eyebrow when Terri emerged from the bedroom dressed in jeans and a loose-fitting shirt that looked too big on her. From the look on Terri's face, it had been a satisfying afternoon. The sounds that had emerged from behind the bedroom door had been impossible to mistake. A part of Cage knew they had been connecting in the most primal way known to humans. She'd seen it many times before in the hours before a potential battle. She couldn't blame either of them. If she'd had anyone with her, she would have been making similar sounds.

Cage wrestled with all the comments that skittered through her brain. Any one of them would do to cause a monster blush, but for once she decided that she would say nothing. There was something entirely too sweet in Terri's face.

"There's coffee made," Cage said without giving anything away.

Terri's expression was classic. It was one of those looks that said she was waiting for the punch line. She walked into the kitchen and poured three mugs of the strong-looking brew. She picked up one mug and carried it to the bedroom, only to emerge again a minute or two later. She walked back into the kitchen and grabbed the other two coffees.

"This one's gonna go either way, isn't it?" Terri asked as she handed Cage a mug. She sat on the couch not too far away from her.

Cage nodded absently. "Yeah. Spyder might decide to be an asshole or he might just do business and leave it at that." She brought the mug to her lips.

"Don't let anything happen to her." Terri's words were even.

"Terri, all I can promise is my best." Cage took another sip.

Terri sat back on the couch, mulling over the words

Both women shifted their gaze when the bedroom door opened and O'Malley walked out of the bedroom in leather pants and a tight blue T-shirt, coffee mug in hand. Her relaxed expression did not reach her eyes. The tension lines gave away her apprehension over the coming hours. O'Malley bypassed her favorite chair to deposit a light kiss on Terri's mouth.

"It's gonna be fine, baby. You about ready, Cage?" she asked without looking away from Terri's eyes.

"Yeah. I got the stuff ready." Cage set her mug down on the coffee table.

"Why don't you two just call them guns?" Terri asked, sarcasm evident.

"Force of habit, Ter." O'Malley sighed. "I just have to gear up and I'll be ready."

Terri watched carefully as O'Malley picked the Sig out from its hiding place and stripped it down. She had done the same thing in the past, just before going in for a bust. At least then she had been an active participant and not just an observer. Watching was harder.

Once the weapon was checked and reloaded, O'Malley caught the shoulder holster rig that Cage tossed to her. Her eyes avoided Terri's as she slipped into the leather straps and adjusted the holster until it was comfortable. The closing of the metal snap sounded final to everyone in the room. At a subtle signal from O'Malley, Cage eased her way out of the room.

Terri didn't miss the obvious. She pushed herself out of her seat and walked to the coat rack. Her fingers closed on O'Malley's leather jacket. She stood immobile for a moment, her mind toying with every scenario—good and bad. She heard the sound of boots on the hardwood floor and was not surprised when O'Malley's arms closed around her. The brush of lips on her ear made her shiver.

"I'll be here when you get back from work." O'Malley's voice held a hint of promise. "We still have a lot to learn about each other, Terri Barclay. I plan on learning all I can."

Terri closed her eyes. "That makes two of us, but don't make any promises, O'Malley. Let's just take it as it comes. But so help me, if anything happens to you I'm going to be pissed." There was no teasing or joke in her voice.

O'Malley's eyebrows rose. "I know. I'll be back soon." O'Malley leaned in for one more nuzzle.

After a long moment, O'Malley pulled away reluctantly. Drawing in a deep breath, she turned and walked out the front door and down the steps.

Terri turned away from the window when the SUV turned the

corner. She wrestled with her options. There was a part of her that wanted to make everything but O'Malley go away. Another part of her knew that she was a sworn officer of the law and no matter how much she might want to just hide, she couldn't. She cursed the toll her job took on her life, but she also knew that what she did was more than a job; it came close to being a crusade. The clock loudly ticked away the seconds in the otherwise silent room. Finally she picked up her cell phone. The call was answered on the third ring.

"It's going down tonight at the Dunes. Spyder's buying a shipment of heavy firepower," she said flatly, hating herself as the words passed her lips. "I'll be at Traders until nine." She cut the connection without waiting for George to answer.

Chapter 25

Terri glanced again at the clock on the wall, relieved that she only had five minutes to go in her shift. It seemed to be becoming a habit with her, and she was sure that Maria had noticed. The bar was jumping busy, and the night had been a bartender's nightmare. She was sure that if one more nonregular asked her out, she was going to have to hurt someone or destroy Maria's furniture. She almost cried out in joy when her relief showed up and she was able to pull her cash drawer out of the register.

Recognizing the look on her face as she took the money to Maria's office, the regulars gave her a wide berth. They figured that she and O'Malley had gotten into a spat and they felt sorry for the biker. The look on Terri's face did not bode well for a good night.

Terri counted out her bank in the office, having to check her math three times. Her thoughts were scattered all over the place. She sighed as she heard the office door open. Turning, she expected to find her boss standing there, not two men and one woman in military uniforms, complete with sidearms. Maria trailed behind them using language Terri was sure a mother-to-be wasn't supposed to use.

"Terri Barclay?" one of the soldiers asked in a no-nonsense voice.

She continued to play her role. "Who's asking?" she responded, suspicion in her voice.

"Lieutenant Mueller, Military Intelligence. I will ask you one more time, ma'am. Are you Terri Barclay?"

Terri shrugged. "Never heard of her," she muttered as she picked up her stack of tips.

The lieutenant shook his head. "Sure, and I bet you don't know Callan O'Malley either." There was a measure of disbelief in his tone.

"Look, GI Joe, I'm not who you think I am."

He pulled a photo from his pocket and tossed it on the desk.

Terri's eyes gave nothing away as she recognized the photo. She and O'Malley had been walking around the mall. The photo showed them smiling as they played with ice cream cones. She almost smiled at the fun they'd had that day. Her gaze wandered back up to the soldier.

"Terri Barclay, consider yourself in custody," he stated without any sort of emotion. "You are suspected of aiding and abetting a gunrunning ring that involves stolen military weapons."

Terri's mind blanked out the Miranda warning. There were very few people who knew what O'Malley did for a living. Maria's eyes questioned her, and she subtly shook her head. Whether or not Maria knew, Terri didn't care; she was not about to give her friend up. Not wanting to cause a scene in Maria's bar, she allowed herself to be handcuffed and led out the back door to a waiting unmarked car. The government plates were the only giveaway.

"Where are you taking her?" Maria demanded harshly.

Terri almost laughed. Only Maria would dare to question a military officer with a weapon.

"This is a military matter, ma'am," the lieutenant answered curtly.

Maria's voice reverted back to its command tone. "You better listen up, butter bar. I did twelve years and finished out as a captain in the Air Force. I happen to know military regs, so you'd better start talking before your CO gets a fast phone call." When the lieutenant failed to answer, she fixed the female MP with a withering glare.

"The subject will be taken to the civilian authorities until we can arrange transport," the MP answered. She ignored the stare from the lieutenant. "I will not be busted back down to specialist, sir. Not for Intelligence. I do not break military regs, sir." The female MP turned her attention back to Terri. "In the car, ma'am, and watch your head."

Once Terri was in the car, the female MP buckled her in and slid in beside her. It took only a couple more minutes for the others to follow suit.

Terri watched Maria's worried face as the car pulled out of the parking lot. The only bright side that she could see was that her cover would be safe when she was booked. She half listened to the chatter between the two soldiers in the front seat. She stiffened when they referred to a bust arranged by an undercover intelligence officer.

"So one of your junior spook wannabes is gonna bust this whole thing open?" the MP driving scoffed.

"Don't kid yourself. She's one of the best, and has been for a very long time," the lieutenant boasted, as though it mattered.

The driver laughed. "You hear that, Sarge? A smart spook."

"Shut up, Archer, and just drive." It definitely sounded like an order. The laughter and conversation up front died out fast. The female MP shook her head. For all their training and preaching about operational security, spooks sure did like to talk.

* ~ * ~ * ~ *

Cage pulled the four-wheel-drive knob and waited for a moment before she continued forward. Hearing the hubs lock automatically, she grinned as they rolled through the sand. She glanced at O'Malley and was surprised to see the momentary flicker of fear. She almost kicked herself. She should have known that this location at night might trigger some unpleasant memories.

"You okay, O'Malley?" she asked quietly as she maneuvered the rolls and dips.

"Yeah. Let's just get there and get this over with. Payback's been too long in the making."

It was hard to mistake the cold edge of hatred in her voice. "Hey, just remember: he goes to jail, not the morgue," Cage said.

"I remember." O'Malley turned her face to her friend. "I can't promise it won't happen, but I'll remember." O'Malley's smile was casually chilling, then she turned away to look out the window.

Cage kept her comments to herself, but her mind was rapidly turning over. She was now certain that she was making the right decision. O'Malley was definitely going to be pissed off at her, and her anger would mostly be justified, but if it kept her friend from committing murder, Cage was willing to piss her off.

"What the hell is that?" Cage asked, slowing down and killing her lights.

Ahead of them another vehicle sat in their meeting place. O'Malley quickly opened the glove box and pulled out the small set of binoculars. It took her a second to focus before she could make out Trey and another man whose face she knew. He was surrounded by four men with weapons.

"Looks like Trey is pulling his deal right now," O'Malley muttered. To the right of the deal going down, she noticed movement at the crest of the dune. "Got another player coming in."

"Gimme the glasses," Cage demanded quietly. "Guess the surgery didn't take," she muttered as she refocused the view in the binoculars. "Shit, looks like Boomer. What the hell is he doing here?" She didn't expect an answer. "You feel like screwing up Trey's little party?"

O'Malley thought about the question for all of two seconds. "Why not. It'll give us some pull with Spyder."

With practiced ease they left the truck quietly and each silently checked her weapons, though there was no need; it was just habit. They walked around the dune, checking constantly behind them just in case it was some elaborate trap. Both women listened hard as they sneaked up into position. They heard Boomer interrupt whatever deal was going down.

Cage stepped out into the open, seemingly oblivious to the weapons that swung in her direction. She heard the small snapping sound that signaled to her that O'Malley was going to play hide-and-seek around the dunes until she could get into position behind the armed group.

"Evening, boys," Cage purred with a smile. "Interesting time to show up here."

"Same thing we were thinking," Boomer replied, leaning against Trey's SUV. "Trey, are you fucking up again?" His voice was in no way sympathetic.

To his credit, Trey's voice did not waver. "Who's we?" he shot at Boomer.

"We includes me." Spyder stepped around a dune. He looked at Cjerzoki. "Anton, you know that I own the trade in this town."

The dealer smiled easily. "I sell to whoever has the cash. He's got the cash. I pay you enough of a cut to make sure that happens, Spyder," Cjerzoki reminded him. "Gentlemen, you can lower your guns," he ordered. His men instantly obeyed.

Spyder walked up to Trey, eyeing him warily. "How many keys, Anton?"

"Ten."

Spyder's voice hardened. "Where does a fucking weasel like you get the green for that much white? I know you ain't rich. You live in that shithole, and you don't have shit for money since you lost Terri."

"Fuck you." Trey stripped off his colors. "I ain't part of your fuck-ups anymore. I don't answer to you anymore."

Spyder laughed and suddenly backhanded Trey, then watched as his former associate bounced against the grill of the SUV.

"That had to hurt," Cage muttered without sympathy.

"Looks like it," Boomer agreed.

"Anton, this deal is over. You can leave the white as your apology," Spyder ordered without taking his eyes off Trey.

Anton and his men stiffened. "That's not how it works, Spyder. He made this deal."

"And he's a dead man," Spyder promised solemnly.

"What makes you think you aren't?" the drug dealer returned hotly.

"Because I'm standing behind you and your boys, Anton," O'Malley announced calmly as she stepped into view. Her Sig was pointed at the drug dealer. "I don't care about your little deal with that fuckhead over there, but you're cutting into my time with Spyder. Besides, if you kill him, I don't get my money. I can't let that happen."

Boomer smiled as all the players in their little game were now accounted for. "Hey, Spyder, why don't we all just chill for a minute?" He spoke the signal over his wire, loud and clear.

"I'm cool. I just want what's mine. You can understand that, can't you, Anton?" Spyder smiled and almost looked like a normal human being.

Cjerzoki said nothing. Chancing a look behind him, he saw that Boomer and the woman standing close to him were armed. They had him and his men in a cross fire. At the small flick of his hand, his men lowered their weapons a second time.

"You do know that this will jeopardize our future working relationship," he said, defeated. He could find other clubs to sell his drugs to, but few had the kind of money Spyder did.

"DEA! Everyone drop your weapons and get your hands in the air." A loud booming voice cut into the conversation, and shadowy figures in DEA windbreakers filtered over and around the dunes, weapons drawn and aimed.

For a long moment, everyone froze in surprise. At a subtle nod from their boss, Cjerzoki's men dropped their weapons and lifted their hands in the air. Spyder bolted in one direction as Cage motioned to O'Malley. O'Malley reached Cage as Boomer tackled his assignment, hard. Cage pulled out her military badge and flicked it open.

"Military Intelligence. You are under arrest, O'Malley," Cage announced officially, and watched the betrayal register in her eyes. "Drop your weapon."

Another voice boomed—"Police. No one move"—and chaos broke out.

Instead of following directions, two people took advantage of the confusion. Spyder flipped Boomer off him and took off like the devil was after him. O'Malley planted her shoulder in Cage's mid-section, bowling her over, then disappeared into the dark like she had been trained to.

∼∼*∼*

George moved quickly through the hallway to central booking. For a moment he was glad that he had followed his instinct and placed a tail on his favorite undercover cop. He'd gotten the phone call less than five minutes after she'd been removed from the bar by the military. His only hope was that he could catch up to Terri before they started to process her. Her ID and badge were in his coat pocket. He hoped it would be all he needed to get her out of the hands of the military.

Turning a sharp corner, he came on the booking counter and halted in his tracks. Three uniformed soldiers were doing their best to convince Terri to just go along with the program and quit putting up a fuss. If things hadn't been so serious, he would have laughed. Instead he pushed his way through the group and stood protectively in front of his officer.

"This is not a booking," he grunted at the booking officer as he shoved his ID forward.

The military intelligence officer stepped forward, not about to lose one of the most important arrests of his fledgling career. "That's where you're wrong."

George shoved Terri's credentials in his face and gloated. "She's undercover, you idiot. Now get those cuffs off her," he demanded hotly. Turning his attention to Terri, he could see the tight control she was exerting over her temper. "You okay?"

"No," she answered through gritted teeth as the female MP unlocked the cuffs and replaced them in the carry case. "Thank you. Now get the fuck out of my way." She pushed past the group with George in tow. "Where is it all at?"

George blew out a deep breath. "Most of the players are being rounded up now. Terri, slow down."

Something in his tone caused her to stop instantly and turn to face him slowly. "What is it?" She couldn't help the slight tremble in her voice.

"Spyder and O'Malley got away."

For a moment, she was quiet. "Shit. She's going to go after him," Terri muttered, and her head snapped up as though someone had hit her. She pulled her cell phone from her pocket and dialed as quickly as she could, her feet already taking her closer to the door. "Come on, answer," she pleaded, as George followed her out the doors of the station.

"Quinn." Cage sounded as frazzled as Terri felt.

"It's Terri. I know who you are, Cage. Now tell me where Spyder might run to," she demanded as George tossed her the keys. She listened to Cage explain where they'd already looked. "Damn it, Cage, think harder. She's going after him, and I don't know that she won't kill him."

Suddenly a thought hit her. *Why would a cop call the cops if she was a cop?* Sometimes the most obvious was the forgotten choice. She turned to look at George. "Do we have anyone at the clubhouse?"

"I can check." He grabbed the car mike and called the question in to the station. They both heard the negative answer.

"Cage, he's gotta be at the clubhouse. You have everywhere else covered and I'll bet anything he's there. We're on it." She cut the connection and turned the engine over. She never heard the curses coming from the cops she almost ran over in the process of peeling out of the parking lot.

~~*~*

Spyder pulled the plastic-wrapped cash from the back of the beer cooler and stuffed it in the saddlebag on the floor. He didn't bother to count it; he didn't have the time. He knew more than one way out of town. A sound caught his attention and he turned quickly. Instead of a threat, he saw only the empty room of the club-house bar. He shook his head. He'd survived so long because he was paranoid as hell. Picking up his bag, he walked softly to the windows to look outside. He slowly scanned the parking lot and grassy area and did not find anything out of place.

He walked quietly to the door and eased his way out. He scanned the grounds repeatedly as his feet carried him closer to his bike. *I'm not going to get caught unawares this time.* He was still seething at not having picked Boomer out as a narc. He vowed to get back at the weasel when the time was right. He settled the saddlebags and quickly straddled his bike. When he turned the key and hit the start button, nothing happened. He tried again and cursed softly at the same result. With the toe of his boot, he eased out the kick-start bar. He lunged down on the metal bar again and again, his frustration rising each time the engine failed to turn over.

"You kind of need this." O'Malley's soft voice caught him by surprise. He looked up to find her holding the ignition coil in her hand and opened his mouth to speak.

* ~ * ~ * ~ *

O'Malley's boot sole caught him midchest and cut off his words. She settled from the spinning back kick and watched him lying on the ground, one leg propping up the machine and keeping it from falling on him. She leaned her hand on the seat with a slow smile and dropped the purloined part on his chest.

"Did ya miss me?" she asked without a trace of sincerity.

"Are you fucking crazy? I don't have time for this shit. The cops—" he began as his leg trembled.

"Yes, I am crazy, and I know about the cops, I just don't care." For the first time in three years her words to him were completely honest. "You took from me, so I'm gonna take from you."

"What the fuck are you talking about? Get this goddamn bike off me," he demanded, trying to push the bike forward.

"Moody Gap, Spyder," O'Malley said as she pressed harder on the bike.

"You're tied in knots for some whore who didn't have the brains to know her place?" he asked, almost laughing.

O'Malley pushed hard on the bike and ignored his scream of pain when it crashed down on his legs a second later. Emotionless, she crouched down beside his head.

"I feel sorry for that girl, I really do. She was running from something and found something even worse. But to tell you the truth, she was the lucky one. They say she died on impact." She tapped his forehead, forcing him to look at her and not concentrate on his pain. "I'm more concerned with the other woman in the car that night."

"Nosy...bitch should have...stayed out of...my business."

O'Malley leaned close to his ear. "She was my wife." She eased back to watch the realization cross his face. "My friends made me promise that I wouldn't send you to the morgue. They didn't mention anything about the hospital," she said as she stood. Without warning, she jumped up in the air and let all her weight drop on the motorcycle that trapped the biker. Oddly, his screams were not satisfying. She jumped up again.

* ~ * ~ * ~ *

Terri pulled the sedan into the parking lot and slammed on her brakes. For a moment, neither she nor George could make sense of what they were seeing. None of the scenarios they had talked about had included O'Malley playing springboard on a Harley with Spyder trapped underneath. As much as Terri didn't want to, she knew she had to pull O'Malley off the bastard. She slipped the chain holding her badge over her head and bolted out of the sedan. Dashing the short distance to O'Malley, she pulled her weapon. She didn't think she'd need it, but she never liked to take chances. She could hear George behind her, announcing their presence. When O'Malley gave no indication of hearing him, Terri ran even faster.

"Stop where you are, O'Malley," she ordered in her best cop tone. When O'Malley kept jumping on the bike and Spyder kept whimpering in pain, Terri moved in closer and pressed the barrel of her pistol against the back of the biker's head.

O'Malley felt the cold metal and reacted instinctively. Her hand kicked back and up, wrapping around the wrist holding the weapon. In the time it took her to blink, she had the weapon in one hand and was holding it on the person who had been wielding it. She took in the sight of Terri in her grasp, the badge hanging in the middle of her chest. She stepped off the bike, which forced Terri to move back.

"You're a fucking cop?" O'Malley demanded, sounding every bit as stunned as she looked.

"State police investigator," Terri corrected tightly around the pain in her wrist. "Let go, O'Malley."

"Drop the gun, O'Malley!" George shouted as he settled into a shooting stance. "Release Officer Barclay."

"At least you used your real name." O'Malley's voice was brittle. She turned her attention to George. "Can't shoot me without chancing a hit on her."

Terri tried. "Don't do this, O'Malley. Ellen—"

"Didn't lie to me. She didn't betray me. It seems that you did." O'Malley leaned in close. "Whose idea was it to fuck me, Terri, yours or your boss's? You know, it doesn't matter. You want me to tell him how good you are at your job? You definitely fucked my mind. I never saw it. Congratulations," she sneered.

Whatever Terri was going to say was lost when O'Malley shoved her, hard. Terri hit the ground and looked up to find herself staring at the hubcaps of an SUV. It took a second for her to register the slamming of doors and Cage's voice shouting orders at the ex-soldier.

Cage took a protective stance in front of Terri, her eyes and weapon trained on O'Malley. "Terri, you and your boss need to get out of here," Cage said, low enough so that Terri was the only one who heard.

"This is my bust, Cage," Terri bluffed. She didn't want the bust; she didn't want anything except to make sure O'Malley didn't kill anyone or get herself killed while being taken into custody.

"Listen to me, Terri. You slept with a suspect. That alone would kill this bust. With that information, everyone connected might walk. And quite honestly, there is more going on here than I can tell you about. You just have to trust me. Please." There was a quiet pleading in Cage's voice. "Because of who she used to be, I have to be the one to bring her in."

Terri watched O'Malley move restlessly, as if contemplating escape. Terri made her decision and walked slowly back toward George until she reached his side.

It took a moment before he lowered his weapon. He didn't like it, but one more look at Terri's expression convinced him that he had no choice. Together they turned their backs and walked away.

Terri felt everything inside turn to a quivering mass as George pulled the sedan out of the parking lot.

* ~ * ~ * ~ *

Cage let out a slow breath when the sedan finally left the area. Something in her brain told her that the easy part was over. *Oh, this might hurt,* her ever-helpful brain supplied with something close to dread. She stepped out to the front of the SUV, still aiming her weapon at O'Malley. A quick glance at Boomer told her that he had her back.

"Hated to do it this way, O'Malley, but I had no other choice," Cage called out as she moved forward. "Boomer, no matter what, don't shoot her." She whispered the order and watched him nod slowly.

O'Malley shifted her confiscated pistol to Cage. "Which master do you really serve, Cage?"

"Can't tell you that. It's over, Callan. Drop the gun," she ordered softly as she moved closer. "I know you don't want to shoot me."

After a long silence, O'Malley let out a sigh. "No, I don't. It would break Thomas's heart." She almost smiled.

O'Malley stood still for a moment, then let the semiautomatic pistol fall to the asphalt. As Cage's eyes followed the weapon, O'Malley lunged and made contact. She planted her shoulder into Cage's chest and drove her backward. Cage hit the ground and let her momentum help her flip over and back onto her feet. O'Malley hadn't anticipated the move and was still moving forward when Cage's fist caught her on the chin.

Rage kept her from going down. She drove her knee into Cage's midsection, grabbed her shoulders and spun them back toward the vehicle. She advanced cautiously this time, knowing that Cage was indeed well trained. She wasn't expecting Cage to stomp on her foot, so she was surprised when she felt the punch to her stomach that ripped her breath away. As soon as Cage's fingers tightened in her hair, O'Malley knew what was going to happen.

Cage bounced O'Malley's head off the hood of the SUV and watched her slide to the ground, a trail of blood following her. Cage sucked in several harsh breaths. Looking around quickly, she saw that Boomer was already moving to Spyder. It took a minute to shift the Harley off him, and then the DEA agent rolled the biker onto his stomach to cuff him. Cage and Boomer both ignored the renewed screams of pain. It did her heart good to see Spyder caught, Boomer's knee digging into his back as he was read his rights. Without one shred of satisfaction, she pulled O'Malley's arms behind her back and cuffed her. Leaning against the SUV, she finally caught her breath.

Boomer walked over and settled next to her. He pulled out a cigarette and lit it slowly. "She's gonna be pissed when she wakes up," he said dryly.

"Yeah. Think I broke her nose again."

"Don't let Terri know that. She just might kill you."

"You're just full of good news, aren't you?" Cage almost laughed. "It was better this way. We gotta get them to the emergency room. You want to call in the ambulance?" she asked. She hesitated, then added, "See you later?"

"I think I've got paperwork 'til the Second Coming, but give me a call on my cell. I might be able to cut free for some food later if you're up to it."

"Why do I think this is gonna be a long night?" Cage asked.

"It's gonna get worse before it gets better," Boomer predicted with a frown.

"Tell me about it."

~~*~*

Terri watched as the parade of prisoners continued. In the last several hours since George confirmed her status and all hell had broken loose, she had seen the results of the multijurisdictional effort. She recognized five city leaders, at least ten police officers—including Bates—and several prominent citizens as they were marched in and booked. Each time the booking door opened she held her breath, expecting to see O'Malley. So far she had been disappointed. Her ears still rang from the things O'Malley had said to her. In her heart she knew that she had deserved some of it, but not all. She wanted to explain and she wanted to kick O'Malley's ass at the same time. Not having either option, she merely let out a low sigh.

George handed over a Styrofoam cup filled with hot coffee and sank down next to her. For a while, neither one said a word. Finally George gathered his courage and leaned forward and touched her knee. When she turned to face him, he said, "The Army boys just reported that they're pulling out with one prisoner in tow."

Terri's heart seized. "Who?"

"No word, and no word on where they're going."

Terri leaned back in her chair. "I'm going to O'Malley's. If you need me, call me."

"I can't let you do that; not everyone's been rounded up. We have a safe house set up. I'll take you there."

Terri nodded. "I'm not gonna find out where they took her, am I?"

He owed it to her to answer honestly. "I don't know, Terri. The Army, they do things their own way. C'mon, we're both going to be up to our asses in paperwork hell for the next week at least."

Epilogue

For the millionth time, Terri readjusted the light jacket that accessorized her dress. In the room full of police brass and dignitaries, she felt like an outsider. She was convinced that if she had to smile and shake one more hand, she was going to scream. Part of her decided that if sitting through the dog-and-pony show was a part of a job well done, she would rather have failed. It only confirmed that she was just a cop and would never be one of those big brass officers who could play politics.

It had been a long and difficult five months. When the videotape was aired, the DEA had taken a major black eye for not moving on Spyder sooner. Hank had rolled over hard on his former boss, and both of them were getting used to spending life in the same prison. Most of Spyder's boys had turned state's evidence. Trey, however, had kept his mouth shut and was probably not having a great time behind bars, since his status as a cop had come out early in the media frenzy. Terri had been spared having to testify, since they had the other evidence, but the reunion with her mother had been delayed even though they spoke frequently on the phone. Just as important, she had also been unable to find out anything about O'Malley. Every question and every inquiry had been stopped cold. She could still see those eyes shift from ice blue to a color that she would never be able to describe.

George sat next to her and handed her another mixed drink. She was pushing her limit and they both knew it. Neither cop cared. They just sat there drinking and watching important people fall all over themselves taking credit. They passed the time between dinner and the awards presentation by making snide comments to each other, just out of earshot of anyone who might matter. Occasionally they would have to interrupt the running dialogue to smile or pose for an official picture. Snickering together, they missed most of the presentation.

Terri did sit up and take notice when she saw a figure in full US Army dress blues go forward to accept a special award for under-cover work. She blinked twice, and for a second could not believe that it was Sean who was standing at the podium.

"He cleans up pretty good, huh?" Joan's voice sounded just to her left.

"So, how's Cage?" Terri couldn't help the cutting edge to her voice. She saw the wounded expression for just a second before Joan covered it up.

"Cage is Cage. We don't know where she is right now. How are you?" Joan asked in all sincerity. "We tried to get hold of you, but you were unavailable, as they put it." Joan sat down next to Terri and pointed to the podium. "Before you judge, you should hear it all."

Terri turned her head to watch if not to truly listen. She had to admit that Sean did look good in his dark blue uniform with its gold trim. The four rows of ribbons seemed to give him an importance, as did the chevrons and rocker on his sleeves.

"Several years ago, there was an Air Force officer who stopped by to visit an old friend. On her way out of town she picked up a hitchhiker, a woman running for her life. They both died that night as a result of being run off the road at Moody's Gap. Those of us who knew her, who loved her, and whom she healed, knew we couldn't just sit back and do nothing. We had rumors and smoke to go on. It took two of our best to find out the rest of the truth." Sean paused to take a sip of his water.

"Captain Cage Quinn of Military Intelligence couldn't be here tonight, but rest assured that she was an integral part of taking down Spyder Williams. It was her information that led us to know he was buying stolen military weapons. And we have plenty of weapons in the Army." Sean smiled his boyish smile, which evoked the desired laughter.

"All we needed was one individual who was stupid enough to go undercover for an undetermined amount of time. Fortunately, she had been dropped on her head enough times to not know exactly what we had in mind." The little boy gave way to evil Sean. "Ladies and gentlemen, I would like to introduce the woman who made this justice possible: Sergeant First Class C. G. O'Malley."

Sean stepped away from the mike and had to wait for a moment until O'Malley emerged in her dress blues, a stoic look plastered on her face. A collective gasp rose from the gathered crowd. They had known her as a freelance biker, a womanizer, and a hard drinker who pissed everyone off. As it sank in what O'Malley had given up to bring Spyder to justice, the applause began and it swelled for several moments.

When the applause died down, O'Malley did not move from her spot. Everyone noticed the confused look on Sean's face as he stared at her. When it became obvious that O'Malley was not going to play her part, Sean stepped back up to the mike.

"Ellen Rivers was an angel to a lot of us. One night in February of 1991, we ran over a land mine planted by Iraqi forces. We were hurt, and she helped heal our wounds and our souls," Sean said with a weak smile.

"When she died, we couldn't rest without making it right. Her killers have been brought to justice, and anything we suffered was small in comparison to that accomplishment. I would like to thank Terri Barclay for her efforts in the investigation. If she had not led us to vital information, we would never have broken this case. In Special Investigator Barclay, you have someone who cares more for the people she serves than for herself. Both you and she should be proud of that. Terri, those of us who knew Ellen can only say one thing: thank you." Sean turned away from the microphone.

Terri sank down in her chair, stunned. For five months she had pictured the worst possible things happening to O'Malley. It was astonishing to have her there in person, looking entirely too good as Sean was singing her praises. Terri didn't hear the applause meant for her, nor did she see Joan leave her seat. She flinched when a warm hand touched her shoulder. Instinctively, she knew who was standing behind her and she did not turn around.

Terri barely managed to retain control. "You have one hell of a lot of nerve. You accused me of betraying you, and I won't even mention what else you said to me."

"What do you say we get out of here?" O'Malley asked quietly. "I can explain almost everything then."

"Why not explain right here?"

"Because that would take more than a week." O'Malley smiled gently. "Just give me ten minutes. If you don't believe me, I'll walk out that door and I swear I will never bother you again."

"I thought the worst had happened to you," Terri said bluntly.

"It did. Cage kicked my ass and broke my nose again." O'Malley could tell by Terri's silence that she had crashed and burned. "I can explain if you'll let me, but I won't beg you to listen."

Terri nodded once and rose, then walked toward a more private part of the room as George ran interference with well-wishers. Terri halted once she was sure that there would be no one there to listen in on their conversation. She turned on her heel and glared at the woman she'd gotten to know as a biker. Her biker.

Terri watched O'Malley for a long time. The woman simply stood still in front of her, holding her tongue, looking as if she was having difficulty finding the words she wanted to say. She had never seen O'Malley look so unsure. Even if it was a smart-ass remark, she had always had words to the ready.

Finally Terri took a breath, a chance. "What's that ribbon?" She pointed to one of the military awards.

O'Malley looked down. "That one is the Purple Heart."

"And that one?" Terri asked.

"That one is the Silver Star."

"What do you get that for?"

"Not staying home when you should have." O'Malley's voice held no teasing. "I should have called you, Terri, but part of me was scared to death."

"Why?"

"Because I didn't know if what we had was real, and I wanted it to be real," O'Malley said quietly, staring at her hands.

"So you stayed away for five months? I don't know if I should be insulted or if I should believe you." Terri took a deep breath. "The things I said to you, I meant. The things I did with you and let you do with me, I meant. The one thing I didn't tell you, I couldn't. It works both ways, O'Malley. You never told me who you were, either."

"Like you said, it works both ways. I thought you were just another biker chick. I couldn't tell you even when I wanted to, and then I couldn't tell you because it would have hurt you or gotten you hurt."

Terri wasn't going to fold quite so quickly. "From the look on your face, I'm guessing there's more."

"That night...Cage betrayed me. I think she knew I might kill Spyder, so she changed the game plan. When they put me in a military jail, they believed that I really was a gunrunner, and she let them think it for several days. Fun was not had by all. Today I can admit that she was right, but that night I wouldn't have. All I knew then was that she sold me out, and then you come along with the cavalry, only you're wearing a badge. My mouth overloaded my brain," O'Malley said with quiet honesty.

"Is that it?" Terri demanded.

It took O'Malley several very long moments to answer. "It feels like I've been a soldier all my life, Terri. All I can do is fall on my sword and tell you I'm sorry. Those aren't easy words for me, and what I need to know is if you think...if you want to give this...us a chance. I do this knowing that you will most likely just decide to walk, and honestly, I'm not sure I'd blame you."

Terri took an equally long time to answer. "Only one way to find out, O'Malley."

"And that is?" the soldier asked.

"What's your middle name?" Terri asked in all seriousness.

"I'll tell you if you have dinner with me," O'Malley promised.

Terri smiled. "I have to warn you, Callan G. O'Malley, I'm an expensive date."

"I think I can cover it." O'Malley spoke her heart. "You know, I would kiss you right now, but I think your fellow officers would have a heart attack."

Terri snorted. "What about your people?"

"Them? I retired last week. This monkey suit is to make the brass happy." There was no missing the genuinely mischievous glint in her eyes.

Terri smiled and leaned in close. "That makes me very happy." She pressed her lips gently against O'Malley's. For the first time in months, she felt like she was home.

* ~ * ~ * ~ *

O'Malley finished ordering and handed the menu back to the waiter, certain that the eyes of the other patrons were on her. She knew that a soldier in a dress blue uniform was not the norm in the hotel restaurant.

"A little uncomfortable, O'Malley?" Terri asked after surrendering her own menu. She draped the napkin over her lap.

"Well, to tell the truth I feel like I'm in a fishbowl. I'm not used to being stared at like this," O'Malley said as she fidgeted with the silverware.

"You didn't get stared at when you've been at your Army dinners?" Terri asked with an amused smile.

"Hell no. Who pays attention to some lowly sergeant? The gawking started when the general's wife walked in," O'Malley answered with a grin. She leaned forward. "Tell me what's been going on in your life for the last five months."

Terri let out a low breath. "Are you sure you want to know?"

"Yes. I've missed so much about you, and I know that's my fault. I hope you can forgive me."

"We have a lot to talk about, O'Malley, and I would venture that we have a lot to shout about. You hurt me five months ago with your words, but right now, with you here in front of me, I can let that go for a little while." Terri took a sip of her water.

"My mom and I talk on the phone all the time. With some luck we're going to get together next month. And before you say a word, the delay was not your fault. With her schedule and mine, it just hasn't worked out. George knows that I'm going to castrate him if he doesn't give me some vacation time very soon."

It took a moment, but O'Malley nodded. "I'll just have to accept that one. What else?"

"Would you believe I've been in paperwork hell?" Terri almost smiled, but it was the truth.

O'Malley laughed. "I think I can relate. The day I actually cleared out my office, I was still finishing the paperwork on my last case."

"Do you miss it?" Terri suddenly asked in a soft tone.

"Parts of it, yes, but not at five in the morning when my old unit is out running and I'm in bed, nice and toasty warm." O'Malley's smile was malevolent.

Terri laughed out loud and leaned back. "Somehow I can believe that, but tell me honestly, why did you retire?"

O'Malley sucked in a breath and looked away. "To tell you the truth, I'm tired of going to lousy places in the world where people are trying to ventilate my body. Twice is enough in my book. At least in Bosnia I didn't get hit, but I want to keep breathing so I can prove to you that I'm going to stay around."

Terri reached across the table and wrapped her fingers around O'Malley's. "Good. I'm sure this is selfish on my part, but I want you next to me when I yell at you, when I smile at you, and when I come around your fingers."

O'Malley was grateful that she hadn't taken a drink of water. "You haven't changed, you know that? Always saying shit that takes me by surprise."

"Are you complaining?" Terri laughed. "I'm being honest here, Callan."

"I'm sorry that I hurt you," O'Malley said suddenly. "I know I'll never be able to make that time up to you, but I couldn't stay away any longer." She looked up to find Terri's eyes. "I don't want to stay away anymore."

"I don't want you to stay away, either. Now quit with the kicking yourself in the ass. That's my job. We both admit mistakes were made and go from there."

O'Malley laughed and felt the weight fall away from her shoulders. "I think I can do that."

"Good, so tell me more. What are you doing now? How is everyone?" Terri's questions came in a rapid-fire sequence.

O'Malley shook her head as she chuckled. "Right now I'm just taking some downtime. The last five months have been an adventure, to say the least. I went from being basically on my own to having to act like a soldier again. Five a.m. is such an ungodly hour. Then there was all the paperwork and the legal hoops I had to jump through concerning the case. They were definitely not happy that I broke our suspect; it was touch and go there for a while concerning possible disciplinary action. In the end they couldn't prove I meant to do it, so they just stuck me behind a desk until they could figure out some place to send me. I beat them to the punch with my request for early retirement."

She took a breath. "Maria and Gato are good; she's getting to look like a small beach ball on legs these days."

"I'm going to tell her you said that," Terri threatened with a laugh. "I've seen them both recently. My boss and I took them to dinner about a month ago."

"I'm glad you keep in touch with her. She's a special lady."

Terri nodded. "Yeah, she really is. You should have seen her that night up that Intelligence guy's ass. I didn't figure out that she was military until late in the case."

"Former military. She was Ellen's boss in Germany. After she met Gato, the Air Force no longer meant as much to her anymore. He was a civilian contractor and they literally bumped into each other one day. Once she was done yelling at him, he asked her out. The rest, as they say, is history."

Terri briefly wondered how she and O'Malley would describe their beginning to others. "Now that's romantic. What a great story to tell their son someday."

"A girl, we're having a girl," O'Malley insisted stubbornly.

Terri couldn't help smiling. "Callan, it's going to be one or the other, and if the kid is a boy I don't want you to be disappointed."

"I won't be, really. I just don't want him to look like Gato," O'Malley said with a sheepish smile. "Sean and Joan are good. He's getting out, too, by the way."

"Why the sudden rush to get out? I thought he was happy in the Army."

O'Malley subtly looked around. "Between you and me?" When Terri nodded, she continued. "Cage still has some friends in the Pentagon and when she gets them drunk enough, they give her the heads-up on stuff. Let's just say the new guy in the White House has a major hard-on to rip a certain dictator in the Middle East a new asshole. I'm not saying it's the truth, but neither of us wants to take the chance. We talked about it, and we aren't going back to war for that family. I don't even know how he would pull it off. It's not like we can just kick in a door. That would piss off a lot of countries, not to mention the UN. If I ever go back to war, it's going to be for a better reason."

O'Malley fell silent and suddenly wondered if she had revealed too much of herself. The feeling passed just as quickly as it had surfaced when she looked into Terri's face. She found no judgment or recrimination, just understanding.

"Any idea what he and Joan are going to do?" Terri asked.

"Well, funny you should ask." O'Malley smiled. "Joan is taking a job at a hospital in Montana. Sean is looking at joining the police department there."

"Montana?" Terri gasped. "I'm envisioning visions of Popsicles in jackets."

O'Malley snickered. "Yeah, I had the same reaction. Joan is Lakota and they both want to be closer to her family, but not *that* close, you know?"

Terri was about to respond with one of her trademark smart-ass comments when their dinner arrived. Her mouth watered at the sight of the perfectly pink salmon she had ordered. For a few minutes they ate in silence until the initial edge of hunger had been dulled.

"By the way," Terri began, "my mother asked me to thank you if I ever saw you again."

"Thank me for what?"

"For what you did when my father called," Terri answered. "She loved it."

O'Malley paled. "You didn't tell her all of it, did you?"

"Of course I did. Why wouldn't I, *Daddy*?"

O'Malley dropped her fork. *This woman is gonna be the death of me.* "You are an evil woman, Terri Barclay," she said, knowing full well that her boxers were now soaked.

"You know, Joan once told me that you were like two people. There's Callan, who is the softer, gentler side of you, and there's O'Malley, the badass bad boy. Do you think that's true?" Terri pushed her plate aside and sipped on her wine.

"Sometimes," O'Malley had to admit, unable to determine of the purpose of the question.

"Good, because I love both sides of you. I was introduced to O'Malley, and then I learned who Callan was. I love both sides, but right now I want to come *to* your bed and come *in* your bed."

Terri's gaze never wavered. She removed the napkin from her lap and slowly settled it on the table. "Pay the bill, O'Malley."

O'Malley reached into her back pocket and drew out her wallet. She took her time in taking out a hundred dollar bill, which she tucked under a corner of her plate. Sure that she was going to have a good rest of the night, she felt like sharing the wealth with what would be a happy waiter. Reaching across the table, she took Terri's hand and stood.

They both ignored the overt stares of curiosity and hostility as they walked out of the restaurant. O'Malley chuckled inwardly as an older man began to sit forward to say something, then halted when he caught sight of her ribbons and medals and sank back. His actions indicated that either he was a vet or he knew someone who was, and he'd recognized that she was no weekend warrior. She nodded her head in his direction, a sly smile on her face.

Neither woman said a word as they waited for the elevator, both lost in memories of the times they had shared a bed and their bodies. After a few moments, they were joined by an older woman. She took in O'Malley's uniform and war patch.

"First Cavalry, huh? My grandson was 101st in the Persian Gulf." Her voice was smug.

"I played with them too—dopes on a rope." O'Malley grinned as the woman's eyes lost their superior glaze. "Hope he made it home."

"Oh, he did." She eyed the crossed pistols on O'Malley's lapels. "MP? My Robert was an MP in World War II." She turned and looked at Terri. "And what do you do, dear?"

"I'm a state cop, ma'am," Terri answered, a little in awe of the woman whose family had given so much.

"Well then, I'm feeling much safer." She chuckled as the elevator doors opened.

O'Malley held her arm across the doors as first the older woman and then Terri entered the elevator. She stepped in and punched the button for her floor, noticing that another button was lit. The car lurched upward.

"I hope you don't mind me saying so, but you make a striking couple," the older woman said with a smile. "Don't ever let small minds make you feel like you don't count. My grandson and his partner are happy, and that's all I can ask for." At the surprise evident on their faces, she added, "Thought I was going to be like the others, didn't you?"

"Yes, ma'am," Terri answered. "But I'm learning that sometimes assumptions can be wrong."

"Would you mind telling me how you two met? I love to hear how couples got their start. I may be getting old, but romance is still fun. I met my Robert when I was a nurse on a hospital ship. Old fool got himself shot one day. Of course, back then he was a young fool." Her mischievous smile was infectious.

"If you're keeping track of the most unusual initial encounters, I think we go to the top of your list. She won me in some stupid biker game," Terri supplied with a smile.

"She what?"

Terri chuckled. O'Malley wanted to melt into the carpet.

"It's a long story, ma'am, but if you join us for a late lunch tomorrow, I'll tell you all about it," Terri offered.

"Call me Doris. I'm in room 1986. Just call my room and I'll meet you. This story I want to hear." Doris looked at O'Malley. "Quit turning red. MPs are never embarrassed and they never retreat."

O'Malley stiffened her spine. "No, ma'am. We just commit a tactical advance in the opposite direction." She chuckled. "Lunch it is then. Our treat."

Doris shook her head. "Oh no, I couldn't do that."

"Yeah, you can. There's no way an MP's wife is going to pay for her own lunch while she sits at *my* table."

There was no arguing with the tone of O'Malley's voice. Doris looked over to Terri with a knowing smile. "Get used to that possessive thing. MPs are like that."

Terri matched the smile. "Somehow, Doris, I don't think I'm going to mind."

There was a freshness and charm about the older woman that made Terri and O'Malley want to keep in touch with her. The three spent the remainder of their shared ride exchanging contact information. When the doors opened to let Doris off on her floor, they were all a little disappointed until she flashed a smile and reminded them of their lunch date.

"She's a trip." Terri snuggled into O'Malley's arms. "Are you sorry that I invited her to lunch?"

O'Malley wrapped her arms around Terri and felt a wave of security hit her. "Not at all. She seems like she could be worth all the hell I'm gonna catch when she hears the whole story."

"Hey, look at the bright side. You get a new MP friend out of it." Terri's words were teasing, and so were her hands as she opened the buttons of O'Malley's uniform jacket.

"Terri, you keep that up and you're going to get more of O'Malley than you expected in the elevator."

"To quote Cage Quinn, 'killjoy.'" Terri stood up as tall as she could and pressed her lips to O'Malley's. "I'll take whatever you give me."

By way of answer, O'Malley pushed Terri against the wall of the elevator and ravished her mouth. Her world tunneled down to warm supple lips that were her path to salvation. She teased and promised at the same time. Five months of want and denial rose to a crest and fell over the banks. Her hands easily tugged open Terri's jacket and then she abruptly stopped when her eyes rested on the gold chain around Terri's neck.

"You still wear it." Her tone was a mixture of disbelief and pleasure.

"You gave it to me, of course I wear it," Terri managed just before she drew her lover down for another kiss.

"I want you so bad," O'Malley moaned between kisses.

Twenty seconds later, the ding signaled the arrival of the elevator at O'Malley's floor and the doors opened. Without a word, the former soldier took Terri's hand and led her out of the elevator and down the hall to her door. She pulled the key card out of her inside jacket pocket, then before swiping it, she took a long look at the woman she loved.

"I'm not changing my mind, Callan G. O'Malley, so just get rid of whatever that thought was." Terri punctuated her statement with a light kiss and stepped back a little. "Now open that door and prove to me how much you want me."

Like any good soldier, O'Malley did as she was ordered. She held the door open and watched Terri walk in, her gaze fixed on a perfectly shaped ass. She had to withhold a whistle as she stepped into her room, closed the door, and then turned the dead bolt.

Terri ignored the décor of the room and turned to face the woman who was her love, her life. "What do you want, O'Malley? 'Cause I know what I want."

O'Malley felt her bad boy side take over and she didn't fight it. "I want you." She stepped forward, shedding her uniform jacket as she moved, letting it drop to the floor.

"How?" Terri whispered as she watched light blue eyes turn impossibly dark.

"Any way you ask me for, every way that will make you scream my name when you come, over and over again," Callan promised as she stalked.

Terri knew she was playing with fire and she didn't care. She wanted to experience all the flame that was O'Malley and Callan, knew that if she pushed the right buttons she would have both. There was a certain appeal to having Callan make love to her, but for the moment, the allure of O'Malley claiming her was stronger. Not submissive by nature, Terri still wanted the ex-soldier to own her, and she knew that if she asked on another day, she would have her chance to own O'Malley. It was give-and-take with them, even if O'Malley didn't know it.

"Then take me, I'm yours," Terri said as she stood before her.

O'Malley sat and her voice was raspy as she said, "Strip for me."

As she watched, Terri didn't speak, she didn't think, she just moved. Slowly, she removed each article of clothing and let it fall to her feet. When the cool air of the room made her shiver, she stepped in front of her soldier and pressed her body close. Her fingers moved with purpose, divesting O'Malley of the trappings of service until every bit of skin was exposed, and then she kissed her lover.

O'Malley took several moments to study the warm body that she had missed so very much for the last several months. Strong muscle was disguised by soft skin, and she loved the contrast. Her fingers massaged and rediscovered places that caused gasps of pleasure.

When Terri took her hand and led her to the bed, O'Malley followed willingly. As Terri settled herself on the mattress, she whispered into the near dark, "I love you and I want you. I don't know any other way to let you know what I feel."

"You show me every time you let me touch you, Terri." O'Malley touched and stroked the flesh that was hers for the taking and let out a low moan. "I will take you," she said as her lips played with an earlobe.

"Promises, promises." Terri chuckled and then lost her breath when her thighs were parted suddenly.

"Believe this promise." O'Malley brushed her hand between Terri's open legs as she settled in. She groaned at the feel of wet flesh and a hard clit. Her fingers stroked lips and a hard bundle of nerves. She was loving every minute of it and she was not about to stop. "You are mine," she panted.

"Yes, I am," Terri gasped when O'Malley's fingers spread and filled her. She arched hard and brought her body down forcefully, wanting more. "I'm yours," she promised. "Mark me, love."

O'Malley sucked on the soft skin of Terri's neck and marked the woman under her as asked, as begged. If she lived for a hundred years, she would mark Terri as hers each and every night she was asked. Adding another finger, she gave her lover what she wanted.

"Oh, Goddess!" Terri groaned with pleasure; she was so close to falling over. Her nipple was sucked into a warm and eager mouth and added to her sensory overload. She groaned with disappointment when O'Malley left her nipple. Her disappointment quickly turned to anticipation as she felt her lover kissing and licking her way down.

O'Malley slid her body between Terri's legs without slowing the thrusts of her fingers. She was not surprised when Terri lifted her legs and let them rest on her shoulders. O'Malley leaned forward and ran the tip of her tongue around Terri's clit and felt Terri's fingers suddenly grasp her hair. She repeated the action and slid her fingers as deep inside her lover as she could.

Terri's breath caught in her chest as she came hard, tightening her thighs to keep the sensation going as long as possible. From the feel of O'Malley's tongue still lightly stroking her clit she knew she hadn't broken her neck. A small giggle broke free and Terri looked down her body to watch her lover. She felt O'Malley's fingers leave her body and missed them instantly.

O'Malley kissed her way up Terri's stomach and around her breasts. "I'm not done with you yet, woman," she promised as she settled her body on Terri's and captured her lips in a tender kiss. "There's something I've been wanting for five months."

Terri pulled away slightly. "What would that be?"

"I love you."

Terri couldn't stop the tears that sprang up in her eyes. She'd heard the sentiment many times, but never so sincerely. There was something in O'Malley's voice that told her how deeply she meant it. Terri wrapped her arms around her lover and pulled her close.

"Thank you," she whispered. "For loving me and for coming here to find me."

O'Malley rolled them over so she could hold Terri. "I told you, I couldn't stay away." Her fingertips played along Terri's shoulders. "Do you have to work tomorrow?"

Terri shook her head. "I have the next two whole days off. Makes me wonder if George lost his organizer again. I hardly ever get days off in a row."

"Spend them with me?" O'Malley was almost afraid to ask.

"I would have anyway, but it's sweet of you to ask." Terri let her eyes close as she enjoyed the sensation of O'Malley's fingers.

"You would have anyway? How come?"

"Because someone I know wore me out a little while ago. It's been five months, O'Malley. I have got to work on my stamina."

O'Malley let out a laugh that shook Terri. "You are priceless."

"Just keep thinking that." Terri smiled and settled her head back on her lover's shoulder and closed her eyes.

O'Malley kept swirling her fingertips on Terri's skin until her eyes closed and then together, entangled, they slept.

Roselle is still living in Dallas, driving friends and family just a little crazy and usually enjoying it. When not writing, she's usually reading, desperately trying to find hockey on TV or playing fetch with the Mouse puppy.

Printed in the United States
47860LVS00005B/40-69